The South Boston Savings Bank would like to thank you for your loyal patronage and continued support.

SOUTH BOSTON: MY HOME TOWN contains the sparkle of a good story, as well as fascinating historical nostalgia of our South Boston neighborhood from the early 1600's to present.

I found this book to be both interesting and inspiring. I'm sure you will enjoy it too.

Sincerely Yours,

Alfred W. Archibald
Chairman of the Board

SOUTH BOSTON: MY HOME TOWN

THE HISTORY OF AN ETHNIC NEIGHBORHOOD

BY THOMAS H. O'CONNOR

QUINLAN PRESS
BOSTON

Published by Quinlan Press
131 Beverly Street, Boston, MA 02114

Printed in the United States of America, 1988.

Library of Congress Cataloging-in-Publication Data

O'Connor, Thomas H.
    South Boston, my home town.

    Includes index.
    1. South Boston (Boston, Mass.)—History
2. South Boston (Boston, Mass.)—Ethnic relations
3. Irish Americans—Massachusetts—Boston—History.
4. Boston (Mass.)—History.   5. Boston (Mass.)—
Ethnic relations. I. Title.
F73.68.S7027 1988   974.4'61   88-42935
ISBN 1-55770-101-6

To my South Boston Family:

the Meanys and the O'Connors, the Pages,
the Turpins, and the Schmidts.

ACKNOWLEDGEMENTS

THE BOSTON PUBLIC LIBRARY HAS BEEN INDISPENSABLE IN THE research and writing of this work on South Boston, not only in providing so many of the primary sources and secondary materials necessary for establishing the historical basis for the study, but also in creating the scholarly atmosphere and support that made it possible to bring this project to a successful conclusion. Especially helpful in this respect was the enthusiastic cooperation of Mrs. Helen Maniadis and her staff at the South Boston Branch Library, who provided valuable documentary materials relating to the history of South Boston and sponsored a series of public lectures, funded by the National Endowment for the Humanities, which drew standing-room-only audiences from the Greater Boston area.

From many of the men and women who attended these lectures, I obtained the kind of first-hand recollections and reminiscences that have made this work possible. In approaching a project such as this, the usual written historical sources are seriously lacking among immigrants, who could not write at all or had little time in the painful struggle of their daily lives to reflect upon their surroundings. Accounts of the immigrant past, therefore, are very often drawn from a variety of unwritten sources. Oral interviews and personal reminiscences make up a large part of the twentieth-century story. Elderly citizens, in their seventies and eighties, may often be vague or forgetful about what transpired yesterday or the day before, but I have found them amazingly accurate in furnishing details about what happened half a century ago. My special thanks go to Dr. William Reid, former headmaster of South Boston High School, for his scholarly writings on the history of Castle Island; to Miss Marie Crowley, for her delightful reminiscences of a girlhood in South Boston; and to Mr. Robert Toland, a former attorney and historian of the Castle Island Association, whose remembrances of recent neighborhood history were unfailingly accurate and informative.

And finally, I would like to express my thanks to Kevin Stevens, executive editor at Quinlan Press, for his professional direction and sage advice; and to Henry Quinlan's 85-year-old father, Gene, for persuading his son to accept this manuscript for publication.

Chestnut Hill
Massachusetts
September 15, 1988

CONTENTS

SOUTH BOSTON: MY HOME TOWN

INTRODUCTION

I N *THE LAST HURRAH*, EDWIN O'CONNOR'S CLASSIC NOVEL ABOUT
Boston politics, Mayor Frank Skeffington tells his young nephew
why he brought him to see an old-fashioned Irish-Catholic wake.
"It's a disappearing phenomenon, like the derby hat," the old political
chieftain explains. Yet he concedes that "the wake will still continue
in some form; after all, it takes a long time to get rid of old tribal customs.
And Knocko's was a bit like some of the old wakes; that's why I wanted
you to see it." It is in something of this same spirit of historical nostalgia
that I have undertaken to write a comprehensive study of South Boston,
one of the most distinctive, colorful and controversial of Boston's many
neighborhoods. Like the legendary wake, the old Boston neighborhoods
have also begun to feel the effects of time. Some traditional communities,
like the former Jewish district along Roxbury's Blue Hill Avenue that
has now become predominantly black, have already been transformed
completely. Others, like North Dorchester and Jamaica Plain, are in
the process of changing from what had been heavily Irish sections into
substantial black and Hispanic communities. Still others are beginning
to show the gradual but inevitable altering of the forms and characteristics
with which they have so long been identified. In another decade or two,
most of these traditional neighborhoods may well have disappeared
altogether—or else have changed so dramatically that there will be little left to remind future generations of what these places were really
like, why they were so different from one another, or what particular
role they played in the city's history.

Of all Boston's neighborhoods, South Boston has survived with perhaps the fewest changes in its ethnic, social and religious composition. It is one of the last surviving relics of a distinctive way of life that goes back to the early days of immigrant Irish families and old-time political bosses. Despite its distinctive characteristics, however, South Boston has never been studied or analyzed with the same seriousness of purpose as other Boston neighborhoods. In his *Urban Villagers*, Herbert Gans explored the varieties of the immigrant experience in Boston's West End, a neighborhood whose socioeconomic life was investigated even more intensely by Marc Fried in *The World of the Urban Working Class*. William Whyte's *Street Corner Society* gained national attention for its perceptive insights into the structure of life among Italian immigrants in Boston's North End, a subject that has been updated in more recent years by William De Marco's in-depth analysis of the same neighborhood in his *Ethnics and Enclaves*.

South Boston, by contrast, has never received this same kind of serious attention. The only historical studies of the district are rather antiquarian narratives written nearly a century ago. Thomas C. Simonds produced his *History of South Boston* as early as 1857; C. B. Gillespie published an *Illustrated History of South Boston* in 1900; and John J. Toomey collaborated with Edward P. Rankin to bring out their *History of South Boston* in 1901. These works are valuable for what they tell us about the colonial origins of South Boston, and about developments in the first part of the nineteenth century, but they barely touch upon the later immigrant experience in the peninsula district. More recent publications dealing with the neighborhood are either too subjective to be of interest to the concerned citizen, or too superficial to be of service to the serious researcher. All too often, friendly local writers have told the story of South Boston by indulging in amusing anecdotes and nostalgic reminiscences without sufficient documentary evidence to indicate whether the reader is being presented with fact or fiction, reality or legend. In the hands of such writers, South Boston has come across as a warm, friendly and generous community, populated by poor but honest, hard-working Irish-Catholic people, much in the Horatio Alger tradition, outwardly tough but inwardly gentle. Devoted to their religion, loyal to their country and committed to the sanctity of the family, such people took great pride in the traditional virtues of their neighborhood—especially in the large numbers of young men and women who went into the religious life and the many young men who served their country in the various branches of the armed services. It was a picture of an American home town that could easily rival that of any small, rural, Midwestern community of the same period.

In the hands of less friendly writers, however, South Boston has come across as a much less wholesome neighborhood, with residents far less friendly than its supporters would have us believe. Indeed, through the eyes of a fictional character like J. P. Marquand's Beacon Hill Brahmin, George Apley, as well as through the news reports of out-of-town journalists, the term "South Boston Irish" soon became the classic synonym for almost any kind of unwelcome Irish immigrant. During the nineteenth century most critics emphasized the personal weaknesses and deficiencies of these "foreign paupers," labeling them as "idle bums" and "drunken hooligans." In the early part of the twentieth century, these same people were characterized as "crooked politicians," responsible for undermining the whole democratic system and indulging in all sorts of political corruption. The district of South Boston itself was often described as an impoverished slum, overrun with barrooms and pool halls, where working-class families eked out a meager existence in ramshackle double- and triple-decker houses.

For a considerable period, however, these rather unflattering descriptions were somewhat offset by an element of tolerance and a touch of good humor. Indeed, in the homes of well-to-do Yankee families in Boston and Cambridge, young sons and daughters often shared a warm intimacy with Irish men and women who served as their stablemen, gardeners, nurses and cooks—while at the same time picking up from their parents what Barbara Miller Solomon called "an inward remoteness" from those people who had come "from a mysterious green island far across the sea...bringing many of their strange customs with them."

The eminent Yankee historian Samuel Eliot Morison recalled fondly his own household at 44 Brimmer Street at the foot of Beacon Hill, where the cook, the waitress and the chambermaid were "always Irish Catholics." They were "girls of character whom we loved and they us," he wrote nostalgically, "although they generally stayed only long enough to find a Boston-Irish husband." It was generally agreed that the so-called "South Boston Irishman," despite his thriftless ways, was a jolly, good-natured, well-meaning fellow at heart, a teller of tall tales, full of inoffensive blarney, who was a loyal husband, a good father and a devoted member of his church. "Poor Paddy," in the early days, was much more apt to be a subject for laughter than an object of scorn.

In more recent years, however, especially since the advent of television, the descriptions of South Boston have become much more critical,
if not downright ugly. During the 1950s and 1960s, it was not unusual
to find South Boston men likened to the comic television personality
Archie Bunker—a beer-swilling, cigar-chewing, insensitive chauvinist
and outright bigot. Perhaps one of the most insulting and stereotypical
descriptions of the people of South Boston appeared in a 1967 issue
of *Newsweek* magazine telling about a local political gathering of Louise
Day Hicks supporters. "They looked like characters out of Moon
Mullins," laughed the New York writer, "and she [Mrs. Hicks] was
their homegrown Mamie-made-good." Sitting at long tables at the South
Boston Social and Athletic Club, the people were described as a "comic-
strip gallery of tipplers and brawlers," and after Mrs. Hicks had given
her speech, the men "unscrewed cigar butts from their chins" and lined
up to kiss her noisily on the cheek or pump her arm "as if it were a
jack handle under a trailer truck."

By the 1970s, with the nationwide controversy over school desegregation, the South Boston Irishman was no longer regarded with humor
or even amused tolerance. Because of his opposition to forced busing,
he was singled out as a lawless and violent racist, an ignorant and reac-
tionary redneck who blocked the path of progress and opposed the equality of the races. With the news media concentrating almost exclusively
on the busing controversy, the breach created between upper-class whites
in the suburbs and lower-class whites in the neighborhoods was substantial. Given this attitude, the residents of South Boston felt under assault
not only from the black population of the city, but also from members
of their own Irish-Catholic population in the surrounding suburbs. A
clearly bitter and defensive mentality intensified a neighborhood disposi-
tion that was already definitely parochial, and often xenophobic.

Was this last state of mind merely a temporary condition brought on
by outside forces beyond the control of residents? Or was it the natural
and inevitable result of a long chain of events set in motion by the complicated and confusing structure of the neighborhood system itself? Just
how does one understand a neighborhood like South Boston? Is it really a warm and hospitable community, as its residents insist, or is it a
narrow and parochial district jealously guarding its turf from outside
influences? How is it possible to reconcile the happy and nostalgic
memories of former residents with the charges of lawlessness and racism
raised in the wake of the recent busing turmoil? How can someone
understand a neighborhood that can turn out lawbreakers and criminals

and at the same time produce a major church leader like Cardinal Cushing, a recognized political spokesman like Speaker John McCormack and a highly respected university president like Rev. Michael P. Walsh, S.J., of Boston College? A more detailed account of this particular neighborhood, from earliest times to the present, provides the historical information and the greater sense of perspective needed to reconcile some of these apparent contradictions and achieve a more objective assessment of this neighborhood's role in Boston's history.

While the major focus of this study is South Boston itself, its significance extends far beyond this one locality. In many ways, South Boston is a fascinating microcosm of what took place in many of the nation's immigrant communities during the rapid process of urbanization in the late nineteenth and early twentieth centuries. The influence of the religious establishment in South Boston, the development of the district's economic composition, the organization of its political structure, the formation of its cultural institutions, and the molding of its racial attitudes provide the basis for a comparative analysis with many other neighborhoods throughout the United States. The old ethnic neighborhood, at least as we have known it, is quickly becoming a thing of the past. It will soon become a part of history, along with the various social, cultural and political forces that created it in the first place. The time has come to judge its shortcomings and measure its positive contributions as a lively and distinctive feature of American life during a time when the nation itself was experiencing deep and substantive changes.

1

FROM COLONY
TO COMMUNITY

I
T IS ONE OF THE MANY IRONIES OF HISTORY THAT A COMMUNITY
with a twentieth-century reputation as a major center for Irish-
Catholic immigrants should have started out as a haven for
seventeenth-century Anglo-Saxon Protestants. On March 22, 1630, John
Winthrop's fleet of ships carrying Puritan dissenters left from Southamp-
ton, England, to seek refuge across the Atlantic in the Massachusetts
Bay Colony. About two weeks earlier, two other vessels had set sail
for New England from the port of Plymouth. One was the *Lyon*, with
eighty passengers from the western parts of England, which arrived
in Salem harbor before Winthrop's ships had completed their crossing.
The other ship was the *Mary and John*, with 140 passengers from the
southwestern counties of Devon, Dorset and the remote parts of
Somerset. Sailing directly into Massachusetts Bay, the captain of the
Mary and John ignored orders to take the vessel up the Charles River.
Instead, he put in along a narrow strip of land called Nantasket, which
jutted out into the southern approaches of the bay. After exploring parties had scouted the mainland, the passengers moved into a peninsula
which the Indians called Mattapan, but which the newcomers called
Dorchester after their native town in England.

Here, in Dorchester, the settlers set up crude shacks and cottages,
although for the first few years most families were required to live in
tents. They built a fort on the water side of their settlement, where they
mounted several small cannon for their defense. In contrast to many
other colonial enterprises of the early seventeenth century, the English
colonists operating under the Massachusetts Bay Company found

themselves in a region almost completely devoid of natives. The size
of the original Indian population of New England just before the Puritans
arrived is estimated to have been about twenty-five thousand—most of
them branches of the Algonquin family. During 1616-1617, however,
some kind of still-undiagnosed epidemic decimated the local Indian
tribes, killing at least one-third of the native people and reducing their
population to somewhere between fifteen to eighteen thousand in all
of New England. To make matters worse, in 1633, only three years
after the establishment of the Massachusetts Bay Colony, a smallpox
epidemic broke out among the local Indians and reduced their numbers
even further. As a result, the initial years of this particular settlement
took place without the bloody wars between Europeans and Native
Americans so frequent in other parts of the American colonies.

The first danger confronting the new settlers, therefore, came not
from hostile savages but from their own lack of food. Arriving during
the summer of 1630, they had come ashore too late for the spring planting and were forced to eke out a meager existence during the cold months
of a New England winter with little relief in sight. Although there were
plenty of fish, clams and mussels in the waters around them, the first
inhabitants would have suffered greatly from the lack of bread and other
foodstuffs if Governor Winthrop had not had the foresight to send to
Ireland for a supply of food. The arrival of a relief vessel on February
5, 1631, was the occasion for much celebration, as well as a day of
thanksgiving and prayer the following day—the first officially designated
Thanksgiving Day in Massachusetts. At the governor's order, the
precious cargo of foodstuffs was placed in a "General Stock," to be
distributed to the people of the various settlements around Massachusetts
Bay as it was needed. In the months that followed, several more ships
arrived from England, increasing the number of colonists and adding
to the settlement's stock of supplies and provisions. To guarantee the
future security of their colony, as well as to provide a permanent body
of men to make whatever laws were necessary, the Dorchester settlers
created one of the first town meeting systems with a group of elected
representatives. In 1633 they elected twelve "Selectmen" or "Towns-
men" who would meet once a month, and whose enactments were to
be "of full force and being to ye Inhabitants."

Two years later, in 1635, the Reverend Richard Mather, a well-known
Puritan clergyman, arrived in Dorchester with about a hundred followers,
as well as twenty-three cows and heifers, three calves, and eight mares.
This may have been one of the reasons why the citizens of Dorchester

looked to the peninsula across the way called Mattapannock—later known as Dorchester Neck, and still later South Boston—as a convenient location for them to pasture their own cattle, along with the new beasts Mather had brought with him from England. Early records indicate that a section of the beach at the foot of present-day K Street in South Boston was the place where settlers from Dorchester first came ashore. Refreshed by a fresh-water spring and shaded by a magnificent growth of weeping willows, this location was known as Pow-Wow Point because it was an important meeting place for the region's Indians who probably also used it as a burial ground. These natives were mainly horticulturalists who planted maize, beans, squash and pumpkins; but they were also food-gatherers who collected plentiful supplies of seeds, nuts, berries, fish and shellfish.

Although Mattapannock was actually a peninsula, attached to Dorchester by a thin strip of land, it often became a virtual island when the Atlantic swept over the ''Neck'' and the beaches at high tide. The future South Boston was then covered with a rich growth of grass, ideal for grazing, and dotted with clumps of trees that offered comfortable shade for the cattle. The peninsula was naturally designed to contain large numbers of grazing animals with a minimum of effort. It required only a short length of fencing across the thin neck of land running between the peninsula and the settlement at Dorchester to control the cattle and prevent them from straying. For several years it was customary for all Dorchester settlers to assume the right of pasturing their cows, oxen, mares and goats on Mattapannock. In 1637, however, the town restricted the exclusive privilege of using the peninsula to about 100 prominent colonists. These men would thenceforth have free access to the land, but would also assume responsibility for fixing the fences, repairing the causeway and maintaining the roads. A certain portion of the land, however, was reserved by the town as common pasture. Any person was allowed to graze his cattle on this particular section of land, provided he paid a small tax.

For the greater part of the seventeenth century, the pastureland on Mattapannock remained in the hands of the original Dorchester families. Over the course of nearly a hundred years, however, the landholdings themselves broke up into units of varying sizes and shapes as each generation of proprietors died off and divided the land among its heirs. By the mid-1600s, there were nearly a dozen proprietors who had moved out of Dorchester and who actually built permanent and substantial residences in Mattapannock. The Fosters, the Wiswells and the Birds held title to most of the property in the western end of the peninsula, where their homes were surrounded by magnificent elms and extensive orchards of peach, apple and plum trees. The Mathers, the Withingtons and the Joneses owned land in the central part of the district, while much of the property at the extreme eastern tip of the peninsula—the "Point" that looked out onto the Atlantic Ocean—belonged to Deacon James Blake.

Just beyond the Point, less than half a mile into the outer harbor, was a small knob of land local ship captains had already named Castle Island because of its jagged silhouette. In July 1634, Governor Thomas Dudley, members of his council, several ministers and a collection of townspeople met at Castle Island and agreed to erect a small fortification for which the General Court appropriated the sum of five hundred pounds. When the final structure was completed, Roger Clap of Dorchester described it as "a Castle with mud-walls, which stood divers years." The garrison consisted of a captain, a gunner and an undetermined number of men, with three men enlisting in 1641 for one year's service at ten pounds a year. As the years went by, Bostonians lost interest in the fort until a day in June 1643, when a French vessel suddenly appeared off the coast and sailed boldly into Boston harbor without stopping. It was a good thing that the French captain was friendly, John Winthrop wryly observed, because nobody at Castle Island had even bothered to challenge him. Despite this scare, however, the town continued to neglect the makeshift fortifications until, in the early 1700s, English military engineers moved in, tore down the old structures, and put up a new fortress they called Castle William. By the time of the French and Indian Wars in 1754, Castle William was recognized as one of the most important forts in British North America.

Having done away with the common land and taken over the rest of the property themselves, the proprietors on the peninsula remained for a long time a small, closely knit, self-sufficient group of landholders, largely dependent upon one another for their regular social and recreational needs. The older landholders—the Blakes, the Wiswells, the Birds, the Fosters and the Withingtons—along with such newer arrivals as the Marshalls, the Williamses, the Ferringtons and the Harringtons, spent many happy hours in each other's company at weddings and at christenings, at suppers and at corn-husking parties. Mattapannock, or Dorchester Neck as it had come to be familiarly known during the eighteenth century, might have continued to remain largely unknown and unnoticed—a small, windswept peninsula, composed of rolling hills, fruitful orchards and verdant grazing lands—had its strategic location not given it a prominent role in the conflict that developed between the American colonists and their British rulers.

Relations between England and the American colonies deteriorated steadily after the end of the French and Indian Wars in 1763. British attempts at establishing firm political and financial controls clashed with American desires for greater local autonomy. When General Thomas Gage sent British regulars to confiscate colonial military stores at the town of Concord, the confrontation that took place on Lexington Green on the morning of April 19, 1775, provided the opening shots of the American Revolution. Two months later, British forces overpowered colonial defenders at the battle of Bunker Hill; they then established an effective military occupation of Boston. With their strong fleet and their absolute control of the waters around Boston harbor, the British made it clear that their occupation of the town would be a long one.

Being so close to the British forces in the town, as well as those stationed on Castle Island, the inhabitants of South Boston were in constant fear of attack. Indeed, they had good cause to worry. British soldiers from Castle Island, in the habit of paying frequent visits to the nearby peninsula, had proved so insulting and intimidating to Deacon Blake and his family, whose property was closest to the Point, that he finally decided it was safer to return to Dorchester for the time being. As soon as he left, the British amused themselves by using the Blake residence for target practice with their cannon from Castle Island. A short time later they set fire to the house and burned it to the ground. Fortunately for the people of South Boston, however, as well as for the inhabitants of occupied Boston, relief was not too far away.

When General George Washington arrived in Cambridge in July 1775 to take command of the Continental army, he was already devising a plan to drive the British out of Boston. His determination to force an evacuation was further strengthened when Colonel Henry Knox arrived in Cambridge in January 1776 with a large number of heavy cannon he had dragged through the deep snow all the way from Fort Ticonderoga. Washington's first idea was to attack Boston by sending forces across the bay from several points along the mainland during the winter months, while the ice was still thick and hard. He proposed to press on with this attack even if it meant that Boston "must be destroyed." Washington's generals would not approve such a plan, however, arguing that gaining control of Dorchester Heights, on the nearby South Boston peninsula, would be a safer and much more effective strategy.

Bowing to the decision of his military council ("I must suppose it to be right," he admitted to John Hancock), Washington began preparations to seize and fortify Dorchester Heights. Under cover of a diversionary bombardment from several artillery positions around Boston that began on the night of Saturday, March 2, 1776, and shook the town for three successive nights (Abigail Adams complained that she could hardly get any sleep!), a long train of American soldiers made their way silently and secretly from Roxbury, through Dorchester, and across into the peninsula of South Boston. Working swiftly and effectively through the night, by daybreak on March 5 the colonists had constructed two substantial fortifications on the crest of Dorchester Heights overlooking the town of Boston. To the consternation of the British across the bay, the American cannon menaced not only the British forces in the town and the garrison on Castle Island, but also the numerous British ships riding helplessly at anchor.

Although Sir William Howe considered the possibility of a counterattack, he thought better of it, and decided that evacuation was the only alternative. In return for a British promise not to burn the town, General Washington agreed not to fire upon the British vessels as they left Boston harbor. The English transports—carrying the 9,000-man British garrison, along with nearly 1,100 Americans who had remained loyal to their King—escorted by sixteen warships, sailed out of Boston. As the British reached the outer limits of the harbor, they stopped briefly at Castle Island to set explosive charges and light a series of fires that left the whole island ablaze. Moving quickly out of range of the American cannon, the armada spent about ten days at Nantasket Roads, and then caught the winds that eventually brought them north to Halifax.

Despite efforts by Sir William Howe to dismiss the evacuation of Boston as inconsequential, most authorities back in England saw it for what it really was—an ignominious defeat. Speaking before the House of Lords, the Duke of Manchester summed up the situation without mincing any words. "Let this transaction be dressed in whatever garb you please," he said, "but the fact remains that the army which was sent to reduce the province of Massachusetts Bay has been driven from the capital, and that the standard of the provincial army now waves in triumph over the walls of Boston." An American could not have summed it up better!

On March 17, 1776, General Washington's troops, spearheaded by a contingent of soldiers who had already had smallpox (a precaution taken to avoid having the colonial army exposed to the dread disease that had plagued the British during their months of occupation) prepared to liberate Boston. Once assured that there was no danger of epidemic, Washington's forces marched triumphantly through the streets of the town. But they found Boston a tragic shambles. Trees had been cut down everywhere; fences had been ripped up; barns and warehouses had been razed to supply the town with fuel. Churches and meetinghouses had been used for stables; private houses had been turned into hospitals; monuments and public buildings had been shockingly defaced. Slowly and painfully, however, the town began to pull itself together after the ordeal of siege, occupation and plunder. General Washington took particular pains to restore the fortifications of Castle Island as soon as possible, so that it could be of use to the Americans, and he engaged Paul Revere to do most of the repair work on the ruined structures.

Later, when the war was finally over, Governor John Hancock took back possession of the castle until March 1795, when the state legislature passed a law calling for Castle Island to serve as a place for the reception and confinement of criminals. The use of Castle Island as a prison colony continued until 1798, when the United States government decided to take possession of the island for national defense in the event that the naval clashes with France turned into an all-out war. On October 2, 1798, Castle Island formally passed into the custody of the United States of America, and the following year President John Adams attended a ceremony at which the name was officially changed to Fort Independence. The work of rebuilding the structure was assigned to Lieutenant-Colonel A. Louis Tousard, and when the reconstruction was completed Nehemiah Freeman, commander of the fort, named each of the five new bastions in honor of a well-known New Englander. The northeast bastion was named Winthrop in honor of the first governor of Massachusetts; the bastion on the northeast corner was named Shirley in honor of colonial governor William Shirley; the bastion on the southwest corner was named for John Hancock, the first governor of the Commonwealth of Massachusetts; the north bastion was called Dearborn in honor of Henry Dearborn of New Hampshire, Secretary of War under President Thomas Jefferson; and the bastion at the corner of the fort was named Adams after John Adams of Braintree, "the late President of the United States who bestowed the present name of Fort Independence." Standing like a lonely sentinel in the silent gray waters of Boston harbor, the old fort would go on to have a romantic and often eerie history, with legends of duels, murders, suicides, strange voices, ghostly noises and spectral anecdotes coming down through the years. There was even a story of a young army officer entombed alive in one of the fort's subterranean dungeons that provided the basis for Edgar Allen Poe's story "The Cask of Amontillado." A graduate of West Point, Poe was stationed briefly at Fort Independence while serving a tour of duty.

The long-awaited news that a peace treaty had finally been signed between the United States and Great Britain reached Boston on the night of March 28, 1783, when Colonel John Trumbull arrived with a letter confirming the signing of a general peace between the belligerents. On April 11, the Confederation Congress proclaimed the end of the war; four days later, it ratified the provisional treaty of peace. It took almost a year before copies of the final articles of peace reached Boston, and on February 27, 1784, the happy townspeople organized a public celebration. All day long the town resounded to the clanging of bells and the booming of cannon. In the evening Governor John Hancock lavishly entertained the leading men in town at his house on Beacon Hill, while a grand display of fireworks on the Common illuminated the whole town and dramatized the meaning of this moment of glory.

Along with the rest of the community, Dorchester Neck slowly returned to a more normal existence. Many families which had moved out of the district while the fighting was going on gradually returned to their homes now that the war was over and the danger had passed. The peninsula quietly slipped back to being a bucolic pastureland where cattle grazed contentedly during the week, and where families from Boston came to visit on Sundays for picnics and outings on the town pasture at the Point. Occasionally, however, the grassy meadows on the Point were used for more unpleasant pastimes. On a bright Sunday morning in June 1801, for example, a small group of men arrived in a solemn procession at daybreak, and marked off a piece of ground for a duel between two men named Rand and Miller. After they took up their positions, Rand fired first, but missed his target. At this point Miller tried to settle the dispute, but Rand insisted on satisfaction. Miller fired his shot; Rand pitched to the ground and was carried off by his friends to die a short time later. Residents of the peninsula were greatly shocked when they heard about what had taken place in their district— especially since the shooting had taken place on the Sabbath.

Despite such an unusual episode, there was little indication at this time that South Boston would ever be used for any purposes other than the pleasure of visitors and the grazing of animals—except that some

Boston authorities noticed that the peninsula's fresh salt air, open spaces, prominent hills and isolated location made it particularly well suited to medical care and therapeutic treatments. This was a period when smallpox was still a terrible and frightening disease. Although the process of inoculation had been advocated by Rev. Cotton Mather and Dr. Zabdiel Boylston during the early 1700s, there was still considerable resistance to what many people regarded as a dangerous and highly questionable experiment. As a result, physicians found it necessary to establish hospitals in various towns to accommodate those who had volunteered to be inoculated with the smallpox germs, and to isolate them from the healthy portion of the community as well as from those who feared inoculation itself. In 1792 one of these hospitals was opened in South Boston to take in smallpox patients from the Dorchester region. This was the beginning of a trend that would eventually see the peninsula district become, among other things, a favorite location for schools, hospitals, homes, asylums, workhouses, poorhouses and institutions of all kinds. For the time being, however, there were few indications that South Boston would attract many more permanent residents than already made their homes there.

In fact, the physical attractions of the peninsula would soon draw the attention of a number of Bostonians who saw that this piece of land had considerable potential for profitable development. Although the economic condition of Boston had not immediately improved when the American colonies won their independence in 1783, the local economy did begin to revive perceptibly during the late 1790s and early 1800s. Ship captains, merchants, traders, importers and exporters made great profits from ambitious overseas enterprises in the West Indies, South America, the Pacific Ocean and the China Seas. And population inevitably followed prosperity. From an all-time low of six thousand people during the period of British occupation, the population of Boston had risen to eighteen thousand by 1790. In 1800 it was recorded at twenty-five thousand, and by 1810 it had gone well beyond thirty thousand—a five-fold increase in only thirty-five years. Because the old town was still a very small peninsula, attached to the mainland only by a thin stretch of mudflats, this remarkable growth forced the leaders of the community to look for more room for expansion.

Some, like the entrepreneurs who called themselves the Mount Vernon Proprietors, set about creating more usable real estate property inside Boston itself by the process of landfill. First, they laid out a system of streets in the Beacon Hill area adjacent to the new State House recently

designed by Charles Bulfinch. Then, during the summer of 1799, they
lopped off some fifty or sixty feet from the top of Mount Vernon to
make way for blocks of elegant townhouses. With the use of small gravity
railroad cars, they dumped the fill from the top of the hill into the waters
at the foot of Charles Street, thus creating even more prime real estate
for potential builders in the town. All this provided an enjoyable pastime
for spectators, young and old, who gathered regularly to watch the gravity cars going up and down Beacon Hill.

Other enterprising speculators developed plans for expanding into the
south end of Boston, where the town narrowed down to the thin neck
of land that connected the peninsula to the mainland near Roxbury. In
1801 they persuaded the selectmen to develop a plan for laying out a
system of streets in this area in a rectangular pattern. A large oval plot
in the center would be called Columbia Square, and Washington Street
would run through its center. Investors hoped that this attractive ven-
ture would attract both permanent residents and commercial enterprisers.

Still other Bostonians looked for more residential and commercial
properties outside the town itself—in those towns and neighborhoods
bordering the old Shawmut peninsula. In 1803 several prominent citizens
of Boston, including William Tudor, Gardiner Green, Jonathan Mason
and Harrison Gray Otis, purchased a considerable amount of property
on the nearby South Boston peninsula, which they saw as an obvious
and accessible area for expansion. Early the following year, William
Tudor and a number of his colleagues presented a formal petition re-
questing that Boston annex the entire peninsula and incorporate it with
the Town of Boston. In that way, they argued, the growing population
of Boston would have more room to expand, while the property values
of land in South Boston would definitely go up.

The petition to have Boston annex old Dorchester Neck ran into stiff
and vocal opposition from the inhabitants of Dorchester, who considered
the peninsula theirs and were determined to keep it in their possession.
At their town meeting in January 1804, Dorchester residents formally
protested against South Boston being ''set off and annexed to the Town
of Boston,'' and they drew up a strong ''remonstrance'' which they
promptly dispatched to the Great and General Court. Despite their angry
protests, the people of Dorchester learned at their town meeting the
following month that not only had a joint committee of the legislature
already reported favorably on the Boston annexation proposal, but also
that the report had refused to recommend any compensation for the Town
of Dorchester. They were informed unofficially, however, that the

investors were willing to pay them six thousand dollars if they would give up their opposition to the transfer. Just when it appeared that the residents would accept this offer, one of their members, John Howe, leaped to his feet and made an impassioned plea that the citizens of Dorchester hold on to their property and reject the money offer of the investors. Obviously aroused by this speech, the town meeting members moved to continue their opposition to annexation, even after the offer was later raised to twenty thousand dollars. It was all in vain, however. On March 6, 1804, the General Court passed a bill annexing Dorchester Neck to the Town of Boston. Not only did the people of Dorchester lose their lands, but they also lost the money that had been offered to them for their silence and cooperation.

Investors' expectations that annexation would boost land values in South Boston were quickly and happily realized. Lots on the 600-acre peninsula that were selling the previous year for four hundred dollars an acre now sold for as much as four or five thousand dollars an acre. To attract more settlers to the district and to promote further investment, the proprietors set about providing more convenient access between the town and its new acquisition. Up to this point, South Boston was separated from Boston by a stretch of mudflats and a narrow channel that forced most people to use small rowboats to get from one place to the other. In 1803 construction was begun on a toll bridge running across the channel from the south end of Boston, at what would later become Dover Street, to the western end of South Boston. The bridge was over 1,500 feet long, completed at a cost of fifty-six thousand dollars, and opened with a gala military display on October 1, 1805. Unfortunately, this so-called South Bridge did not prove very successful in attracting more settlers to South Boston. Wanting a bridge much closer to the center of town, residents had urged a structure that would link up somewhere near Summer Street, Federal Street or Wind Mill Point. Such a plan was delayed for many years by a group of private investors called the Front Street Corporation, who feared the effects of bridge construction on their shore-front enterprises. After nearly twenty years of litigation, however, a charter was finally granted in 1826 for a free bridge to be built from the foot of Federal Street across the channel to South Boston. This North Free Bridge proved such a popular route that the investors of the original South Bridge (Dover Street) had to sell off their properties to the city in 1832.

Once assured of more convenient access, landholders and investors in South Boston quickly set about arranging for a rational system of

streets and roadways. Prior to annexation in 1804, little or no consideration had been given to street planning in South Boston. The main
thoroughfare that ran the length of the peninsula was not much more
than a pathway made by cattle on their way to and from the grazing
lands at City Point. Eventually this pathway became a public street,
and today Emerson Street follows the original course. The other main
highway was the Causeway—a road that crossed the marshy flats connecting Dorchester and South Boston. From written accounts of repeated
complaints and petitions voiced by the residents, it is clear that the
Causeway was always in poor condition and frequently under water.
This long-standing colonial street pattern was illustrated in a map drawn
for the British high command by Henry Pelham, Loyalist engraver and
cartographer, and half-brother of the famous painter John Singleton
Copley. This map outlines in detail the topography and military installations of the American and British forces in the Greater Boston area and
makes it apparent that these two roads were the only thoroughfares on
the South Boston peninsula during the colonial period.

After they had succeeded in annexing their new property in 1804,
the South Boston investors took steps to avoid the unplanned and
haphazard street system that had prevailed in Boston for so long. They
engaged Mather Withington, a well-known surveyor from Dorchester,
to design a street plan for the district. This plan, which was completed
and approved in 1805, laid out two main roadways, eighty feet wide,
for the district. One was Dorchester Street, which ran south-to-north
from the town line of Dorchester to Broadway; the other was Broadway itself, which traversed the peninsula west-to-east from the
Dorchester-to-Boston Turnpike on the Boston side to City Point. Using
Broadway as one axis, Withington plotted a series of streets in numerical
order. First, Second and Third Streets ran parallel to the north side of
Broadway; Fourth, Fifth, Sixth and Seventh Streets ran parallel to Broadway on the south side. On the western side of South Boston he added
Eighth and Ninth Streets, each fifty feet wide. Withington then lined
up a series of streets running parallel to Dorchester Street in alphabetical
order. There were six on the western side—A through F Streets—and
ten on the eastern side—G through Q Streets. All the lettered streets,
also fifty feet wide, were designed to intersect the numerical streets
at regular intervals. The original plans also included two other streets—
Old Harbor Street and Telegraph Street, which were located at the south
end of Dorchester Street. Except for a number of smaller streets that
were added later, the basic street pattern designed for South Boston
remained essentially the same for the next century and a half.

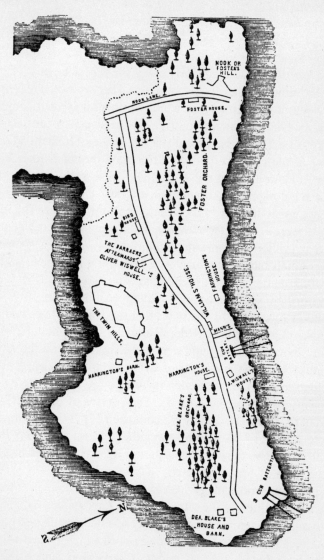

Henry Pelham's plan of Dorchester Neck, drawn for the British Army's use in 1775.

After the rectangular street pattern had been worked out, the South Boston investors set about promoting real estate development and building construction. In 1805 Judge William Tudor constructed a large and well-appointed block of brick buildings at the corner of Broadway and A Street which was familiarly called the Barracks, or Brinley Block. About the same time, a Mr. Murphy built what eventually became known as the South Boston Hotel, but which started out as a public house with a large golden ball hanging outside advertising its wares. It was also in 1805 that a Mr. Ross, a local soap manufacturer, built a large brick building at the corner of Fourth Street and the main road from Dorchester to Boston called the Turnpike. These buildings, along with a residence belonging to Abraham Gould near the corner of Fourth and E Streets, were the only brick structures in the district. The remaining buildings were constructed of wood, some occupied by newcomers from Boston and others by workmen employed in Mr. Ross's soap factory or other small businesses that were beginning to appear in the lower part of the district closest to Boston.

Any further real estate development on the peninsula was halted abruptly in June 1812 by the news that the United States had declared war against Great Britain. Federalist leaders throughout New England had serious reservations concerning the morality and the advisibility of "Jimmy Madison's War," however, and made it clear that they did not intend to provide either men or money to support such a conflict. Massachusetts troops did not enter the service of the federal government, but put themselves under the command of militia officers appointed by the governor of the Commonwealth. Because they were paid from the state treasury, they assumed they were not required to serve outside the state of Massachusetts.

Despite their serious misgivings about the war, Bay Staters were aware of the practicalities of the situation, and took immediate steps to defend themselves against the possibility of attack by British military or naval forces. Governor Caleb Strong issued a proclamation for troops, the militia gathered in great numbers in Boston, and Massachusetts soldiers took up positions at the various forts in Boston harbor. The inhabitants of Boston were in constant fear of invasion, and a wave of panic swept through the town whenever elements of the British fleet were sighted off the New England coast.

Because of its strategic position guarding the water approaches to Boston, South Boston was singled out for particular attention and soon took on all the appearances of an armed camp. Several regiments of militia were stationed on the peninsula, wooden barracks were erected on a large field near D Street, and a replacement depot was opened on the corner of Broadway and A Street where soldiers were billeted until they received their travel orders. Troops were drilled regularly every morning and afternoon, guards were stationed day and night along the stretch of beach running from South Boston to Dorchester, and nobody was allowed to leave the peninsula during the night. Tension continued to remain high, and when British troops were reported to be advancing down the Maine coast in September 1814, there was great concern in Boston. The selectmen issued a public appeal to the residents of the town and the surrounding neighborhoods for help on the fortifications for the harbor. In response, a number of volunteer organizations representing various civic, fraternal and religious groups worked from the middle of September to the middle of October at different military installations in and around Boston. Even the popular Roman Catholic Bishop of Boston, Jean Louis de Cheverus, worked on the fortifications on Dorchester Heights in South Boston, along with 250 of his parishioners. They constructed a new powderhouse near the redoubts and erected platforms to hold a number of cannon ready for action if they were needed.

Fortunately, these elaborate defense precautions did not prove necessary, because by the closing months of 1814 serious peace talks were in progress in Europe. Early in 1815, even while they were celebrating the news of General Andrew Jackson's dramatic victory over the British at New Orleans, the American people learned that a peace treaty had been concluded some six weeks earlier. It was now time for things to return to normal.

Over the course of the next decade and a half, the patterns of religious, social and cultural development in South Boston followed those of almost any other Anglo-Saxon-Protestant community of this period. As in any such society, of course, religion was uppermost in the minds of the people, and South Boston was no exception. During the colonial period, inhabitants of Mattapannock would have to get up very early Sunday mornings to make their way across the low-lying causeway to Dorchester to attend religious services in some unheated Congregational meetinghouse. Not long after the district was annexed to Boston in 1804, residents of South Boston indicated their desire for a meetinghouse of their own, much closer at hand. Mr. John Hawes, a well-known philanthropist and a public-spirited citizen, donated a piece of land upon which he and his neighbors built a wooden, one-story structure in 1810 as

a temporary place of worship. At first they employed a Methodist
clergyman from Milton as their preacher; later they used the services
of a young Congregational minister named Zephaniah Wood. In 1818
the group became incorporated as the Hawes Place Congregational Society, and the following year they organized themselves into a regular
church consisting of fourteen members. When John Hawes died in 1829,
the Society was able to use the substantial legacy he left to the church
to erect a new and larger meetinghouse close to the site of the original
structure near Dorchester Heights.

After the unexpected death of young Mr. Wood in 1822, a majority
of the small congregation voted to bring in a minister who professed
the newer and more liberal Unitarian views that were becoming popular
in New England at this time. Without questioning the authority of Scrip-
ture or the existence of a personal God, this new sect rejected old-time
predestination, emphasized the goodness of God, and proposed the
perfectibility of man. Characterized by a humanitarian spirit, the new
religious movement appeared capable of combining successfully the
scientific and rationalistic views of the new age of Enlightenment with
the theological faith and intellectual commitment of traditional
Puritanism.

Unitarianism spread very quickly; by the early 1800s nearly every
Congregational pulpit in and around Boston had been taken over by
Unitarian preachers. Nathaniel Frothingham had taken over at the First
Church; Henry Ware was preaching at the Second Church; John Gorham
Palfrey was serving at the Brattle Street Church; Francis Parkman was
holding forth at the New North; and the eloquent William Ellery Chan-
ning was attracting followers at the Federal Street Church. By 1820
the intellectual and theological force of Unitarianism had swept through
Boston and was obviously making its influence felt in the South Boston
peninsula.

The decision to move to Unitarianism caused the remaining Congregational members to leave the Hawes Church. For a while, some attended services at other places of worship. Others felt they should continue
to worship according to their more fundamentalist beliefs, and they began
holding private prayer meetings that gradually attracted a greater number
of people each week. The group moved from one meeting place to
another to accommodate their growing membership at prayer meetings,
Sabbath schools and religious services. In 1823 the leaders of the group
decided to form the Evangelical Congregational Church in South Boston,
formally incorporated two years later as the Phillips Church Society

in Boston in honor of John Phillips, the first mayor of the newly created City of Boston. In 1835 the brick building that served as the church's original meetinghouse on the corner of Broadway and A Street was taken down and replaced with a much larger wooden structure capable of seating about nine hundred persons.

The multiplication of religious denominations that followed in the wake of the War for American Independence was nowhere better illustrated than in the appearance of different church groups in South Boston during the early nineteenth century. In March 1816, for example, St. Matthew's Episcopal Church was formally organized, and proceeded to hold public services in the local schoolhouse. The following year, the membership began construction on a brick church on Broadway, between D and E Streets, which was finally consecrated as St. Matthew's Church in June 1818.

Baptists, too, although their numbers were still small, wanted a church of their own in South Boston. For a while, they held services at the Phillips Church, until one of their own members purchased a small building on the corner of Broadway and C Street. Despite the fact that the more prominent Federal Street Baptist Church in downtown Boston threatened to absorb most of the local groups, the South Boston members continued to retain their independence. Indeed, when the Boston group decided to replace their wooden meetinghouse with a larger brick building, the South Boston Baptists dismantled the original downtown structure, carried the timbers back to the peninsula, and used the wood to build their own church. In 1831, with their own building and their own membership, the local group obtained official recognition as the South Baptist Church. Although there were several years in the mid-1830s when a succession of controversial pastors and a series of conflicts over financial policies appear to have divided the church membership badly, by the early 1840s the situation had become stabilized and the conflicts resolved.

Members of the Methodist persuasion also desired to have a permanent congregation in South Boston, and in 1843, after holding services in various local halls, they finally erected their own meetinghouse on D Street. This was actually the third major attempt to start a Methodist Church on the peninsula. The first had taken place back in 1810 when a young Boston carpenter called "Father" Pierce had been brought in for a brief period to preach to a handful of followers. The second attempt had occurred in 1825 when a number of Methodists, many of whom were employed in local glass factories, put up a place of worship on

the corner of Broadway and C Street. When the glass factories suddenly failed, the workers were forced to go elsewhere in search of work,
and the congregation soon evaporated. This third effort was much more
productive, and by 1840 the Methodists had become a recognized part
of the South Boston community. This variety of religious expression—
Congregational, Unitarian, Universalist, Episcopal, Baptist, Methodist—not only showed how the varieties of new religious experiences
were breaking down what had once been an exclusively monolithic structure, but also of the growing acceptence of a more pluralistic society
by the American people.

Just as religious organizations in South Boston grew and expanded
during the first half of the nineteenth century, so too did its schools
multiply. The question of adequate schooling was a serious matter for
the residents of South Boston. An essential consideration in the Puritan
environment of the Massachusetts Bay Colony, education passed on traditional cultural values and enabled people to read and understand the
Holy Bible.

Throughout most of the colonial period, the inhabitants of old Dorchester Neck had received no funds at all from the Town of Dorchester
for educational purposes. As a result, they were forced to maintain a
small local school at their own expense. In 1761 Dorchester did vote
the sum of four pounds for the support of a school in the peninsula
district; thirty-three years later it raised the amount to six pounds, a
sum hardly enough to meet even modest expenses.

Once the war with Great Britain was over and the new nation had
won its independence, Boston began to take stock of an educational
system that had been largely neglected during years of occupation and
hostilities. A town committee appointed to look into the current state
of schooling was forced to report that during normal school hours too
many children were out in the streets "playing and gaming" instead
of indoors learning their lessons. This condition, commented the committee in terms that would be familiar to modern social critics, was due
either to the "too fond indulgences of parents" or to the "too lax government of the schools." In either case, determined to rectify the situation, the town fathers began immediate steps to improve the school
system.

Even after their annexation to the Town of Boston in 1804, the inhabitants of South Boston were supporting a single school out of their
own pockets. In 1807, assuming they were entitled to the same educational privileges as those citizens who lived in other parts of town, they

requested the school committee to provide a suitable school for the instruction of their children. Although the school committee ignored the petition, Boston selectmen voted to grant three hundred dollars for the support of a school for one year. Although this was still not enough to meet all expenses, the people of South Boston gladly agreed to pay the difference. A schoolhouse large enough to accommodate about ninety pupils was constructed at a cost of four hundred dollars on the south side of G Street, and finally came under the jurisdiction of the Boston School Committee in 1811.

As the population of the district continued to increase, and especially after the tensions of the War of 1812 receded into the past, the residents decided that the small wooden structure on G Street was no longer large enough to meet their needs. In April 1821, they sent another petition to the school committee, and early the following year the committee agreed that it was "expedient" for a new schoolhouse to be built, with two rooms large enough to accommodate at least 150 pupils each. A site was selected, and the brick structure known eventually as the Hawes School was erected on Broadway, between F and Dorchester Streets. In the fall of 1823, the building was ready for occupancy, and the schoolmaster proudly marched his pupils from their old school on G Street down the hill to their new home on Broadway as groups of residents watched and cheered.

For some unexplained reason, a wave of unrest and unruly behavior developed among the pupils of the Hawes School during the late 1820s and the early 1830s. The youngsters may well have been reacting to some of the worst effects of an unregulated and essentially haphazard system of common schools just before the educational reforms of the late 1830s and 1840s. Most schools were overcrowded, with rows of desks with backless benches placed against four bare walls. There were few windows, little heat, no blackboards and no provisions for ventilation or sanitation. Textbooks were few and dull, and the curriculum was restricted to the traditional three R's and whatever additional subjects an untrained teacher happened to know. Under the direction of Horace Mann, who became the first secretary of the Massachusetts Board of Education in 1837, a series of wide-ranging reforms would gradually change both the nature of the school curriculum and the training of the teachers. For the time being, however, education consisted of a deadly recitation of facts and dates, committed to memory and delivered by rote.

Whatever the reason, the correspondence of the headmasters during this period complains of the lack of discipline and obedience among students they came to regard as incorrigible. "Truancy was very common," writes an early historian, "and the boys and girls were perfectly lawless." One headmaster after another resigned his post at the school after failing to resolve the frustrating impasse. During 1832-33, Mr. Moses W. Walker resorted to a program of whippings to subdue the "insubordinate spirit of the young South Bostonians," but failed either to convert the rebellious students or to placate their angry parents. Walker's replacement, Mr. Joseph Harrington, Jr., proved to be a man of more humane and imaginative instincts. He set up a series of programs, activities and associations that effectively channeled the energies of his young students into more positive directions. By the time Mr. Harrington left teaching in 1839 for a career in the ministry, most of the more serious disciplinary problems seem to have been resolved and the tenure of succeeding headmasters made much more routine.

By 1840, however, the major educational problem in the district had become one of numbers, not behavior. The population of South Boston had grown substantially, and the Hawes School quickly filled to overflowing. Already there was a total of 563 pupils—292 boys and 271 girls—in a building originally designed to hold four hundred students at the very most. The school committee authorized the administrators at the Hawes School to rent another building for temporary use and to hire more teachers. When the number of students continued to increase at a remarkable rate, however, the school committee agreed to authorize the construction of a new, three-story schoolhouse on Broadway, on the corner of Third and B Streets. This was named the Mather School in honor of Richard Mather, but the name was later changed to the Lawrence School in honor of Amos Lawrence, the well-known Boston textile magnate and philanthropist.

At first, all residents living east of C Street were required to attend the Hawes School, while all students living west of C Street were to attend the new Mather School. Enrollment at the Hawes School soon became so great, however, that the dividing line was changed to D Street. Indeed, by 1849 these two South Boston grammar schools had become so crowded that more schoolhouses were clearly needed. The first to go up was the Bigelow School, a brick structure on the corner of E and Fourth Streets, designed exclusively for girls and named in honor of the incumbent mayor of Boston, John P. Bigelow. A few years later, the Lawrence School on Broadway was moved to a new four-story brick building on the corner of Third and B Streets. This handsome new structure was formally dedicated on March 17, 1857—the anniversary of the Evacuation of Boston—with prayer, pomp and ceremony to mark what was regarded as the latest step in the educational and cultural progress of the district.

The rapid increase in the number of churches and schools in South Boston during the 1820s and 1830s reflected a characteristic American devotion to the moral values of religion and the cultural advantages of education. Similarly, the appearance of a remarkable number of medical and correctional facilities in the area during this same period showed the growing concern with serious social and communal problems. The actual selection of South Boston itself as the site for these facilities, however, derived in great part from its geographical location and its environmental advantages.

On February 23, 1822, Governor John Brooks officially approved an act "establishing the City of Boston" under the direction of a mayor, an eight-person board of aldermen, and a forty-eight-person common council. With this transformation of Boston from an old-fashioned town to a more up-to-date city, a number of the city's more aristocratic leaders once again became active in local political affairs and also turned their attention to new forms of humanitarian enterprise. The Brahmins had always provided philanthropic support for what they regarded as good and noble causes—Harvard College, the Boston Athenaeum, the Massachusetts Historical Society, the New England Genealogical Society and the like. After the War of 1812 had demolished their party, a younger generation of Federalists like Josiah Quincy and Harrison Gray Otis sought to reestablish themselves as the natural leaders of Boston. They continually emphasized the responsibility of the "happy and respectable classes" to safeguard the interests of the working classes and the "less prosperous portions of the community." Sickness, disease, mental illness, blindness, poverty, alcoholism and prison reform now attracted the time, talents and attention of city leaders.

In these endeavors, South Boston played a significant role. Town authorities had already seen the advantages of the peninsula's fresh salt air and broad expanses of green pasture when they established a special hospital there in 1792 to isolate smallpox patients and those who had submitted to inoculation. Prominent Bostonians continued to show an interest in the physical attractions of the district, and in the years that followed a number of well-known institutions appeared in South Boston. One was the famous Perkins Institute for the Blind, established by Dr.

Samuel Gridley Howe and originally located at the Pearl Street residence
of Colonel Thomas Handasyd Perkins, who had donated his estate to
the cause. Early in 1839 the Mount Washington House on the corner
of Broadway and H Street in South Boston, a structure built only a few
years earlier as a hotel at a cost of over $100,000, was offered to the
trustees of the Perkins Institute in exchange for the estate on Pearl Street.
The hotel investors proposed an even exchange of the land and building
on the in-town Boston site for the lot on which the Mount Washington
House stood, along with all the buildings. The exchange was agreed
upon, and in May 1839 the clients were removed from one site to the
other, with the moving expenses paid by the private contributions of
Samuel Appleton and several other prominent Boston gentlemen. From
that time on, the Perkins Institute became a well-known feature of the
South Boston landscape, frequently visited by people from other parts
of the country and from many parts of Europe who observed the various
mechanical experiments Dr. Howe used in educating blind persons and
who marveled at the progress he had made with Laura Bridgman, a
child born without hearing or sight. In 1849 a large, three-story workshop
was erected adjacent to the main building where clients could be provided with occupational training in such skills as furniture upholstery,
mattress stuffing and the manufacture of a particular kind of fiber mat
which became a popular item of sale. In 1862, while Dr. Howe was
director of this South Boston institution, his wife, Julia Ward Howe,
at the request of President Abraham Lincoln, put new words to an old
drinking song the Union soldiers were using to sing about John Brown's
body and called it the "Battle Hymn of the Republic."

Dr. Howe was also named superintendent of what was called the
Massachusetts School for Idiots, a residential facility in the City Point
section of South Boston that accommodated some fifty retarded and emo-
tionally disturbed young people ranging from seven to fifteen years of
age. Under Dr. Howe's direction, the clients followed a carefully
regimented program, rising at 5:30 each morning, eating breakfast at
6:30, dinner at noon, and supper at 5:00, with a period set aside every
day for exercises in a gymnasium located in a separate building. In between, the clients attended school classes for a total of six hours a day.
Those who were educable were taught the basics of reading, writing
and speech; those with more limited abilities were instructed in "form,
color and size." The girls were also given lessons in needlework.

Already famous throughout the world for his involvement in liberal
causes and his pioneering efforts on behalf of handicapped people, Dr.

Howe made his home for a number of years in South Boston with Julia and his children, four girls and a boy. They lived in an old colonial home with a large new addition on four and a half acres of land at the end of Story Street (a dead-end lane off G Street) not far from the Perkins Institute. The household also included a gardener, a cook, a governess, a nurse and several servant girls. It was a happy and lively home they called Green Peace. While Julia played the piano, taught the children all kinds of songs in all kinds of languages or supervised small family recitals and plays, her celebrated husband worked in the garden, pruned the fruit trees, tended the roses or greeted the procession of important visitors who came from all over the world to visit the social reformer.

One of the last major medical institutions erected in South Boston in the decades before the Civil War was the Carney Hospital. Andrew Carney, an Irish-born businessman and philanthropist who had helped build the new Holy Cross Cathedral and Boston College in the South End of the city, purchased the J. Hall Howe Estate on Dorchester Heights in South Boston for $13,500 and converted what had been a frame house into a hospital building. The hospital fell on bad days when Carney died quite suddenly in 1864; it was discovered that he had not signed a codicil to his will that would have endowed the hospital he had built. The task of maintaining the hospital fell to Sister Ann Alexis, Sister Ann Aloysia and the other members of the Daughters of Charity, St. Vincent de Paul, who staffed the institution. For nearly four years these nuns begged daily in the streets of Boston for enough money and food to keep the hospital open and the patients fed. Archbishop John Williams finally heard about their plight and sponsored a charity bazaar that realized the enormous sum of twenty-five thousand dollars. The Sisters constructed a new four-story hospital building capable of housing more than 100 bed-patients. Despite almost constant financial problems, the Carney Hospital continued to grow in size and reputation, and became a landmark in South Boston until well into the twentieth century.

In addition to serving as a site for these private hospitals and training schools, South Boston also became the location for a number of public institutions. The first of these was a facility for the poor. Since colonial days, the care of Boston's poor and homeless had been the responsibility of a popularly elected Board of Overseers of the Poor. This board either gave sums of money (called "out-of-door" relief) directly to those who remained at home with their families, or provided shelter in an almshouse for those who were homeless, destitute or disabled. Questions about the proper approach to poor relief began to rise during the early 1800s as the population of Boston increased dramatically, as the first wave of immigrants made their appearance felt, and as local tax rates rose perceptibly. Between 1801 and 1820, reports showed that treasury payments for the care of paupers had already gone up 60 percent. Many public officials felt the time had come to review old policies. In his role as chairman of a special committee to study poor relief in Boston, state representative Josiah Quincy called for an end to "indiscriminate charity" and the start of what he regarded as a more sensible approach to public welfare. While he was content to extend municipal charity to what he called the "impotent poor"—infants, the aged, the sick, the disabled—he recommended that the so-called "able poor" be required to work for their keep at a facility he called a "house of industry." The results of their labor would help defray city costs. In this way, Quincy boasted, the town would be able to separate the "respectable and honest poor" from the "idle and vicious" elements of the community.

The town accepted Quincy's report and voted to establish such a house of industry according to his recommendations. Deer Island was first considered as a site, but eventually South Boston was selected as more agreeable and much more accessible. This would put the institution only two and a half miles from the center of Boston by land, and only one and a half miles by water. For their purposes, the town leaders purchased a tract of fifty-three acres of land in the City Point section, running from the corner of L and Fourth Streets to the corner of O and Fourth. After Josiah Quincy was elected as Boston's second mayor in 1823, he proceeded to sell off the old almshouse on Leverett Street near the Charles River, and by 1825 he had completed moving the poor and unfortunate inmates to the new house of industry in South Boston. In coming years, the tract known as the City Lands became the site of a cluster of large brick institutions that included the original house of industry, along with a poorhouse, a lunatic asylum, a house of correction for adults found guilty of misdemeanors and a separate house of reformation for juvenile offenders.

As the number of people in the district continued to increase, however, and as the population began to move closer to the City Point area, local residents came to resent the construction of so many institutional structures in what had formerly been a pastoral expanse of grazing lands, fruitful orchards and lovely houses. A formal expression of this resentment demonstrated the district's emerging spirit of political solidarity. When South Boston had first become part of the Town of Boston back in 1804, it was made part of Ward 12, which consisted of substantial parts of the South End as well. Although Boston was transformed from a town to a city in 1822, South Boston continued to remain politically linked to the South End. There was little love lost between the residents of these two districts, and trouble flared into the open when a meeting was called to nominate four representatives to the newly formed common council. The South Boston residents felt that they should have at least two of the four councilmen; the South Enders argued that South Boston should get only one. When the controversy could not be resolved, both groups went into the elections supporting four-man slates of candidates from their respective districts. The South Enders succeeded in electing all four of their candidates for the council, much to the chagrin of the South Boston people, who found themselves totally unrepresented.

Over the course of the next decade, however, South Boston became so thickly settled that the district was able to send a member of its own to the council, even though the position involved certain risks. On Thursday evening, February 14, 1833, Josiah Dunham, the representative from South Boston, arrived in Boston to attend a council meeting at Faneuil Hall. He left his horse and sleigh at a stable in the rear of the Mansion House Hotel on Milk Street with a man who identified himself as the hostler. When the council meeting adjourned about 9:00 P.M., Mr. Dunham called for his horse and sleigh—only to find them gone and the hostler nowhere in sight. Not only did the owners of the stable deny any knowledge of the affair, they also laughed at the poor man's embarrassing predicament. He was finally obliged, according to a newspaper account, "to proceed home on foot." A few years later, city authorities finally agreed that the peninsula had become large enough to form a separate ward. On December 10, 1838, South Boston became Ward 12, and its citizens were allowed to elect four members to the city's common council.

In 1847, indicating that their sense of political expression was beginning to take root, residents of South Boston sent a strongly worded "Memorial" to the mayor, the aldermen and the common council complaining that the leaders of Boston were turning their district into a dumping ground for the impoverished and the disabled—another "Botany Bay" they called it, after the infamous British penal colony in Australia. The politicians, they claimed, were forcing into the peninsula those establishments that the city fathers themselves would look upon as "nuisances" if they were put into "the neighborhood of their own private dwellings." Signed by prominent members of Ward 12 with such obviously Yankee names as Cranston Howe, Samuel Perkins, Isaac Adams, Seth Adams and Joseph Smith, the memorial reflected the concerns of a predominantly Yankee leadership that looked forward to developing a quiet, solid, conservative middle-class community of its own. Although later in the nineteenth century the residents would force several of the facilities to move to Deer Island and other locations, for the time being it looked as though they would continue to be a permanent part of the peninsula. At this point, the direction of South Boston seemed pretty well defined for the future, but the unexpected arrival of large numbers of foreign immigrants would make unique and unexpected changes in those plans.

If the colonial period, with its celebrated victory at Dorchester Heights as its focal point, had established a sense of South Boston as a uniquely patriotic community, the early national period established another important theme in the district's history. As the community struggled to develop its new political identity after its annexation to Boston in 1804, it began to resent what it saw as indifference and neglect on the part of Boston authorities regarding the needs and desires of South Boston residents. Congregationalists on the peninsula had been obliged to build their own place of worship; Baptists had to fight against being swallowed up by the larger in-town church. Even after annexation, parents were forced to maintain their own schools when the school committee ignored their petitions for financial support. After the city had constructed a cluster of hospitals, reformatories, poor houses, asylums and other public buildings on choice lands in the area, this resentment spilled over into the memorial of 1847 that summarized a long list of complaints against the city government. This notion of independent action in the face of municipal neglect, this resentful spirit of "us against them," was a theme that would continue on through the long history of the community and help explain episodes in that history when residents of South Boston would fail to cooperate with city authorities or withhold their support from municipal projects.

2

THE
IMMIGRANT TIDE

T HE STEADY RISE IN SOUTH BOSTON'S POPULATION DURING THE late 1830s and early 1840s was in good part due to the movement of Irish immigrants into the peninsula district. Contrary to early accounts, many people from Ireland arrived in New England long before the Great Famine of the mid-nineteenth century. Shipping records, passenger lists, town records, church registers and graveyard epitaphs during the colonial period list family names that are distinctly Irish. By far the greatest number of Irish immigrants during the eighteenth century came from the northern regions, descendants of Scottish settlers planted in Ulster by the English monarchs. As dissenting Protestants, mostly Presbyterians, they were not only despised by the Catholics of Ireland but also discriminated against by loyal Anglicans. Suffering from high rents, repressive taxes and periodic famines, these Ulster Scots started to leave Ireland in large numbers during the early 1700s. By the end of the century an estimated 200,000 to 250,000 Scotch-Irish had entered America.

Yet shipping records and passenger lists also show that a significant number of immigrants left Ireland from such ports farther south as Waterford, Cork and Dublin. Most of these emigrants undoubtedly started out as Roman Catholics, but the majority soon turned to the religion of the colony in which they found themselves. This was particularly true in New England, where "papists" were not only denied liberties extended to most other settlers, but were also subjected to penalties similar to the Penal Laws already in force throughout the British Isles.

In Massachusetts especially, Catholics were placed under unusually severe limitations, and their priests were subject to life imprisonment if found in the colony—and to death if they tried to escape. In most cases, immigrants from southern parts of Ireland during the 1700s were poor and hard-working. Since money was scarce, most people were unable to pay for their transportation across the Atlantic, so many were "bound out" as indentured servants under an agreement to work off the cost of their passage when they got to America. Among those recorded on the passenger lists were artisans, masons, bricklayers, carpenters, tailors, shoemakers, stonecutters, hatters, weavers and blacksmiths, as well as husbandmen, farmhands and common laborers. Some of the women were described as cooks, dressmakers, seamstresses and household servants. Marriage license records of the time show that Irish men and women usually ended up with Congregational partners, and town records indicate that the children of such marriages were brought up in the prevailing religion.

It was not until the War for Independence produced a treaty of friendship and alliance with France that people in Boston began to assume a more tolerant attitude toward foreigners in general and Catholics in particular. Numbering perhaps a hundred, mostly French and Irish, Boston Catholics felt free enough to attend Mass in public in the years after the Revolution in a former Huguenot chapel on School Street in Boston, just off Washington Street. In 1799, when the lease on the old chapel was about to expire, the Catholics purchased a site on nearby Franklin Street for their own place of worship. Here, on St. Patrick's Day, March 17, 1800, ground was broken for the first Roman Catholic church in Boston—the Church of the Holy Cross. This became a cathedral in 1808 when the popular French priest, Fr. Jean Louis de Cheverus, was appointed as the first Bishop of Boston.

Although the number of Catholics in Boston slowly increased over the course of the next decade, they were still small enough in numbers, and productive enough in the services they provided, to insure their continued toleration. Many of the French, for example, served as skilled watchmakers, candy-makers, cooks, caterers, waiters, musicians and dancing teachers. The Irish usually functioned as blacksmiths, wheelwrights, bakers, tavern-keepers, marketmen, shoemakers, tailors and clothiers. With the end of the War of 1812, however, and especially after the collapse of grain prices in the wake of Napoleon's defeat in 1815, the landlords in Ireland sought to sustain their prosperous wartime incomes by jacking up rents to impossible levels, or converting their fields into larger tillage holdings or pastureland for the grazing of cattle. This preemptive postwar land policy markedly accelerated large-scale emigration of bankrupt tenant farmers and displaced laborers from all parts of Ireland, but especially from the southern and western counties. From 1825 through 1830, upwards of 125,000 people emigrated from Ireland to the United States—an average of twenty thousand a year. Over thirty thousand of these arrivals came to the state of Massachusetts, and by 1830 the Irish-Catholic population in Boston alone had swollen to over eight thousand, double that of only five years earlier.

The sheer number of Irish Catholics coming to the city during the 1820s and 1830s was frightening enough; the numerous social and economic problems they helped intensify caused even greater alarm among established inhabitants, whose recently acquired veneer of religious and ethnic tolerance was already beginning to wear thin. Certainly the issues of poverty, unemployment and religion played a very great part in the rapid deterioration of relations between the immigrants and the native population of the city. When the War of 1812 had threatened to wipe out the commercial basis of the entire New England economy, Boston entrepreneurs managed to salvage their financial fortunes by diverting their idle capital into the manufacturing of cotton textiles. This move to industrialization established a much more healthy and diversified basis for the region's economic structure, but it only further complicated an already difficult labor situation for the central city. Since water was the only source of natural power capable of operating looms and spindles before the advent of the steam engine, factories had to be constructed in such outlying areas as Waltham, Lowell and Lawrence, where adequate waterpower sites were available. This created jobs for the daughters of farm families in the rural areas of Massachusetts, but it left the city of Boston itself with few economic opportunities for the large numbers of unskilled workers now coming in from Ireland.

With little money, few skills and no prospects of meaningful labor, most of the newcomers moved in with friends and relatives in congested districts along Boston's waterfront, close to the docks and wharves, the shops and markets, the countinghouses and stores, and the workshops and stables, where unskilled men found occasional work and extra scraps of food. Forced to rely for a time upon the assistance of such private groups as their own Charitable Irish Society, or upon the more substantial support of local municipal agencies, unemployed Irish Catholics were viewed with growing resentment by the natives of the city. The newcomers were denounced as "lazy paupers" or "vicious criminals" who would flood the almshouses, the poorhouses and the jails, raising the tax rates and lowering the moral standards of the entire city.

By the late 1820s Boston newspapers were carrying regular reports of the extensive damage being done by roving gangs of local toughs who repeatedly invaded the Irish sections of town—Broad Street, Pond Street, Merrimac Street, Ann Street—breaking windows, damaging homes, looting shops and beating up Irish workmen. In August 1834, the community was shocked when a mob of local workmen smashed their way into the Ursuline convent in Charlestown and burned the structure to the ground. Three years later, on June 11, 1837, a company of Yankee firemen, returning from a call, clashed with a Catholic funeral procession in the Irish section of town along Broad Street. The resulting fistfight eventually mushroomed into a full-scale riot involving some ten thousand people. The so-called Broad Street Riot was finally brought to a halt only when Mayor Samuel Eliot brought in eight hundred of the state militia with fixed bayonets, headed by a mounted force of National Lancers. It was obvious that relations between the native population of the city and the new immigrant settlers would soon reach the breaking point.

It was at this stage that many Irish—hard-pressed for living space and desperate for work—began to notice the potential advantages of the good-sized peninsula just across the channel. Fast becoming a prime site for heavy industry and manufacturing, South Boston was especially attractive to unemployed immigrant workers. The Dix and Brinley Chemical Works had been established near A Street in the early 1800s, and during the same period a skilled metallurgist named Cyrus Alger located an iron works on Fourth Street near the Dover Street bridge. At first, workmen commuted in rowboats across the channel from Boston to avoid paying the tolls across the South Bridge. Later they formed a settlement of their own on the South Boston side, living in William Tudor's tenements on A Street. Despite the economic slowdown throughout New England caused by the War of 1812, local industrial production continued, and during the course of the war a Britisher named Thomas Cains started up an establishment for the manufacture of flintware—the first flint-glass factory in the United States. Located on the corner of B and Second Streets, Cains's Phoenix Glass Works (so called because although the buildings of the plant burned down with annoying regularity, new buildings were always erected on the ashes of the old site) specialized in tableware, chemical apparatus and apothecaries' supplies. After the war, the manufacture of quality glass products became a major industry in South Boston as the Phoenix Glass Works was joined by the American Flint Glass Works and the Mount Washington Glass Works, which all together employed over three hundred workmen.

In addition to the glassworks, the chemical works and Alger's rapidly expanding ironworks, several other manufacturing establishments came to be located in South Boston. In 1836 the Adams Printing Press and Machine Shop began operations in the district, turning out not only fine printing presses but also steam engines and boilers. In October 1844, the *Boston Pilot* announced that it had purchased a new printing press from the "manufactory" of Isaac Adams, Esq., of South Boston for the sum of $1,600, pronouncing it to be "a splendid machine." The Fulton Iron Works, also incorporated in 1836 and specializing in building steamships for the United States government, was reputed to have one of the most efficient plants of its kind in the country. The Loring Works specialized in producing stationary and marine engines and boilers; the Bay State Iron Company, located at City Point, manufactured railroad iron; and the Globe Locomotive Works began operations in 1846. Besides these heavy industries, there was a varied collection of smaller enterprises in South Boston, including a brewery, a wagon factory, a plow factory, a leadworks, two soup factories and two ropewalks.

The construction of ships, both commercial vessels and pleasure craft, also became a prominent part of the South Boston economy. As early as 1822, Captain Noah Brooks established his shipyard at the foot of F Street. In 1847, at their yard at the northern end of K Street, the Briggs brothers began work on clipper ships that would gain national fame for their speed in setting passage records throughout the world. The *Northern Light*, launched in South Boston in 1851, became famous for making the fastest passage from Boston to San Francisco, covering the distance around Cape Horn in only seventy-six days. Many years later, South Boston-built ships would sail the seven seas and carry on trade with major ports throughout the world.

The development of so many and such varied industries so close to where they lived was obviously a powerful attraction to the increasing number of Irish immigrants packed into the waterfront area of the old city with no prospects of work of any kind except cutting fish and sweeping stables. In 1826 the state legislature approved plans for the construction of the new North Free Bridge, which went directly from the heart of the city into South Boston, greatly facilitating the almost in-evitable movement of the Irish across the channel into South Boston. By the 1830s, with two bridges available to them—one from the South End, and one from the North End—the Irish began to move into South Boston in ever-increasing numbers. Several prosperous businessmen and retired gentlemen had earlier sought out the pleasant rural environs of South Boston, settling in fashionable residences along East Broad-way and City Point, but most of the new inhabitants were Irish im-migrants. Some were small businessmen, middle-class shopkeepers or skilled craftsmen who had left Ireland because there were few outlets for their talents and ambitions. Others were laborers, mechanics or sim-ple day laborers who moved into the area bounded by Broadway, C Street, Fourth Street and the Dorchester Turnpike, close to the factories, glassworks and foundries.

Since an increasing number of the Irish moving across the channel into South Boston by the early 1800s were Roman Catholics, it was obvious that plans would have to be made for the preservation of their religious faith. Catholic priests were interested in the area at least as early as June 12, 1802, when Abraham Gould and his wife, the former Susanna Foster, sold Father Jean Louis de Cheverus a piece of land "on or near Nook Hill lying in South Boston" for the sum of four hun-dred dollars. According to the deed, this property was located between lower Fifth and Sixth Streets. Just what Fr. Cheverus planned for the land is not at all clear, although one historian suggests he may have wanted to construct a small school similar to the one later opened by the Ursuline nuns in nearby Charlestown. But Fr. Cheverus's main con-cern at the time was working with his friend and fellow curate, Fr. Fran-cois Matignon, to complete work on the Church of the Holy Cross on Franklin Street, which was finally dedicated in 1803.

When Matignon died unexpectedly in September 1818, Cheverus had his friend's body placed in the Old Granary Burying Ground on Tre-mont Street, in a tomb belonging to a prominent Catholic layman named John Magner. Up to this time, Catholics were buried alongside their Protestant neighbors in such local cemeteries as the Granary Burying Ground, Copp's Hill in the North End or the Central Burying Ground on Boston Common. Bishop Cheverus, however, took steps to move Fr. Matignon's body to a more appropriate site. In November 1818, the Board of Health of the Town of Boston gave permission to "that group of Christians known as Roman Catholics" to erect a cemetery of their own in the South Boston peninsula. Fr. Philip Lariscy, an energetic Irish Augustinian who had come down to Boston from the Canadian provinces, began a campaign to raise money to buy land in the district on which to build a tomb for the remains of Fr. Matignon. Through his efforts, Fr. Lariscy was able to raise $680 for the purchase of the uppermost portion of the land at the corner of Dorchester Street and Sixth Street. More than two hundred parishioners of Boston's Holy Cross Cathedral subscribed to the new cemetery and made arrangements to transfer the bodies of a number of Catholic relatives and friends buried in local cemeteries to the new Catholic burial ground in South Boston.

Almost three months to the day of his death, the body of Fr. Matignon was taken from the Old Granary Burying Ground to its final resting place in South Boston. A procession of more than a thousand persons attended the cortege as it made its way from Tremont Street through the south end of the town, and then crossed over the South Bridge at Dover Street into South Boston. The remains of the French priest were placed in a large vault standing above the ground, covered with a heavy marble slab, and then consecrated by Bishop Cheverus. "The services, in the open air, were very impressive," commented the *Columbian Centinel*, "and the assemblage of members of the church and citizens large." "We learn," added the paper, "that the land cost over $500."

The successful fund-raising activities of Fr. Lariscy enabled Bishop Cheverus also to build a mortuary chapel in the cemetery the following year, just behind Fr. Matignon's tomb. On July 4, 1819, Cheverus blessed the small chapel, measuring only eighteen by thirty feet, and named it in honor of St. Augustine, founder of Fr. Lariscy's order. Constructed of hard-burned brick, cruciform in shape, with a slate roof and high Gothic windows, the chapel is believed to be the oldest Gothic-style building in New England. There have been suggestions that the famous Boston architect, Charles Bulfinch, who had already donated plans for the construction of the Holy Cross Church on Franklin Street, provided the design. As the Irish population in South Boston gradually increased, the little chapel was used more and more for Sunday Mass whenever a priest could be spared from his duties at the in-town church. To accommodate the growing number of parishioners, Bishop Fenwick authorized an enlargement of the tiny burial chapel from thirty to seventy-six feet in length, although he kept the width of the structure at its original eighteen feet. The new St. Augustine chapel, equipped with sacristies and choir, was formally dedicated on October 16, 1831.

But one small chapel was not enough. When Benedict Fenwick, Boston's second Catholic bishop, came to South Boston in July 1841 to administer the sacrament of Confirmation, he found the small chapel at St. Augustine's cemetery "crowded to suffocation." Buying a site on lower Broadway between the turnpike (now Dorchester Avenue) and A Street, only a short distance from where most of the laborers lived, Fenwick authorized the construction of a new church. The cornerstone of this new edifice was laid on July 27, 1843, after a procession marched from St. Augustine's chapel to the site of the new church on West Broadway accompanied by a "splendid band of music." Two years later, the church was completed and dedicated to Saints Peter and Paul. At a cost of sixty-four thousand dollars the Gothic structure had a seating capacity of one thousand, and was one of the handsomest churches in New England. In this respect, South Boston was a microcosm of a Church that had started out with no places of worship and few members, but which had grown with amazing speed in the course of a single generation. Even though the Boston diocese had lost ten thousand Catholics when Connecticut and Rhode Island were detached in 1844, there were still nearly seventy thousand Catholics in the remaining four New England states of the huge diocese. The city of Boston was clearly the most populous urban center, however, with nearly thirty-five thousand registered Catholics—most of them from Ireland.

Despite the growing number of people coming into Boston from the southern parts of Ireland, until 1835, according to Oscar Handlin, Ulster (particularly county Tyrone) was still the principal source of emigrants. Most of those who arrived in the early nineteenth century were displaced artisans and fairly well-to-do farmers—"in general, the wealthiest elements of the population." The balance would not shift until ten years later, when the larger waves of emigrants came from the counties in the south and west of Ireland, especially Cork, Kerry, Galway and Clare. These were the "poorest peasants," assisted in making the transatlantic crossing by the bounty of others. "From this group above all," declares Handlin, "Boston got its immigrants."

This change is refelcted in the patterns of immigration into South Boston. In the decades before the Great Famine, the number of Irish laborers and workmen coming into South Boston was small compared with the number of Irishmen of middle-class occupations who established themselves in the district as persons of some means and prominence. Of the six physicians ministering to the people of South Boston, Dr. C. B. O'Donnell, with an office at the corner of B and Fourth Streets, was one of the most highly respected. His colleague, Dr. Dennis McGowan, a druggist as well as a physician, had an apothecary shop on the corner of Broadway and the Dorchester Turnpike, and advertised regularly in the pages of the *Boston Pilot*, the Catholic weekly. Thomas Murray was the first Catholic undertaker in South Boston, and he also maintained the first Catholic bookstore, on Boston's Cornhill. He had come to Boston from Ireland in 1810, was enrolled as a funeral director in 1817, and was appointed sexton of St. Augustine's chapel in 1819. At a time when there were only a handful of houses in the City Point area, Murray built himself a home on the north side of East Fourth Street, between O and P Streets, where Bishop Cheverus was a frequent visitor. Not too far from Murray's fine house was an entire block of greenhouses, running from M to N Streets, between Fourth and Fifth. These were owned by a well-known horticulturalist named William McCullough who in 1847 was placed in charge of the Boston Public Gardens. McCullough's greenhouses were certainly "worth a visit," wrote the *South Boston Gazette*. "The old gentleman is so polite that half an hour may be spent very agreeably with him, and then you can purchase such a beautiful bouquet!"

Patrick Lally, who had come over from Ireland in 1825, was one of the earliest successful Irish businessmen in South Boston. After learning the blacksmith trade at the Hinckley Locomotive Works, he was able to purchase a blacksmith and wheelwright business of his own within a few years. His machine shop at the corner of Dorchester Turnpike and First Street soon grew into such a prosperous manufacturing enterprise that during the Civil War he supplied the United States government with gun carriages and paddle arms for war vessels. Other early businessmen of Irish descent in the peninsula included J. W. Sullivan, the only cigar-maker in the district; John Kirkpatrick, who owned a dry-goods store on Fourth Street between A Street and Dorchester Turnpike; Thomas O'Malley, who operated a tailor and drapery shop on Fourth Street; and C. Cunningham, who ran a blacksmith shop on the corner of the Turnpike and Second Street.

The middle-class character of South Boston was obvious in the memorial residents presented to the City of Boston in 1847 complaining about the way the city was turning their district into another "Botany Bay" with construction of public institutions. In the course of this formal letter, residents drew attention to the remarkable progress of their district, the prosperity of their citizens, and the amount of taxes they paid regularly to the city government. They demanded paved streets, more public squares, better lighting, more adequate police protection, a fresh water supply, and similar public improvements. The people of South Boston, the Memorial emphasized, were not "scum, thrown out from purer material." On the contrary, they were a community of "intelligent and respectable persons of narrow means, but independent spirits, who wished to dwell in their own houses and have elbow room about them and pure air to breathe, and a wide prospect to enjoy." Furthermore, the petitioners boasted, there was not "a single colored family" in the entire district, and not as many "foreigners" as in other wards of the city. And those foreigners who did reside in South Boston were, for the most part, of that "better class" of immigrants who did not remain content to "live in cellars, or congregate together in order to keep warm"—an unkind reference to those poor immigrants who lived packed together along the polluted waterfront in Boston.

Except for a rather steady diet of crude "paddy" jokes the *South Boston Gazette* ran in a weekly column called "The Junk Shop," which ridiculed the Irishman as a dull bumpkin given to drinking and fighting, there is little evidence to indicate that the early Irish had not been accepted into the everyday life of the local community. They purchased homes, operated small businesses, went to the polls, attended whist parties, took part in the dances that were so popular during the summer months, and joined in sleigh rides during the winter. They participated in civic celebrations, became members of local military associations, and joined in volunteer social organizations of various kinds. Men signed up with the Pulaski Guards, the local military organization, while women joined the South Boston Samaritan Society, which "sought to relieve all the suffering poor of the district."

The Boston Irish also tried to keep in close touch with developments back in Ireland and subscribed to the *Boston Pilot* for getting reliable information not only about religious matters, but also about political events, agricultural reports and shipping news. Of particular interest during the early 1840s was the struggle of the famous Irish patriot Daniel O'Connell to obtain a greater measure of justice for Ireland by forcing Great Britain to repeal the Act of Union (the 1801 act that merged the two kingdoms) and reestablish an independent parliament for the Irish people. Along with their fellow countrymen, both in Ireland and in other parts of the United States, the Boston Irish followed this "Repeal" movement very closely, and on June 8, 1841, a notice appeared in the *Boston Pilot* announcing that a meeting of the Repealers of South Boston would be held at Harding's Hall on the corner of Fourth Street and the Turnpike. At this meeting, marked by "exuberant patriotism and high-souled firmness of purpose," forty-one persons, representing seventeen of the thirty-three counties of Ireland, contributed a total of thirty-seven dollars to the cause of Repeal, an average donation of about a dollar per person—a generous sum considering that many of these people were earning no more than eighty cents a day. A list of the contributors and their home counties showed that county Wexford was most heavily represented, with nine Repealers claiming it as their place of origin. This distribution underlines the middle-class character of the early pre-Famine population of the district, since Wexford not only had a strong tradition of political activity, but was also a southeastern county whose people were generally better educated, more Anglicized, and more prosperous than in most western counties at the time. At subsequent meetings of what was soon formalized as the South Boston Repealers' Association, county Wexford continued to dominate the membership list, although Cork, Longford, Kilkenny and Tipperary—some of the less industrialized, potato-dependent counties in the south and west of Ireland—had strong representations as well.

Interest in the Repeal movement in South Boston reached its peak at the July 1843 meeting of the association when the sum of ninety-one dollars was collected from over 100 members—twenty-three of whom were women. That the Repealers were allowed to hold their meetings in the Free Will Baptist Meetinghouse on the corner of C and Fourth Streets indicates some measure of the tolerance for the Irish that still existed. After 1843, however, with the arrest and imprisonment of Daniel O'Connell, interest in the Repeal movement began to decline. Although a group of young militant nationalists, members of a group called "Young Ireland," attempted to take over the movement when it became clear that O'Connell's health was shattered beyond repair, the Boston Irish could not generate the same degree of enthusiasm for the cause. Collections fell off badly, membership started to dwindle, and many Irish turned their attention to more immediate problems and issues among their own people.

One issue that occupied much of the time and energy of the early Irish inhabitants of South Boston was intemperate drinking. As early as the sixteenth century, travelers through the British Isles invariably commented upon the hunger, deprivation and grinding poverty of the malnourished and half-naked peasants of Ireland. Without fail, visitors expressed shock at the crippling effect of drunkenness on the lives and society of these poor people. In recent years, scholars have attempted to analyze the various factors that contributed to making alcohol such an unusual part of Irish culture. Economists emphasize the depressing aspects of a rural society in which there was a minimum of land, a scarcity of work and a woeful lack of incentive. Sociologists point out the behavioral influences of a society where the shortage of land discouraged early marriage, where the sexes were carefully separated, and where male bonding was encouraged by horseplay and drinking. And historians underline the serious consequences of what one writer has called the "creeping Anglicization" of the late eighteenth and early nineteenth centuries. Throughout many parts of Ireland, the growing distinction between the poorer classes, which clung to the Irish language and traditional customs, and the more affluent classes, which adopted the English language and a more rational worldview, produced a general feeling of discouragement and malaise among the depressed people of the Irish-speaking counties in the west. Confined to shacks on barren land, regarded by many English-speaking easterners with contempt, they could not compete economically, function socially or succeed academically. In his *Emigrants and Exiles*, Kerby Miller suggests that the resulting "cultural demoralization" of this process may well help explain why in the 1820s and 1830s whiskey drinking among the poor people of Ireland appeared to have assumed almost "pathological proportions."

To a great extent, Irish emigrants brought their traditional drinking habits with them when they came to America. In short order, grog shops, barrooms and saloons sprang up in the East Coast cities populated by the Irish. Boston felt the impact almost immediately. In 1846 the city had 850 licensed liquor dealers; in 1849, only three years later, there were 1,200 dealers, most of whom were Irish. The following year, Boston's mayor reported that two-thirds of the local grog shops were owned by the Irish, and that almost half of those shops were concentrated in the North End and Fort Hill.

Conditions in America increased the Irish propensity for drinking. The saloon was "the poor man's club," a transfer of the familiar pub that had always played such an important role in Irish country life. It was one way of humanizing the cold and impersonal urban environment. For emigrants without work, money or status, the saloon was the social center of the neighborhood, a meetingplace where the talk, camaraderie, songs, stories and brogue were friendly and familiar. It was a place where a poor, tired Irishman could go, rest his bones, forget about his problems and obtain a few hours of joy and laughter. And in most American cities, the saloon was also a key center of political activity—a veritable "political powerhouse." Party leaders recruited new voters, indoctrinated inexperienced ward-heelers, and prepared newcomers for eventual citizenship. Bartenders handed out application forms for naturalization, provided free legal advice, and loaned money to those in need. In the new world, emigrants found that alcohol was an acceptable, universal and almost essential part of their social and political environment.

In Boston, local Catholic leaders were very aware that frequent intoxication, promoting the unsavory Irish reputation for riotous behavior and criminal activity, posed a serious obstacle to acceptance and assimilation. The *Boston Pilot* constantly warned about the dangers of intemperate drinking among Catholics, and on one occasion described the disgraceful effects of alcohol at some Irish wakes, where crowds of people stood around "drinking and smoking as they would in a common barroom." Just as bad were the hack drivers returning from funerals roaring drunk, driving at a furious, "neck-breaking speed," singing and screaming at the top of their lungs. The road to success, advised the Catholic weekly, was not through talking, singing and dancing, but through hard work, perseverance, prudence and, above all, sobriety. These editorials echoed the sentiments of Bishop John Fitzpatrick, who encouraged temperance and regularly urged members of his flock to become good Americans and to behave in such a manner that other ethnic groups in the city would not be able to sneer at them for being lazy, apathetic or careless. During the 1830s and 1840s, Catholics established a number of temperance societies in Boston and many other East Coast cities where there were substantial numbers of immigrants. Preferring to conduct their own campaigns, with an emphasis on free will and personal abstinence, Catholic temperance leaders tended not to join forces with the various Protestant groups that were increasingly inclined to work for state-legislated prohibition.

The temperance movement found many supporters in South Boston who were obviously influenced by the remarkable work being carried on in Ireland during this period by Father Theobold Mathew, a Capuchin friar who traveled throughout his Irish homeland lecturing on the evils of liquor and administering total abstinence pledges in churches and at huge outdoor rallies. In America, temperance organizations used similar evangelistic techniques, often selecting St. Patrick's Day, with its numerous parties, banquets and celebrations, as an appropriate occasion to demonstrate publicly for abstinence and to persuade men and women to "take the pledge." The *Boston Pilot* reported that on

March 17, 1842, for example, Irish and Catholic temperance societies paraded through the main streets of Boston, marching across the bridge into South Boston where, "in the open air," they listened to an "eloquent Temperance oration" delivered by Father Terence Fitzsimmons, the newly appointed pastor of SS. Peter and Paul Church.

A native of county Cavan, Fr. Fitzsimmons was a vigorous advocate of temperance. He was particularly concerned about the curse of liquor among the laborers who worked in the factories and foundries behind his church. St. Patrick's Day and the Fourth of July were favorite occasions for an "oration" by that "zealous, laborious and indefatigable clergyman and Apostle of Temperance, the Rev. Mr. Fitzsimmons." He also organized special gatherings to promote temperance in South Boston, including the one in November 1842 at which he spoke for two and a half hours tracing the course of "the fruit of the bewitching glass" from pleasure to "remorse to self-abasement" with such dramatic effectiveness that all who were present took a "pledge of total abstinence." "The community at large owes much to this gentleman," commented one parishioner in the pages of the *Boston Pilot* in September 1843. Because of his "untiring zeal and energy," the writer said, more than seven thousand of the "poorer classes" had been able to take the temperance pledge directly from his hands and thus be rescued from the "premature grave of intemperance."

By 1845, then, the early Irish immigrants had come to form a small, cohesive and distinctive part of a peninsula located just across the channel from Boston. What had started out as a quiet, pastoral area with only a handful of rustic settlers had developed into a thriving, bustling community of slightly more than ten thousand residents. In the eastern half of the peninsula, called City Point because it looked out upon the wide expanse of the Atlantic Ocean, a number of well-to-do older families had constructed fashionable residences with attractive lawns, colorful gardens and well-kept orchards. In the western half, closer to the south end of Boston, were the factories, glassworks and foundries for which the district had already become famous, along with small wooden homes, boarding houses and brick tenements, where most of the Irish laborers lived. Although they were occasionally ridiculed because of their national characteristics or religious beliefs, their hard-working contribution to the district's economy (and the rural character of much of the peninsula) allowed the Irish to be accepted into the community without serious problems. Within a year, however, this generally tolerant relationship would change dramatically. Tragic events in Ireland sent shock waves across the Atlantic, setting in motion a series of changes that would permanently affect the future of the Irish in Boston and throughout the world.

When a strange fungus first attacked the potato crop in Ireland during the summer of 1845, most observers, certain it was only a temporary phenomenon, predicted a bountiful harvest the following year. By the summer of 1846, however, the deadly fungus had struck again, and by the fall it had ruined the country's entire crop of potatoes. This was a catastrophe of enormous proportions, because the potato was the absolute mainstay of the Irish diet. Although the farms of Ireland produced large quantities of foodstuffs, dairy products and meat, farmers had to sell these products at market to make enough money to pay the rent and avoid eviction. Because they lived off the potato, anything that endangered that basic crop promised starvation and disease. To make matters worse, during 1846-47 the European continent experienced one of the most terrible winters in recorded history. Drenching rains and icy gales made outdoor work impossible, while driving snowstorms blanketed the fields and closed the roads. Without land to work or money to spend, without food to eat or firewood to burn, the poor people of Ireland began to die by the thousands of hunger, disease and exposure.

To many Irish, there seemed no future, for themselves or for their devastated country. In their helpless desperation, they could see only one possible road to survival—emigration. Before the Famine, leaving Ireland was the most terrible of fates, and the departure of early immigrants was marked by the weeping and wailing of relatives and friends—the dreadful "keening" usually heard at wakes. But the trauma of the Famine years had undermined the traditional faith of the Irish people in the land and utterly destroyed their powers of resistance. They scraped together what money they could, turned their backs on their native soil and headed for a country that would offer them the opportunity denied them in their "doomed and starving land."

By February 1847 what had started out as a steady trickle had taken on all the characteristics of an uncontrollable flood. Reports told of particularly heavy emigration from towns in the southern counties like Sligo, Westport, Galway, Tralee, Bantry, Skibbereen, Kinsale and Wexford. Many left in vessels so poorly outfitted that they were called "coffin ships." By the tens of thousands, the Irish poured into America during the "Black Forties," huddled together as human ballast in the dark, stinking holds of lumber ships. Their small savings completely used up by the price of passage, they landed sick and destitute at Boston and

other East Coast ports, too poor to move on, too desperate to care. In
the single year of 1847, for example, the city of Boston, which had
been absorbing immigrants at the rate of about four or five thousand
a year, was inundated by over thirty-seven thousand new arrivals, most
of whom were officially categorized as "Irish labourers."

The immigrants who had come over during the 1830s and early 1840s
had been physically strong enough to work on the canals, roads and
railways, thus making an important contribution to the region's economic
development. Indeed, many of the pre-Famine immigrants often had
mechanical talents and technical skills that were welcome additions to
the local economy. Most of the "Famine Irish," however, came ashore
pallid and weak, half-starved, disease-ridden and impoverished. Few
had any skills at all, except a most rudimentary knowledge of farming.
There was little they could contribute to the Boston community, and
almost nothing the community could do for them. Boston offered few
economic opportunities to those without skills. At a time when other
American cities were developing industrial centers, manufacturing
outlets, and railroad concentrations capable of employing large numbers
of unskilled workers, Boston's capital investments still remained in such
outlying areas as Waltham, Lowell, Lawrence and Manchester, where
the textile factories had been located earlier in the century. Within the
city itself there was little call for the abundant supply of cheap Irish
labor now at hand. Without the schooling to be clerks, the training to
become craftsmen or the capital to become shopkeepers, the Boston
Irish became, as Oscar Handlin expressed it in his *Boston's Immigrants*,
"a massive lump in the community, undigested and undigestible." Most
men were forced to rely on the meager earnings of their wives, daughters,
and sisters, who worked as domestic servants in the hotels, boarding
houses, and private homes of the city. The income from the women
could tide the men over until they scraped up temporary jobs as day
laborers sweeping streets, tending horses, cleaning stables, unloading
ships, cutting fish or lugging crates.

In addition to a bleak economic picture, Irish Catholics also faced
a social climate that was definitely and unabashedly hostile. Boston was
already an old city in 1845, with more than two centuries of history
and tradition. In confronting this new wave of immigration, the native
community responded in ways that were uniquely different from most
other urban centers of the period. For one thing, the city's Brahmin
aristocracy was understandably proud of its distinctive past and fierce-
ly determined to fight against any changes that could threaten its future.

Boston had retained its distinctively Anglo-Saxon-Protestant character long after eastern cities like New York and Philadelphia had become cosmopolitan centers, and newer western cities like St. Louis and Chicago were rapidly absorbing frontiersmen and immigrants. The possibility that Irish Catholics, with their alien culture and detested religious practices, would ever be welcome or even admitted into the exclusive ranks of such a long-established and highly self-conscious social system as existed in Boston was extremely unlikely.

Generating, then, a greater degree of fear and suspicion than ever before, the new wave of Irish immigrants joined their relatives and friends in a largely segregated and isolated community. Most of the newcomers continued to live along the waterfront area of Boston itself, from the Fort Hill district to the North End. But a substantial number also moved across the channel to the South Boston peninsula, which was rapidly increasing in size. The district had fewer than four hundred residents as late as 1810. By 1835 there were nearly six thousand living in South Boston; by 1845 the figure had risen to ten thousand; and by 1855 there were over sixteen thousand people living in the peninsula, a significant number of whom were recent immigrants. Like their fellow countrymen in other parts of the city, the Irish inhabitants of South Boston also suffered from the bigotry of the native population during the late 1840s, as well as the intimidation of the so-called Know-Nothing movement in the early 1850s.

The contempt of many native Bostonians for the newcomers created all sorts of obstacles and annoyances. Those immigrants who had already become citizens were discouraged from exercising their political rights, and more recent arrivals faced the prospect of legislation that would reduce immigration quotas and lengthen the period of residency necessary for naturalization. Catholic priests were forbidden to enter hospitals, poorhouses and other public institutions in South Boston and on Deer Island to comfort the sick and minister to the dying. Children were forced to read Protestant versions of the Bible and recite unfamiliar hymns and prayers at the public schools. Their churches were vandalized, their religious ceremonies disrupted, their convents inspected by local authorities and even their burials subjected to all sorts of petty rules and annoying regulations. In March 1849, for example, Bishop John Fitzpatrick was informed that the sexton of St. Augustine's had received an order from the Board of Health closing the historic cemetery. Claiming that it had received numerous complaints about an oppressive stench emanating from the property because the graves had allegedly not been sunk deeply enough, the board said the cemetery constituted a serious health hazard and banned any more burials in that plot of consecrated ground.

Convinced that these complaints were merely smokescreens for the crafty designs of a few greedy men who wanted to close the cemetery so they could buy up the adjacent property for profitable real-estate speculation, the Bishop sent an indignant letter to the grand jury investigating the case. The South Boston cemetery had been free of trouble since Bishop Cheverus first purchased the small plot of land in 1818, he argued, denying that there had ever been an instance where the depth of a coffin top had been less than three feet from the surface, the current health regulation. Reports to the contrary were "very unjust and exceedingly obnoxious to Catholics," the prelate charged boldly, since all the "old families of Boston" (including his own mother and father) had their graves in that historic cemetery. He recalled that a reported stench from the summer of 1848 had come not from the cemetery itself, but from the carcass of a dead dog that vandals had hidden near the mortuary chapel. He flatly denied any health menace at the South Boston site and insisted that all the graves were in strict compliance with the law. Although he emphasized that he had neither legal nor financial responsibility for the South Boston cemetery, he clearly put the city on notice that he was prepared to use all the powers at his command as Bishop of Boston to protect his people from further illegal harassment.

Although the mayor and the common council finally revoked the order closing St. Augustine's, they still felt it necessary to stipulate that a city inspector be on hand to supervise all burials to certify that all graves were dug to the required depth. Bishop Fitzpatrick claimed that the bills regulating the cemeteries were not being passed to protect the public health or safeguard the public welfare. The real reason, he said, was an attempt to distress and annoy Irish Catholics by Protestants of the city who did not want to have "paddy funerals" passing in front of their fine houses.

On the night of September 7, 1848, flames appeared on the tower of SS. Peter and Paul Church on the western end of Broadway. With most of the firemen across the channel fighting a large fire on Sea Street, the blaze quickly got out of control, and within three hours the structure had been reduced to smoldering ruins. Nearly every house between A and B Streets had its roof set afire by showers of burning embers, and two nearby Protestant churches were also set ablaze by flying sparks. In the current atmosphere of bitterness and tension, many Catholics in

South Boston suspected arson, and although it was finally decided that the fire had been caused by sparks carried through the air from the Sea Street fire, many people maintained their suspicions. The pastor, Fr. Terence Fitzsimmons, took part of his congregation to hear Mass in a hall on Sea Street at the foot of Fourth Street and sent others back to St. Augustine's chapel. Meanwhile, the new young Bishop of Boston, John B. Fitzpatrick, set about the task of rebuilding the church. Fortunately, he had enough insurance on the building to start reconstruction almost immediately, although a prevailing debt reduced his insurance payment to the point where he had little more than eighty thousand dollars with which to work. Nevertheless, he went ahead with the project with great determination.

The process of rebuilding SS. Peter and Paul produced more than just financial problems, however. Apparently judging Fr. Fitzsimmons no longer capable of handling the complicated details of financial investments, insurance claims and construction operations, Bishop Fitzpatrick replaced him with Fr. Patrick Lyndon. Many residents of South Boston were indignant at Fr. Fitzsimmons's removal, and dissension became rampant. The newly appointed pastor was denounced publicly by a group of irate parishioners during Sunday Mass on April 17, 1853. Cooler heads finally prevailed, and further trouble was headed off after a parish committee held a meeting with the bishop, who explained the reasons for his actions. After Fr. Lyndon completed the rebuilding of the church, Bishop Fitzpatrick rededicated it on Thanksgiving Day, November 24, 1853, with the most elaborate ceremonies ever held in the diocese up to that day. But the bishop's troubles were by no means over. A number of pew-owners insisted that their ownership rights carried over to the new church. Bishop Fitzpatrick maintained that their original rights had perished in the fire and did not carry over to the new structure, which had been built with insurance money, not pew money. The parishioners disagreed strongly with the bishop's interpretation, and one of their number brought suit against the Church under the title *Field v. Tighe*. The case was heard in a Court of Justice in January 1854, and a decision was handed down supporting the position of the bishop, although a number of the parishioners fumed for some time.

The social and religious antagonism between Irish Catholics and native Bostonians that raged throughout the 1850s was further fueled by the issue of racism. After William Lloyd Garrison issued his call for the total and immediate emancipation of slaves in 1831, his abolitionist

movement remained for a long time confined to a small group of
dedicated zealots. The conservative Brahmin aristocracy, which still
had strong social and financial ties to the slave-owning, cotton-growing
establishment of the South, held most of the early reformers in contempt. As time went on, however, and especially as slavery followed
the sweep of Manifest Destiny during the 1840s into the vast lands of
the Southwest, the mood of New England became less hostile to abolitionism and much more critical of slavery. The final straw came with
the passage of the Kansas-Nebraska Act in 1854, which allowed slavery
to spread north of the 36° 30' line into the territories of Kansas and
Nebraska. Northerners quickly formed the Republican party to prevent
the further expansion of slavery and preserve the northern lands for
"Free Soil, Free Labor, and Free Men." From that point on, every
week and every month seemed to intensify the opposition of Bostonians
to slavery as an American institution.

Not so with the Irish, however. As newcomers to the American scene,
preoccupied with their own immediate survival, most immigrants had
given little thought to the country's "peculiar institution." They generally
assumed it to be a local phenomenon, officially supported by state laws
and sanctioned by the Constitution of the United States. Although they
gave little indication of wanting such an institution for themselves, they
generally conceded the right of citizens in other parts of the country
to hold slaves until that institution could be eliminated in some gradual,
peaceful and equitable manner.

Racism in Boston is by no means a modern phenomenon; nor was
it introduced by foreign immigrants. The attitude of Irish immigrants
regarding the nature and character of the black race was almost exactly
that of most native Americans in the early nineteenth century. They
shared the widespread belief of white people in both the North and the
South that black people were members of an inferior race—ignorant,
savage, brutish, given to emotional impulses and animal passions—
who were far better off under the enlightened and paternalistic direction of the white race. Expressing the belief that the Founding Fathers
had acted wisely in 1787 when they sanctioned slavery and deliberately left it "undisturbed," the *United States Catholic Intelligencer*, shortly
to be renamed the *Boston Pilot*, echoed the sentiments of most of its
readers when it said that it was best to keep the institution intact so
that no injury could "fall upon the public from the colored population."
If blacks were freed from the restrictions of slavery, the "maddening
spirit of revolution" would be let loose from the "prison of the African

heart" with all its "brute and ferocious force" in a more "bloody spectacle than St. Domingo ever displayed." Slavery was part of the law of the land and therefore had to be obeyed. "We have not attempted any defense of antislavery principles," said the *Pilot*. "We presume not to meddle with negro slavery."

These clearly racist sentiments were made even more intense by the strong feelings of Irish Catholics against certain white people, especially those who loudly advocated the emancipation of slaves. Boston Irishmen regarded most of the liberal, upper-middle-class, native American Protestants who made up the membership of the local abolition movement as bigots and hypocrites who pretended to be concerned with human rights and the plight of poor black people (about whom they cared no more about than the "fifth wheel of an omnibus," the *Pilot* scoffed), but who joined the anti-Catholic forces of the Know-Nothing movement and campaigned against the interests of poor white immigrants.

The Boston Irish saw what they regarded as a typical example of the hypocrisy of white northern liberals after the Massachusetts legislature enacted a law in April 1854 stating that no child, on account of "race, color or religious opinions," could be excluded from any of the public schools of the Commonwealth. Following passage of this statute, a number of boys from the all-white Phillips School in Boston were walked across town to the Smith School, a separate primary school for black children, while a corresponding number of black students from the Smith School were walked over to the Phillips School. The *Pilot* urged that the new law be given a fair and lengthy trial, pointing out to its readers that none of the Catholic parents involved had raised any objections to having their children take part in this exchange process. But the paper did maintain that a number of well-to-do Protestant families, which had been among the loudest supporters of abolitionism, were now sending their own children to private schools so that the youngsters would not be "polluted" by black children in the same classroom. The parallel with the school desegregation crisis over a century later is obvious and instructive.

The Irish also considered William Lloyd Garrison and his abolitionist supporters disloyal and antisocial. When they fled the oppression and deprivation of Ireland and sought refuge in America, the newcomers transferred their collective allegiance to the government and Constitution of their adopted country. With simple, total and sometimes almost childlike dedication, they devoted themselves to supporting the Union and idealizing the nation that had given them a home. To such people, the militant rhetoric and the exaggerated posturing of the abolitionist leaders appeared as an offensive affront to the government of the United States and a dangerous threat to the stability of the Union. To hear Garrison publicly denounce the Constitution of the United States as a "covenant with death and an agreement with hell" because it sanctioned the institution of slavery was shocking to immigrant people who viewed that same document as a sacred guarantee of their political rights and religious liberties. Such insulting words and provocative language, according to the Irish, could only serve to promote civil disorder and public violence. They rejected this behavior as contrary to the American ideals of social harmony and community responsibility. The concept of "higher law" was inconceivable to people who believed that individuals must subordinate their personal views to those in lawful authority—both in matters of state and religion. Immigrants had little respect for supposedly highly educated people who said that a citizen had to obey the laws of the country only as far "as they agree with his or her individual notions of right or wrong." The idea of selective obedience was generally abhorrent to the immigrant mentality.

If the Kansas-Nebraska Act of 1854 was a turning point in the minds and hearts of native Bostonians, persuading them to take a much stronger stand against the further expansion of slavery, it had no such effect among the Irish. Contrary to prevailing sentiment, they persisted in their outspoken support of slavery and their attitude of contempt toward the black race. As good Democrats, they emphasized the right of individual states to decide the question of slavery for themselves, and they gave such overwhelming support to the candidacy of James Buchanan in 1856 that the *Boston Bee* remarked that the Pennsylvanian's election was one of the greatest victories for Rome "since the days of the Reformation." And when Chief Justice Roger B. Taney handed down the Dred Scott decision the following year, the Irish welcomed the document as a vindication of their traditional views of the status of the slave and the ultimate power of sovereign states in regulating slavery in the United States.

Massachusetts Irish continued to cling firmly to the banner of the Democratic party, especially after the Republican-dominated legislature passed two amendments to the state constitution in retaliation for the Irish vote against Buchanan's opponent, John C. Fremont. In 1857 they passed a literacy requirement for voting; in 1859 another measure kept foreigners from voting for two years after naturalization. Furious over these discriminatory amendments, large numbers of Irish cast their votes for Stephen A. Douglas of Illinois in the election of 1860. Indeed, the

Democratic candidate was so clearly the favorite among Irish-Catholic voters that local Republicans even suggested Douglas was Catholic. The *Bee* asserted that members of the Republican party would be much wiser if they would simply accept the fact that the Roman Catholic Church in the United States was their "declared and uncompromising foe." "Catholicism and slavery," declared the paper, "are twin sisters." For Boston Democrats the highlight of the local campaign came in July 1860, when Douglas himself paid a visit to Boston and spoke to a crowd of thousands in the square on Bowdoin Street. Even though they recognized it was a lost cause, the Irish supported his candidacy up to the last moment, declaring that any "naturalized citizen" who voted for a party that proscribed his race, did "not deserve the rights of citizenship."

When Lincoln's election touched off the secession of seven Southern states and fighting broke out in April 1861 after the bombardment of Fort Sumter, the Irish were suddenly confronted with a bothersome dilemma. On the one hand, for nearly thirty years they had consistently praised the Democrats, denounced the abolitionists, defended slavery, and sympathized with the Southern point of view. On the other hand, as loyal and patriotic citizens, devoted to the sanctity of the Constitution and committed to the permanence of the Union, how could they possibly defend the secession of the Southern states and the disruption of the Union?

In the final countdown, their devotion to the Union prevailed. "We Catholics have only one course to adopt, only one line to follow," the *Pilot* said. "Stand by the Union; fight for the Union; die by the Union." Fully admitting that the South had suffered much at the hands of "northern fanatics and pharisees" and legislatures that represented "those blind and wicked disturbers of the national peace," the newspaper nevertheless insisted that nothing serious enough had happened to justify secession and civil war. The South had put herself "in the wrong," the paper concluded, announcing that henceforth it would support the national government. "We have hoisted the American Stars and Stripes over the *Pilot* Establishment," the editor wrote, "and there they shall wave till the 'star of peace' returns."

By the time of the Civil War, immigrant residents of South Boston had been accepted with surprisingly good grace by the original Yankee residents of the peninsula district, who acknowledged the entrepreneurial spirit of those with trades and professions and accepted the ambition of the less fortunate who had left the dismal environs of the waterfront to seek hard work across the channel. In their 1847 memorial, the leaders of the community had spoken in positive terms about the "better class" of immigrants who had come to South Boston rather than remaining closeted in "cellars," and who were already adding to the district's growing population. For their part, the immigrants quickly integrated themselves into the local community and made the story of Dorchester Heights especially a distinctive part of their own sense of place and history. Every year, generations of school children wrote Evacuation Day essays commemorating the great event that had already become part of their community education. Irish fraternal societies took great pride in Brigadier John Sullivan, whose father had emigrated from Limerick, Ireland, one of the officers on General Washington's staff during the evacuation. Every Irish family in the district repeated the legend—assumed to be an indisputable fact—that since the actual evacuation had been scheduled to take place on March 17, 1776, General Washington made General Sullivan officer of the day and authorized "St. Patrick" as the official password. "Thus, on the most eventful day in the history of our city," James Cullen wrote in his popular *Story of the Irish in Boston*, "did the commander in chief of the American army pay a graceful compliment to the Irish people." This valuable piece of folklore served as a nostalgic bond for generations of old-timers and newcomers who would make their homes in South Boston as this stable and manageable base of immigrant residents suddenly mushroomed during the late 1840s and early 1850s. By the mid-1850s, as their numbers climbed to nearly one-third of the city's total population, there could be no question as to the overwhelmingly Irish and Roman Catholic character of the community. It was stamped upon the district as clearly as the churches that had sprung up, the pubs that were doing a thriving business, and the lilting brogues that could be heard in the houses and on the streets.

Whether this particular neighborhood would survive the Civil War, retain its distinctive characteristics and be assimilated into the larger Boston community remained to be seen. For the time being the newcomers had grudgingly taken their stand with Abraham Lincoln and his Republican administration in the hope that the war would not last too long, that the slavery issue would not become involved, and that the Union they loved would eventually be restored—that is, "the Union as it was."

3

FORMING A
NEIGHBORHOOD

OR A BRIEF PERIOD AFTER THE CIVIL WAR BROKE OUT, TENSIONS between Yankee and Celt in Boston lessened as the problem of controlling immigrants became secondary to the task of saving the Union. For the first time, Irish immigrants had an opportunity to show loyalty to their adopted country, either by joining the Union army or doing war work in the nearby armories and factories. For the first time, too, they had an opportunity to make a little money, improve their poor economic status, and gain a greater degree of acceptance in the community.

Local Irish leaders formed the 9th Regiment, Massachusetts Volunteer Infantry (the "Fighting Ninth,") in the spring of 1861, and within a few months formed a second Irish volunteer unit, the 28th Regiment, which was sworn into active service in December. Both of these units won recognition on the battlefield. At Gaines' Mill and Malvern Hill, the 9th Regiment was in the thick of the fighting, and in the spring of 1864, the Irish suffered heavy losses on the Orange Turnpike and at Spottsylvania during Grant's Wilderness Campaign in Virginia. The 28th Regiment, too, established a reputation for courage and valor, first at the Second Battle of Bull Run in September 1862, and two weeks later at the bloody battle of Antietam. Just before Christmas, the 28th was heavily engaged in Burnside's suicidal assaults against Lee's veterans at Marye's Heights at Fredericksburg, and during the next two years it saw almost continuous action at Gettysburg, in the Wilderness Campaign and on the Petersburg front below Richmond in the last stages of the conflict.

The loyalty and courage of the Irish under fire won them the respect
and admiration of the Yankee community and gained them tolerance
and acceptance unthinkable only a few years earlier. The newspapers
of the city reported regularly on the formation of the Irish regiments
and their brave accomplishments in the field. "When the foster-sons
of old Massachusetts are making such sacrifices," the conservative
Boston Daily Advertiser reported, "it is the least we, her own sons,
can do to give them our countenance and encouragement." Perhaps
the most symbolic gesture of approval came in July 1861, when Harvard University conferred upon Bishop John Fitzpatrick the honorary
degree of Doctor of Divinity. "This is probably the first time it was
ever bestowed on a Roman Catholic Ecclesiastic at Cambridge," observed Amos Adams Lawrence, a member of the Harvard Corporation, "and this would not have been done were it not for the loyalty
shown by him and by the Irish who have offered themselves freely for
the army."

Although the Irish made clear from the outset their willingness to
die for the Union, they made it equally clear they were not fighting
for the freedom of slaves. Secession and civil war did not alter their
opposition to emancipation or their attitude toward the black race. "The
white men of the free states do not wish to labor side by side with the
Negro," the *Pilot* said. "Not one volunteer in a hundred has gone
forth...to liberate slaves." Emphasizing the political and military aspects
of the war, the Irish supported the administration as long as President
Lincoln insisted the war was being fought to restore the Union and not
to free the slaves. When the President appeared to change his policy,
issuing a preliminary Emancipation Proclamation after the Battle of Antietam in September 1862, the Irish immediately leaped to the attack.
Along with other Democratic groups and antiadministration critics in
the North, the Boston Irish denounced the proclamation as one more
blunder by the "incompetent, fanatic, radical administration of Abraham
Lincoln." They were certain that the Republicans had betrayed the poor
people of the country by selling out to the abolitionists. Such a proclamation, the *Pilot* warned, would not only stiffen Southern resistance,
prolong the war, and ruin any chance for a negotiated settlement; it
would also cause a massive flood of black workers into the North who
would take jobs away from white laborers. Most blacks would not accept emancipation anyway, the Catholic weekly claimed. They were
devoted to their owners and satisfied with their lot in life because "ser-
vile plantation life is the life nature intended for them." The paper

bitterly deplored the efforts of "negrophilists" and "nigger-worship-pers" to convince blacks that they were the equals of whites, and called upon its readers to withdraw their support from President Lincoln. "At one time we did support Lincoln," the *Pilot* admitted, but "he changed, and so have we."

The angry reaction of the Irish to the Emancipation Proclamation in-tensified their bitter complaints about the conscription law that Con-gress passed in March 1863. The vagueness of the law and the many abuses in its administration caused widespread protest, organized op-position and outright violence. Its provisions were particularly unfair to poor people and immigrants, because the sons of rich Yankee fathers were allowed either to hire substitutes to go into the army in their place or to purchase outright exemption for three hundred dollars. The heavy casualties suffered by Irish regiments (at Antietam, for example, the 28th Regiment lost almost a quarter of its members) made the Irish feel they were poor men fighting a rich man's war.

Throughout the North—in Ohio, New York, New Jersey, Penn-sylvania, Wisconsin, Indiana and Illinois—there were many disturbances and "insurrections" against the ways the conscription law was being enforced. During the hot summer of 1863, a New York City mob of predominantly Irish workmen went on a three-day rampage, turning their anger first against the enrollment officers and members of the police department, and then exploding against the rich by plundering fine houses and looting prosperous shops and stores. Finally, they lashed out at the blacks, whom they blamed for causing the war, for taking jobs away from white workers, and for avoiding conscription themselves. Order was not restored until federal troops were brought up from the Get-tysburg campaign to stop the looting and put down the rioting.

The city of Boston, with an Irish population now well over fifty thou-sand, seemed a likely arena for violence. There were discernible rumbl-ings in the poorer sections of the city, and one priest complained that this "most iniquitous and despotic administration" was doing what no other government had ever done before—"drafting poor people, our Irish people." Officials at both state and local levels were extremely worried that anger at the Emancipation Proclamation and resentment against the conscription laws would cause disorders in Boston similar to the riots in New York, especially with Bishop Fitzpatrick away in Belgium.

Trouble did break out in the working-class district of the North End late in the afternoon of July 14, only a day after the outbreak of New

York's bloody riots. A group of irate women attacked two provost marshals who had come to serve conscription papers. A number of men joined in, beating the local policemen attempting to rescue the marshals. The melee soon expanded into a wholesale riot as more men came home from their jobs and joined in the fighting. By that time the crowd had swelled to such proportions that the police retreated to their station house, only to find themselves surrounded and barricaded by the screaming mob. At this point Mayor Frederick Lincoln ordered three militia companies assembled at the Cooper Street armory, where they were reinforced by regular army troops from outside the city. The rioters quickly surrounded the armory and tried to break through the doors, but the troops inside opened fire with rifles and cannon, driving the attackers off. Determined on further mischief, the rioters headed for Dock Square, where several gun shops offered an arsenal of weapons. An advance detachment of police arrived at Dock Square first, however, and held back the mob until the main body of militia arrived and cleared the area. This marked the end of the Boston riot for the night; yet no one knew for certain whether trouble would break out again the following day. For two or three days following the rioting there was still "great apprehension" in the city. All kinds of rumors had the Irish planning new disturbances in other parts of the city, and there were reports that nativist vigilante groups from neighboring communities were ready to come in to help local authorities deal with any new outbreaks of violence. Fortunately, however, there was no further trouble. The tensions began to ease, and the city gradually returned to normal.

Compared with the three-day orgy of looting and killing in New York City, the spontaneous and essentially leaderless riot in Boston was brief and ineffective—it was all over by 11:00 P.M. that same night. The prompt use of military force by Mayor Lincoln and the city authorities squashed the trouble before it became really ugly. The Catholic clergy, by expressing their displeasure, also helped maintain calm. The diocesan chancellor, Rev. James Healy, instructed priests to use their influence to keep people at home, and local curates walked the streets of the North End breaking up gatherings of restive young people. Furthermore, contrary to what some recent writers have suggested, in the Boston incident there is no evidence that the rioters directed any violence against the black people of the city. During the confrontation with local authorities, no racist slogans or banners were observed, no attempts were made to move into the black neighborhood in the West End, and no black people were reported among the dead or wounded.

Although Boston's immigrant population objected to many aspects of the Civil War, it welcomed the much-needed jobs and incomes the war provided. The Civil War was a modern war, an industrial war. The armies of the North required huge quantities of manufactured goods to support their offensive operations, demands that called for greater numbers of unskilled laborers than ever before in history. Never had industry been called upon to produce such a volume of goods for so many customers in such a concentrated period of time. Heavy industries expanded dramatically as larger factories, greater investment and increased productivity filled the need for large guns, powerful artillery shells, ironclad vessels, mobile bridges and railroad locomotives. In the peninsula district, smaller industries kept pace with industrial production. Here, iron was shaped into bars and drawn into wire; ship chains were hammered and tempered; bricks were turned out of kilns; rope was produced in ropewalks. Local factories supplied castings of brass and copper, wagons and carriages, hard and soft soap, kerosene and oil. As a major center of industrial production in the Northeast, South Boston responded readily to the unparalleled demand for manufactured goods. It kept foundries and machine shops in operation around the clock, and its busy factories attracted even greater numbers of artisans, mechanics and laborers to the district to enjoy the high wages of wartime prosperity.

The South Boston Iron Works, which had started out in 1809 as Cyrus Alger's foundry business on West Fourth Street and was continued after his death in 1856 by his son Francis, was extremely active during the Civil War. Over the years, this plant had become a particularly valuable source of military equipment. It had produced the first rifle-cannon in 1834; in 1836 it had turned out the first malleable-iron cannon; and it was Cyrus Alger who had improved time-fuses for spherical shells. When the Civil War broke out in 1861, the ironworks doubled its capacity and made extensive additions to its plant. With wartime contracts, the plant turned out large orders of guns, cannon, ammunition and an experimental missile called the "schenkle projectile," while Francis himself was kept busy consulting with government engineers on questions of ordnance. According to one source, government orders kept the ironworks operating "day and night," producing guns and projectiles that were an "important factor" in defending the Union and bringing hostilities to a successful conclusion. "Their guns sank the *Merrimac* and the *Alabama*," he wrote, "and played a conspicuous part all along the coast from Norfolk to New Orleans." So great was the wartime demand that early in 1863 Francis built an additional foundry, a large machine shop and three additional forty-five-ton air furnaces to take care of war orders.

Another South Boston plant the government kept busy filling war orders was the City Point Works. Founded in 1847 by Harrison Loring, the plant originally manufactured marine engines, boilers and paper-mill equipment, but by 1857, seeing the long-range possibilities of ocean-going steamships, Loring purchased from the city of Boston the seven-acre estate where the House of Industry had stood before it was moved to Deer Island. Here he began the first permanent iron shipbuilding establishment in New England, starting out with two 1,150-ton iron steamers—the *South Carolina* and the *Massachusetts*—that he built for the Boston and Southern Steamship Company. In 1857 and 1858 he also built vessels for contractors in India, and was able to remain in full operation at a time when many other industries were forced to cut back production during the depressed economy following the Panic of 1857. When the Civil War broke out, Loring's company increased its output, and in March 1862, after the momentous clash between the two ironclads, the *Monitor* and the *Merrimac*, the government urged him to build as many monitors as could be completed in the shortest time possible. He immediately began to work on one named the *Nahant*, the first monitor ever built in New England, after which he turned out an improved model called the *Canonicus*.

Still another South Boston concern that contributed significantly to the Union war effort was the Globe Works Company, incorporated in 1845 by John Souther. Souther had worked for the Boston Locomotive Works for many years, and his new operation specialized at first in the manufacture of railroad engines, turning out twenty to thirty locomotives a year. At some point, however, perhaps after a fire destroyed the works in 1860, the company turned to the manufacture of steam excavators, which were used in the United States and in Europe for the construction of railroad lines. During the Civil War, the Globe Works was also pressed into wartime service by the government. It constructed the U.S.S. *Housatonic*, provided the hull and machinery for one of Loring's monitors, and furnished the machinery for a sloop of war and two side-wheel steamers. South Boston-built excavators, steam shovels and locomotives saw service by the hundreds in every state of the Union as well as Canada. The locomotive used on California's first railroad had been made in South Boston, shipped around Cape Horn in 1849, and driven from Sacramento to the bustling gold fields. A little less than two decades later, a pair of South Boston-built locomotives were also shipped to California. One of them drew Leland Stanford's private parlor car to Promontory Point, Utah, where the famous Golden Spike was driven into the last railroad tie, joining the Union Pacific with the Central Pacific and completing the first transcontinental railroad in the United States.

The employment created by the Civil War increased the population of the peninsula from about twenty-two thousand in 1860 to over thirty thousand in 1865. With increased employment producing a greater level of prosperity, several prominent citizens, including Zibeon Southard, Henry Souther and D. McB. Thaxter, petitioned the General Court for a charter to establish a local savings bank. Once the legislation was approved by the governor, the South Boston Savings Bank opened its doors for business on September 1, 1863. On opening day, the president of the bank, Henry Souther and five other members of the corporation demonstrated their faith in the new undertaking by depositing a combined total of $550. The next name in the ledger was that of a twelve-year-old, Frank D. Morse; his name was followed by other depositors whose occupations were listed in the ledger of that first day as "Broker," "Dep. Sheriff," "Brewer," "Merchant," "Physician," "Grocer," "Lumber Dealer" and "Gentleman." The growth of commercial activity represented by this increase in financial investment produced so much traffic between South Boston and the city that lower Broadway had to be brought across the inner channel to link up with Washington Street. A short time later, Congress Street was extended across the Fort Point Channel to connect with L Street to provide an additional means of access from the in-town area to the peninsula. The legislature also set aside a large sum of money to reclaim the flats along the waterfront from the Fort Point Channel to City Point—some twenty-five acres of which were subsequently used by the New York and New England Railroad for storage and commercial purposes. The same appropriation was used to deepen the outer channel around City Point and dredge the inner harbor so that it could accommodate large ocean-going vessels.

But the Civil War did more than expand the property, improve the economy and increase the population of South Boston. Though a small core of well-to-do Yankees still controlled most of the wealth and owned most of the large houses in the City Point area, the war had taken a rather amorphous and undistinguished peninsula of land and transformed it into a unique Irish-Catholic neighborhood that would shortly become one of the most colorful districts surrounding the central city. The transformation was clearly distinguishable in the sharp decline in the number of Protestant churches in South Boston during the last part of the nineteenth century. Nearly every Protestant denomination lost a number of members, and many churches had to merge with other groups or disband completely. The Dahlgren Post, Grand Army of the Republic, took over the building on D Street where the Congregationalists formerly worshiped, and it became a popular meeting place for veterans to discuss wartime experiences and Boston politics. Before long the local chapter of the Ancient Order of Hibernians began to meet every second Sunday in Dahlgren Hall, giving recent immigrants an opportunity to talk about former times in the "old country" and learn about new customs in their adopted land. In the structure where the Methodists used to gather, the Presbyterians now held their services. And the building on the corner of Broadway and F Street, where the South Baptist Church had been located for many years, gave way to a large brick business structure.

The number of Catholic churches, by contrast, multiplied at a remarkable rate. In 1863, for example, even while the Civil War was still going on, the Gate of Heaven Church was constructed on the corner of Fourth and I Streets, a plain brick structure to accommodate the growing number of Catholics who were slowly beginning to make their way up from the western end of the peninsula (now called "the lower end") and into the City Point section of South Boston. At the turn of the century, this original building would be replaced by a much more magnificent Gothic structure, but for the time being the smaller church served its purpose adequately.

In 1868, only three years after the end of the war, Bishop John Williams authorized the construction of a new church on Dorchester Street to meet the needs of those parishioners who could no longer fit inside the small cemetery chapel of St. Augustine's. Under the vigorous direction of Fr. Denis O'Callaghan, who would remain as pastor for nearly half a century until his death in 1913, a large and beautiful Gothic church was constructed out of red brick. Only a short distance from the old cemetery grounds, the new St. Augustine's Church was formally dedicated in August 1874. To provide for the people of nearby Washington Village, a few years later Fr. O'Callaghan purchased a small wooden Unitarian church (Unity Chapel) on the southern end of Dorchester Street near Andrew Square and converted it into the mission chapel of St. Monica's.

While some of the Irish were gradually making their way up toward Dorchester Street and beyond, the most densely populated section of South Boston was the lower end, between A and F Streets, where SS. Peter and Paul's Church still handled the greatest number of parishioners. The population in this area, overwhelmingly Roman Catholic, had grown so large since the Civil War that church authorities decided to ease the pressure by establishing two new smaller churches in what had originally been the original parish of SS. Peter and Paul. St. Vincent's Church, on the corner of E and West Third Streets, was dedicated in July 1874. This church was actually the successor of the old St. Vincent de Paul's Church, a former Unitarian church Catholics had bought on Purchase Street in Boston's Fort Hill district. The great Boston fire of November 1872, which broke out on the corner of Summer and Kingston streets and swept through the downtown commercial district, also burned down many of the tenements of Fort Hill, where the poorest Irish immigrants still lived. Displaced by the fire and the extensive renovations that followed, many of these people came across the Summer Street bridge to take up "temporary" lodgings with friends and relatives in South Boston—and stayed forever. To preserve a sense of continuity, they brought the bell from their old church in Fort Hill and placed it in the small cupola above the front of the simple, gray-granite church that now served their predominantly immigrant community. The other new addition, a small, wooden structure called Our Lady of the Rosary, was dedicated in May 1884. Made up out of a heavily populated triangle formed by Dorchester Avenue, D Street and West Sixth Street, this parish relieved a little more of the pressure on nearby SS. Peter and Paul. Immigration from Ireland had picked up briskly after the Civil War, and by 1880 there were nearly sixty-five thousand people of Irish birth living in Boston—nearly double the number of Irish-born residents living in the city thirty years earlier.

Like the social and religious makeup of the district, the economic structure of South Boston also underwent extensive changes during the postwar decades. For nearly half a century, the area had become well known for its heavy industries—iron foundries, locomotive factories, glassworks, machine shops, shipyards, and so on—which had contributed substantially to the district's economy and attracted many immigrant craftsmen and laborers. By the 1880s, however, many of the larger plants in South Boston had moved to other parts of the country or closed down completely. In what became known as the Age of Big Business, when large-scale industrialization capitalized on new mechanical inventions and modern technological processes, many of the older factories found it impossible to keep pace with new techniques that made many of their own operations obsolete. The old chainworks on Broadway and F Street, for example, had employed large numbers of workers for many years turning out massive anchor chains for shipyards, but it was put out of business by the invention of machinery that did the work faster and more cheaply than it could be done by hand. The manufacture of glass, for many generations a major South Boston industry with no less than six plants in operation at the same time, was quickly abandoned as a result of new mechanical techniques. And the district's iron factories, once the most extensive in New England, also began to close down during the 1880s. With the rapid decrease of government orders after the Civil War, for example, Alger's ironworks had to close its doors in 1883. As widespread industrialization increased demand for iron and steel throughout the nation, industrial centers like Pittsburgh set up their blast furnaces as near as possible to the coal and iron mines, reducing the cost of transporting raw materials. Unable to compete with these larger, more productive and more efficient factories in Pennsylvania and Ohio, the smaller plants in the Northeast rapidly disappeared.

A broad range of factories, shops, businesses and other enterprises maintained a modest economy in South Boston and continued to attract workers. The Standard Sugar Refinery, for example, employed well over a thousand men, maintaining both a day and night shift that turned out about six hundred barrels of fine granulated sugar a day. There were at least two major breweries in the district, an asphalt company, a roofing company, companies manufacturing fabrics and buttons, a plant that made barrels and belts, and a new firm, Walworth Manufacturing Company, which would become a major employer in the district. But most of the truly heavy industries were on their way out, and by the end of the nineteenth century South Boston was essentially a manufacturing area whose residents were mainly artisans and mechanics. Concentrated on the lower end of the peninsula, they worked only a short distance from where they lived.

South Boston was slowly becoming much more of a residential district, with inhabitants spread throughout a broader portion of the district. Many residents made their living in small industries on the lower end of Broadway, in the new leather and wool houses along the new roadway connecting L Street and Summer Street, or on the wharves and piers across the channel in Boston itself. Most men worked nine- or ten-hour days on Atlantic Avenue unloading the freight boats of the various steamship lines. Others maintained all kinds of stables in the outskirts of the district—livery stables, boarding stables, private stables—in those days when anything on wheels that was not drawn by hand was pulled by horses. And every evening after supper, groups of Irish women walked across the Broadway bridge to the business section of Boston to scrub floors and clean offices until midnight, and then walked home again across the same bridge. One contemporary historian estimated that four-fifths of the working population of the peninsula was employed outside the territorial limits of South Boston.

Fortunately for immigrant workers, a series of new public-utility companies were being incorporated just as heavy industry was fading out—the New England Telephone and Telegraph Company, the Boston Edison Electric Company, the Massachusetts Electric Company and the Boston Gas Company. These industries brought gas, electricity and telephone lines to the homes, schools and businesses of Boston and the surrounding neighborhoods of Charlestown, Dorchester, East Boston, Roxbury and South Boston.

Transportation was an essential ingredient in this industrial change-over, and the city's transit system changed considerably during this time. For a long time, all forms of transportation in Boston and its environs had depended on horsepower. Ephraim Dodge operated the first public conveyance between South Boston and the city during the 1830s. Since Broadway was not yet paved, Dodge usually drove his hack across the old South Bridge and up Fourth Street—although his carriage wheels occasionally got stuck in the spring muds. Before long, he had enough passengers to warrant the purchase of two omnibuses, which ran back and forth to the city once every hour. Dodge was forced out of business in 1839, however, when members of the Warren Association began running a coach from the Old State House to their Mount Washington Hotel in South Boston, reducing the fare to six cents and adding another coach to the Boston run. Although ownership changed from time to time, the new omnibus line continued to grow until it had some twenty coaches, 105 horses and forty drivers. Running trips every five minutes from its office near I Street to the Boston terminal at Cornhill, it became known as the White Line after all its coaches were painted white.

A commercial stagecoach in those days usually had three inside seats: one at each end of the coach and one in the middle called the "strap seat." Each seat accommodated three passengers, making room for nine in all. In some of the larger coaches there were outside seats as well. The back part of the coach was used to store baggage. As a rule, stagecoaches running to distant points left very early in the morning. The normal starting time was 5:00 A.M., but several lines started at 4:00 A.M., and some as early as 2:00 A.M. Josiah Quincy, telling about a journey he took in 1826 with Judge Story from Boston to Washington, recalled that his stage was scheduled to leave Boston at 3:00 A.M. At 2:00 A.M., a man was sent around to the houses of those people who were booked for the ride. His instructions, wrote Quincy, were to "knock, pull the bell, and shout and disturb the neighborhood as much as possible" so that the passengers would be up and dressed by the time the stage pulled up in front of their doors. When the coach did arrive, it was still pitch dark, and since there was no light inside the coach the passengers had to wait until daybreak before they could see who their fellow passengers were.

The streets of South Boston were gradually paved at mid-century, making it possible to lay the steel rails needed for horse-drawn street-cars. The first road paved in the district was Turnpike Street—later renamed Dorchester Avenue—from Fourth Street to North Street Bridge. Starting in 1849, Fourth Street itself was paved, first from B to C Streets, then all the way from Turnpike to Dorchester Street at the St. Augustine cemetery. Work on Broadway began in 1850, from B to D Streets, and over the following years the heavy cobblestone paving extended up past Dorchester Street to K Street, and then all the way to City Point. One of the first new horsecar lines belonged to the Dorchester Avenue Railroad Company, which had been incorporated early in 1854. Its first stretch of track extended from Lower Mills in Dorchester to the foot of State Street in Boston, using South Boston's Dorchester Avenue (old Turnpike Street) as its main thoroughfare. From its terminal at State Street, the company then laid a single track over the Federal Street Bridge along L Street into South Boston. At the same time, a second enter-prise, the Broadway Railroad Company, was incorporated in April 1854 to construct another streetcar line, with a set of tracks running east-to-west the length of South Boston from City Point to Dorchester Avenue, where it formed a junction at lower Broadway with the line being pro-jected by the Dorchester Avenue Company. Over the next two decades, the horse-drawn railroads of Boston gradually stretched farther out of the city until five hundred miles of streetcar lines brought the outer edge of a reliable and inexpensive transportation system some four miles from City Hall. Starting in 1889, the streetcar system was electrified and fur-nished with newfangled trolley cars that went underground when the city began construction of its subway under Tremont Street in 1898.

This development added even more lines to the system and extended the outer transportation radius to six miles.

These new public utilities and municipal services opened up badly needed sources of employment that had never really existed before in the Boston area on such a massive scale. These jobs were not already preempted by native workers, and Irish-Americans considered themselves eminently qualified. In filling this labor vacuum, they provided services in a quasiofficial capacity and attained a definite feeling of social status and a gratifying sense of economic security. At first the tasks were more menial—ditch-diggers, hod-carriers, pile-drivers, cement-mixers and maintenance men. In another generation, their sons would be working at more skillful and better-paying occupations as plumbers, pipe-fitters, carpenters, linemen, motormen, conductors, firemen and policemen.

South Boston also felt the impact of extensive ethnic changes in the late nineteenth century. In the 1860s, almost 90 percent of all immigrants had come from northern and central Europe—Great Britain, Ireland, Germany and the Scandanavian countries. In addition to its Irish population, for example, South Boston also had a small but closely knit community of German immigrants, some of whom had arrived at the same time as the Irish, fleeing bad harvests, economic depression and political upheaval. Others came over nearly fifty years later, during the 1880s and 1890s, in an effort to escape enforced military service in the Kaiser's army. They quickly became a quiet, well-ordered and hard-working part of the community, serving as carpenters, mechanics and electricians, working in such breweries as the Boston Beer Company on Second Street or the Suffolk Brewery on the corner of Eighth and G Streets, and operating the numerous and very popular German bakeries that could be found on almost every street corner in the district.

But the 1880s saw a drastic change in the national character of immigration, and by the 1890s most immigrants were coming from southern and eastern Europe—Italy, Austria-Hungary, Greece and the Balkan countries, as well as Poland, Lithuania and Russia. Fleeing from high taxes, low wages, political oppression and religious persecution, the "new immigrants" were no longer from easily assimilable groups whose cultural traditions and political institutions were similar to those of the United States. Drawn by America's celebrated image as a nation of freedom and a land of opportunity, they were determined to build for themselves a new and more hopeful future. Most came to the Northeast, and Massachusetts received its share. In the decade between 1899 and

1910, over eighty thousand Poles entered the Bay State, along with nearly twenty-five thousand Lithuanians and over 150,000 Italians. Most of them headed for the major urban centers of Boston, Brockton, Lowell and Lawrence in search of jobs and homes.

By the turn of the century, ten thousand Poles had located in the Boston area, most of them settled near the boundary between South Boston and Dorchester, just off Andrew Square. In 1893 Archbishop Williams assigned a Polish-born priest, Rev. John Chmielinski, to work among these predominantly Roman Catholic people, who had been attending religious services at the in-town German church on Shawmut Avenue or at St. Margaret's Church in Dorchester. Fr. Chmielinski purchased a tract of land extending from Dorchester Avenue to Boston Street as a site for a national church, and the following year, in November 1894, a wooden structure was dedicated to Our Lady of Czestochowa. The Polish population in the area continued to grow, quickly becoming a small but active part of the peninsula district.

Around the same time, about one thousand Lithuanian immigrants arrived in Boston, most of whom made their homes in South Boston. Reflecting the strong nationalist impulse of the 1880s that called upon Lithuanians to cultivate their language and preserve their traditional customs, the newcomers settled together in the lower end of the peninsula, along C and D Streets, directly across town from where the Polish immigrants had settled. The archbishop assigned a young Lithuanian priest, Rev. Joseph Gricius, to care for this new settlement, and in 1896 Fr. Gricius purchased property on Seventh Street, which he remodeled into St. Joseph's Church. Unfortunately, difficulties between the inexperienced young curate and his parishioners became so bitter that when his church burned down in February 1899, they refused to help him rebuild it. Instead, they built another church of their own (St. Peter's), and pressured the archbishop into appointing a new priest, Rev. John Zilinskas, to serve as their pastor. Once this difficulty was resolved, and Fr. Gricius had moved to another part of the country, things gradually settled down, and the Lithuanians became a distinct and very closely knit community in South Boston. Because they conducted virtually all their numerous publishing and cultural activities in Lithuanian, however, they were much slower to become assimilated into the general society of the district.

Although most of the Italian immigrants who flooded Boston during the late 1800s and early 1900s congregated along the waterfront in Boston's North End, a surprising number moved into South Boston and settled along East Third Street between H and L Streets, perhaps because in 1868 Archbishop Williams had appointed an Italian Franciscan, Rev. Emiliano Gerbi, OSF, as pastor of the newly constructed Gate of Heaven Church. Until his death five years later, Fr. Emiliano served the parish, regularly assisted by one or two other Italian Franciscans who undoubtedly influenced a number of Italian families to make their homes near the church. Before long, Italians had become an important part of South Boston, serving as barbers and hairdressers, working as cobblers and leatherworkers, and operating nearly all the fruit stores in the district. Residents who enjoyed a cut of beef known as "skirt steak" patronized Cataldo's Meat Market on Dorchester Street and Broadway; Paino's Fruit Store at the corner of Emerson Street and Broadway became known for its excellent range of fruit products; and Tony Buongiorno operated a popular fruit market on the corner of M Street and East Fourth. Invariably these newcomers became known familiarly as "Mickey," "Sully" and "Pat" to the predominantly Irish population, who were unable to pronounce names like Minichiello, Solimini or Pasqualucci.

There was even a small colony of Jewish people in the lower end of South Boston. They lived on West Fourth Street between A and B Streets, close to their places of work as junk dealers and rag-and-bottle collectors. Jewish families gradually moved to several other locations in the district, such as Pleasant Place on the east side of Broadway, and later they established a Hebrew School in the old Bird schoolhouse on East Fourth Street, just up from Dorchester Street.

Despite the influx of new immigrant groups, however, by the closing years of the nineteenth century the life and society of South Boston had become almost completely dominated by the patterns and customs of Irish-Catholic culture, particularly below Dorchester Street—the so-called lower end—where most of the Irish still congregated, and to which newly arrived immigrants (called "greenhorns") made their way across the channel after landing at Boston's waterfront. There was a tendency for people to group together by county of origin—people from Galway lived around A and B Streets, the Cork people around D Street and so on—but this clannishness quickly broke down as residents moved to other areas of the district and people from other parts of Europe arrived. In a fairly short time the various immigrant groups, old and new, settled into a bustling neighborhood that took on a vibrant life of its own as it extended along the peninsula from the lower end to City Point. By the 1890s Broadway had become the main thoroughfare of South Boston, with streetcars rattling along the principal line of tracks

all day long. At either end of the most populous stretch were two
firehouses: one at the corner of Dorchester Avenue and the lower end
of Broadway (Engine 15); the other on Dorchester Street, just below
Dorchester Heights (Engine 3). The joy of any young boy's life was
to be passing one of these fire barns when the alarm came in. The doors
flew open, the snorting horses came charging out into the street, and
the brightly polished steam engine belched great clouds of smoke. It
was an inspiring sight, but modern technology soon had these same boys
watching a new phenomenon. During the fall of 1918 the neighborhood
was deafened by the roar of engines as firemen learning to handle the
district's first motorized ladder truck assigned to the station house on
Dorchester Street drove through the streets. Groups of children and adults
gathered on the street corners to admire the huge truck and watch the
gyrations of the tiller man sitting atop the ladders as he strained to turn
the rear wheels of the great machine.

In the block between F Street and Dorchester Street, people shopped
on Saturdays at the two department stores, two furniture stores, stationery store and florist shop. For the remainder of the week, however,
most people patronized the scores of small shops and variety stores that
also served as places for political debates and local gossip. Dan Kiley's
drug store offered five-cent sodas; Tom Quinn's hat store provided the
latest in derbies; Berlo's meat market featured ground beef every Saturday afternoon; Eicardi ran a popular Italian fruit store. There was a
Chinese laundry, a German bakery, a tobacco shop, a barber shop and
several well-attended barrooms. These barrooms, one former resident
recalled, were generally well supervised and well cared for. "There
was never any trouble, never any rioting." They were usually patronized
by hard-working men who took the five-cent ride home on the streetcar, got off at the local barroom (Bill Kirby's bar on the corner of D
Street and Broadway, for example), had a glass of beer or two while
they talked with friends and neighbors for twenty or thirty minutes,
and then walked home to supper. The owner of the bar was generally
a leader in the community, and a man of considerable influence. "He
was part saloonkeeper, part bartender, part doctor, and part father-
confessor," a longtime native wrote. "His word went far, and he was
respected." It was no coincidence that a number of future Irish political
leaders in the city, like Patrick J. Kennedy of East Boston, started out
their influential careers as saloonkeepers. Occasionally, of course, things
got out of hand, especially on the weekends. The cells at Police Station
Six on D Street were usually filled by midnight on Saturdays by those

who had taken "just a drop too many." On Monday morning most of them were carted off to the South Boston District Court, sentenced to a few days at Deer Island, and then back on the streets again.

A bowling alley on West Broadway provided a new source of entertainment for the people of the district. Francis E. Birmingham recalled a night in 1897 when this new "get-up" was filled with patrons. A gigantic figure suddenly filled the doorway and announced in a loud voice: "I'll treat the house!" It was John L. Sullivan, the "Boston strongboy." Although he had been defeated by James Corbett for the championship five years earlier, he was still a local favorite, and the wild tumult that greeted the popular boxer was quieted only when the great John L.'s "stentorian voice" called for order. He then brought forward his friend Darby Noonan to sing his favorite song, "O'Donnell Abo," with everyone joining in on the chorus. It was one of those "unforgettable nights," Birmingham said, when the bowling alley rocked with a "clarion call of survival from the days of the Kings of Ancient Tara."

Determined that their children would have a brighter and more prosperous life, immigrant fathers and mothers instructed their children in the virtues of personal morality, the importance of a sound education and the values of thrift and sobriety. Obvious attributes sought by poor, working-class people forced to raise nine or ten children on an average salary of ten or twelve dollars a week, these qualities were also remarkably close to the old-time American Protestant ethic. Irish immigrants had developed a love-hate relationship with the traditional Yankee-Brahmin culture, admiring many of the natives' personal characteristics and emulating a number of their economic views and social attitudes, even while they went to great lengths to blame the Yankees for the hardships of their climb up the socioeconomic ladder. To their own children they held up the best of the Yankees—the Cabots, the Lowells, the Lawrences, the Lodges, the Saltonstalls—as models of honesty and integrity. This kind of admiration appears frequently in reports and reminiscences of the many splendid Yankee teachers who taught in the schools of South Boston at the turn of the century. The Yankees themselves seemed more than conscious of this grudging admiration, and many of them worked diligently to transmit their own traditional values to the newcomers in an attempt to minimize the social and cultural differences. "What we need is not to dominate the Irish, but absorb them," one Boston Brahmin declared. "We want them to become rich, and send their sons to our colleges, and share our prosperity and sentiments." Only nine years later the *Atlantic Monthly* took obvious pride in the tangible steps in that direction: "the Irish will, before many years are past, be lost in the American, and...there will be no longer an 'Irish question' or an 'Irish vote,' but a people one in feeling and practically one in race."

In achieving this acculturation, the Yankee community put a great deal of faith in the successful operation of its public school system as an agency of progress. Since a formal parochial school system was not established in Boston until 1880, and since poor immigrants could not afford even the modest tuition for private schools, most Irish families in the lower end sent their children to one of the public schools in the district. In the early years, the children would attend either the Lawrence Grammar School, on B Street between Broadway and Third Street, or the newer Bigelow School, on E Street between Broadway and Fourth Street. As the school-age population increased, a new district was formed out of the Lawrence and Bigelow districts. The boys remained in the Lawrence and Bigelow schools, and the girls were moved into the new Norcross School on the corner of D and Fifth Streets. The following year, the Shurtleff School was constructed on Dorchester Street in order to accommodate girls from the Bigelow School. The movement of the population across Dorchester Street toward City Point called for the construction of even more schools. The Lincoln School, named after Mayor Frederick W. Lincoln, was a large brick structure built in 1859 on Broadway between I and K Streets. By 1873 the Lincoln district had grown so fast it had to be divided up. Girls were sent to the new Gaston School on the corner of L and Fifth Streets; boys were later assigned to the Thomas N. Hart School on the corner of H and Fifth Streets.

Classroom teachers during the latter part of the nineteenth century were predominantly women, severe in appearance, modest in dress and completely dedicated to their profession. Respecting the attitudes of the local community and developing close relationships with the parents of the district, they worked hard to raise the educational and cultural levels of their disadvantaged pupils. Strict disciplinarians who ruled their classes with an iron hand—women of "significant glances and few words," as Sam Bass Warner aptly described them in his *Province of Reason*—they refused to compromise what they regarded as the traditional standards of scholarship and excellence. They not only insisted upon such basic essentials as correct spelling, proper grammar, legible handwriting, clear diction and accurate calculation, but they also managed to convey to many of their restless charges an appreciation of the elements of poetry, music and the fine arts. Many years later, men and women who attended these schools could still vividly remember some particular lines of verse, some special musical composition, or some thoughtful gesture of kindness on the part of these devoted teachers. Most students completed the nine grades of grammar school, but few went on to any of the high schools located in Boston. At this time boys could leave school after the sixth grade, and for those with neither the desire nor the ability to pursue studies any further—and those obliged or eager to go to work—this was probably a blessing. But for more talented youngsters who might have gone on to high school, and possibly even college, the necessity of contributing to the needs of a poor family often brought an abrupt end to formal education.

Before children could start out for school each morning, they had to await the completion of a unique and impressive daily event. All the heavy trucking of freight throughout the city was still done on huge four-wheeled wagons called drays, about the size of a modern ten-ton truck and drawn by two, four or sometimes even six great horses, which were kept stabled in South Boston. Every morning at seven o'clock, the noise of clopping hooves resounded loudly on the cobblestones of the lower end as hundreds of drays rumbled down Third Street on their way to the Broadway bridge. Once the parade had passed, the children would get up, have their breakfast of oatmeal and cocoa (fresh milk was a scarcity), and leave the house about 8:30 to make it on time for school, which started at nine. Once the children were in school, the streets filled with the sounds of peddlers, each with his own distinctive cry, calling out their wares and rousing the housewives of the neighborhood. The vegetable man yelling "fresh tomatoes!" made his way through the streets with fresh vegetables for the kitchen table. The fish man bawling "haddock and mack-er-ellllll!" was a popular figure on Thursdays and Fridays, although his wagon usually attracted every cat on the street because he butchered the fish as he sold them. The rag man, with his broken-down wagon and worn-out nag, rattled along shouting, "Any rags, any bones, any bottles today?" The scissors-grinder, with his complicated contraption of wheels, levers, foot-pedals, pulleys and bells, was always a fascinating sight. The soap-grease man sliced off a bar of very heavy, dark-brown laundry soap and gave it to the housewife who handed over her used fats and grease. The piccalilli man went around with two or three different kinds of relish on his cart, ladling it out for a modest price. Frequently, the tinkling sounds of "O Sole Mio" or "Funiculi Funicula" brought people into the streets. Sometimes it was the organ-grinder, balancing his portable organ on its single wooden leg; sometimes it was the hurdy-gurdy man, pushing his large upright organ along on two wheels. But almost always it was the antics of the monkey that captured the attention as he went through the crowd at the end of a long chain collecting pennies and nickels in his little red cap. On hot summer days, the watering cart sprinkled water on the broiling streets; and in days before refrigeration, the ice man was always in great demand as he lugged huge cakes of ice on his back up two or three flights of stairs to the icebox in the kitchen. A constant patrol of beer trucks went up and down the streets—huge trucks driven by huge men delivering barrels to the various corner barrooms.

There was also the insurance agent who went from house to house, floor to floor, from door to door, day after day, collecting nickels and dimes on small insurance policies that might amount to three or four hundred dollars, guaranteeing poor families a decent funeral for their deceased members. Many Boston Yankees found this practice particularly distressing. Samuel Eliot Morison, the distinguished Harvard historian, recalled how his mother and father supported efforts by the Society for the Prevention of Cruelty to Children to stop insurance agents from going into the "slum areas" and persuading parents to take out policies on "babes and sucklings" for a few cents a day so that they could have a "swell funeral" if the child died. In effect, wrote Morison, children were being denied food so that they could be buried in style. But for most immigrants, a respectable funeral was an important matter of family pride, and so the practice continued for many years. Indeed, most Protestants, accustomed to dealing with the shock of grief in their own families with stoic calm and solemn reserve, were often at a loss to understand the apparent callousness of immigrants at the time of their greatest sorrow. They were especially horrified at the typical Irish wake, where women congregated around the corpse in the living room to exchange the latest gossip, and men gathered in the kitchen to talk politics, puff on big cigars, and drink liberal amounts of whiskey. While outsiders usually regarded such activities as insensitive and barbaric, Irish Catholics did not see it that way at all. The wake was adapted from the old-country custom of friends and neighbors sitting up all night with the bereaved relatives in their cottage during the usual two days before the funeral. Tobacco and liquor were generously provided, and enthusiastic conversation helped keep everyone awake (hence the name "wake") during the long hours before the break of day. The Irish brought this ritual with them when they came to America, where it quickly became a familiar characteristic of neighborhood life in districts like

South Boston. For poor, hard-working people, leading dreary lives, the wake offered a singular opportunity to socialize with friends, catch up on the latest neighborhood news, and exchange family information with their many relatives, who could be counted on to attend. After mourners expressed personal condolences to the family of the deceased and said five decades of the rosary commemorating the Five Sorrowful Mysteries, they spent the remainder of the night in a steady round of conversation, stories, reminiscences, introductions, arguments and general joviality. Recalling the virtues of their departed friend, the visitors also took considerable satisfaction in keeping the family members occupied in their hour of trouble and helping the widow forget her sorrow for at least a short while. Most residents of South Boston would agree with the reaction of one of Edwin O'Connor's fictional characters when he learned that an acquaintance had allowed himself to be cremated. "I wouldn't want nothin' like that to happen to me!" he cried out. "When I go I'm damned sure I mean to stay around the house a few days and nights so's some of the old pals can come in and have a drink and the last look! What the hell's wrong with that, now?" What, indeed! At a time when there were few outlets for pleasurable activity, and even fewer occasions when friends and neighbors could get together and talk over old times, the old-fashioned Irish wake continued to be a standard fixture throughout South Boston.

Beyond such occasional events as a wake or wedding, however, opportunities for leisure and recreation were decidely limited for the people of South Boston. Formal vacations were practically unheard of. Without radio, motion pictures or television, poor people made up their own simple pleasures—walking, singing, dancing, swimming and playing all sorts of games. Organized athletics became an almost essential part of the life of the community, particularly after the City of Boston set aside a large tract of filled land, between the northern end of D Street and the inner harbor, as a recreational area called Commonwealth Park. Covered with a coating of hard black cinders instead of grass, the park contained as many as six baseball diamonds, at least two oval tracks and a good-sized municipal gymnasium that offered hot showers for people who had neither showers nor bathtubs in their homes. When the youngsters returned home from school at four o'clock every afternoon, they would have a piece of bread and jam or molasses and then play baseball or football in the park until suppertime. During the summer months, when the work day was over and the horses had been led back to the stables, the streets also became a playground as children

played Kick the Wicket, Prisoner's Bar and Relievo. The automobile
had not yet made its appearance, and there was practically no evening
traffic to injure children or disrupt their games until the familiar
lamplighter came along at twilight to reach up with his long stick and
turn up the yellow gaslight atop each lamppost, sending most of the
youngsters in for the night. When the young Irish immigrants (the
"greenhorns") came back from longshoring all day at the docks or handling freight at the railroad yards, they enjoyed getting together at the
same park for a game of Gaelic football or a vigorous "hurling" match
with a stick and a hardball until after dark. On Saturday afternoons in
the summer, crowds gathered to watch local favorites play baseball,
and in the cool autumn months they cheered an amateur version of "college" football by teams of various neighborhood groups.

But if there was one thing that drew the people of South Boston
together and gave the neighborhood a distinctive quality of life, it was
the Catholic Church. Everything revolved around the Church, and the
Church, in turn, became an integral part of almost every aspect of family
life, from the cradle to the grave. Unlike many other parts of Europe,
where the Church was identified with the ruling aristocracy and the
political status quo, in Ireland the Catholic Church was publicly identified with the cause of Irish nationalism and against the oppressive im-
perialism of Great Britain. Most of the Irish who came to America retained an intense faith in their religious beliefs and looked to their priests
and the Church hierarchy for guidance and support. Pictures of the
Sacred Heart of Jesus, the Blessed Mother and St. Joseph—the model
Holy Family—decorated many homes in South Boston, and no Irish
home was complete without a crucifix, "the Alphabet of Spiritual
Knowledge," as Dennis Ryan called it in his study of the social history
of the Boston Irish during this time. Religious pamphlets and inspirational literature were prominently displayed throughout the house; many
people went to daily Mass in the dark hours of the morning before going to work; and entire families knelt together every night to recite aloud
the decades of the rosary.

Sunday was the big day of the week. The parents usually went to
early Mass so that the mother could prepare the breakfast while the
youngsters went to the "childrens' Mass" at 9:30 A.M. There was
always a lengthy sermon at Sunday Mass, usually centering on one of
three major topics: the importance of the Blessed Sacrament and the
benefits to be derived from attendance at the Holy Sacrifice of the Mass;
the loyalty and obedience Catholics owed to the Holy Father in Rome

as the successor of Saint Peter; and the special devotion all Catholics should have to the Blessed Virgin Mary, Mother of God. These themes were repeated from the pulpit over and over again during the course of the year until they became, in the words of one elderly parishioner, "part of the mental and religious furniture of our minds." The children returned from Mass to a large breakfast of fried eggs and bacon or ham on a huge platter. A short time later, usually around 2:00 P.M., the children returned to the church for Sunday School. The girls went upstairs, the boys downstairs. For about an hour the children recited their catechism and received instruction in the basic tenets of the Catholic religion. Although most of these young people never received any further formal education after graduating from the local grammar school, the question-and-answer format of their catechetical instruction (Q. "Who made you?" A. "God made me."; Q. "Why did God make you?" A. "To know Him, to love Him, and to serve Him in this world, and be happy with Him in the next.") remained with them the rest of their lives. About three or four in the afternoon, after the children had returned from Sunday School, the whole family sat for the main meal of the day, which almost always featured a roast beef, a roast chicken or a baked ham. In most Irish homes, this large Sunday meal was an absolute necessity, and practically nothing was allowed to change the time of the meal, the character of the menu or the attendance of every member of the family.

But the influence of Catholicism was not limited to the sermons at Mass or the routines of Sunday. This period formed the high-water mark of what Thomas Wangler, a modern church historian, has termed the "romantic era" of American Catholicism. The late nineteenth century, he says, was characterized by the widespread proliferation of religious devotions and a semireligious affirmation of civic identity. Throughout the entire week, men and women engaged in activities that kept them closely involved with the extended Catholic culture well beyond the Sunday requirement. Almost every parish had a Rosary Society and a Scapular Society. Some had a St. Vincent de Paul Conference and a Confraternity of the Sacred Heart, while an increasing number had Sodalities for both married and single women. May devotions to the Blessed Mother, June devotions to the Sacred Heart and First Friday devotions were extremely popular. The Forty Hours Devotion to the Holy Eucharist was regularized by the Chancery in 1882, and in 1899 Pope Leo XIII designated the month of October as a time for the daily recitation of the rosary. Through these and similar devotional activities,

Catholics unwittingly created what Wangler calls a "second" devotional calendar, which competed with (but did not conflict with) the regular church calendar with its traditional Easter-Christmas focus. These rituals provided Catholic communities like those in South Boston with a distinctive socioreligious society of their own.

The involvement of the Catholic Church in the daily lives of all its parishioners went even further. In addition to saying Mass every morning, the parish priests heard confessions regularly every Saturday afternoon and evening, and usually stayed late into the night until the last penitent had been heard. They operated small clubhouses close to the church, where they held various religious and social activities during the week. They organized choirs for the church and arranged plays, minstrel shows and operettas, where members of the parish could display their musical talents once or twice a year. They ran colorful outdoor bazaars during the spring months to pay off the parish debt and give members of the parish a chance to get together after the long season of Lent. And the priests also took a strong personal interest in encouraging sports, not only for its importance to the health and well-being of the parishioners, but also because of its moral value in keeping vigorous young men away from the temptations of crime and the attractions of sex. Before long, every parish in South Boston—SS. Peter and Paul's, St. Vincent's, the Rosary, St. Augustine's and the Gate of Heaven— had its own baseball team that drew large crowds on Saturday afternoons at Commonwealth Park. And these same priests were constantly on the streets of the neighborhood, plainly visible at all times, talking to parishioners, buying penny candy for the little children at the corner store, and making sure that teenagers were not loitering in the doorways after dark.

South Boston was gradually being transformed into a unique and distinctive neighborhood, intensely proud of its own traditions, customs and way of doing things. In the thirty years after the Civil War, there was a consolidation of those ethnic and religious factors that had begun to make their appearance during the antebellum years, when Irish immigrants first began to move into the peninsula district in significant numbers. It was during this period that South Boston became less a heavy-industry district and much more an integrated community where its own residents lived and worked. It was also during this generation that the district changed from a refuge for other people into a neighborhood of its own, with an ability to function effectively in its own interests.

The Catholicism of the district, already apparent during the pre-Famine years, began to take on some its own unique characteristics in the latter half of the nineteenth century. The public and fervent devotions of its people to the Blessed Virgin Mary each May and October, to the Sacred Heart on every First Friday, and to Michael the Archangel after each low Mass "bespoke a view of reality," Thomas Wangler wrote, "unlike that of either Boston's Congregationalists or Unitarians." The Irish were showing signs of moving out of a time, as an essentially minority and oppressed people, when they had been emphasizing their similarity and compatibility with other Christian denominations in Boston, and into a time when they were much more secure in demonstrating their differences.

These commonly accepted rituals provided Catholic neighborhoods like South Boston with a unique socioreligious society, clearly distinct from that of their non-Catholic neighbors; but it also supplied them with a set of moral ideals and ethical principles that would serve to guide their own community for generations to come. The Holy Family—with the obedient Jesus, the devoted mother Mary and the strong carpenter Joseph—became the universal ideal for all working-class families. The ideals of the sacredness of life, the sanctity of the home, and the permanence of the matrimonial bond were constant themes in church and in the home. The importance of unqualified sexual abstinence outside the formal married state was both a social and religious tenet of the community, and the virtues of purity, modesty and virginity were accepted as articles of faith without question or condition.

So, in its moral aspects, the Irish-Catholic community of South Boston developed a culture that had certain distinctive characteristics— characteristics uniquely representative of the neighborhood itself but decidedly separate from the larger community of traditional downtown Boston. Its people clung tightlt to their church, revered their priests, memorized their catechisms, obeyed their doctrines, and followed their rituals to the letter. Perhaps because of their special devotion to the Blessed Virgin Mary, they adopted an unusually unyielding attitude regarding matters of a sexual nature that some defined as Jansenism, and others called puritanical. They might tolerate fighting, swearing and intemperate drinking as unfortunate but understandable weaknesses in the human condition, but they found it almost impossible to countenance such abominable "sins of the flesh" as premarital sex, birth control or the birth of illegitimate children without benefit of marriage.

The importance of such spiritual values is that they were by no means restricted to a purely religious or denominational context. They became a deep and integral part of the whole cultural fabric of the community, shared by the young and old, men and women. They were reinforced by song and story, by sermons in church, by lessons in school and by instruction in the home. The people's strong sense of ethnicity reinforced their devotional practices, and their religious beliefs infused the traditional pride of their national spirit. It was precisely this interrelationship of ethnicity and morality—this distinctive socioreligious culture—that would cause residents of South Boston to react violently and self-righteously to anything they regarded as a challenge to their ethnic pride, their religious beliefs and their moral principles.

4

PENINSULA POLITICS

T HOUGH THE BOSTON IRISH ACHIEVED SOME SOCIAL ACCEPTANCE
and financial security by the end of the Civil War, if they were
to advance their interests and become a significant force in the
affairs of the city they would need political influence. When they first
arrived in the middle of the nineteenth century, the Irish did not have
a political machine of their own, and they certainly were not invited
to join any of those already operating in Boston. Unlike most other
American cities of that time, where newcomers were welcomed into
the existing political structure almost as soon as they got off the boat,
the Boston Irish were forced to build their own Democratic organization virtually from the ground up.

Denied any access to political power in the "old country" for centuries, the Irish often found themselves despised in their adopted land
as well, and they were determined to achieve a measure of unassailable
personal security and ethnic solidarity. Most avenues for rapid economic
advancement were closed to them, especially in a city with a traditional,
rigidly controlled financial establishment. Politics, therefore, provided a ready-made road to power and influence for those who were quick,
shrewd and tough enough to seize opportunity. Those who took the
leadership in Irish politics were strong men who ruled their wards with
gentle smiles and iron fists.

Known as "bosses," these men established themselves as centers of
patronage and influence and turned out the votes of "their people" with
almost mathematical precision. In the West End's Ward 8, Martin

Lomasney, known to his friends as the great "Mahatma," exercised extraordinary power, and in the nearby North End, the cocky John F. "Honey Fitz" Fitzgerald ruled the roost. Joe Corbett was kingpin in Charlestown; Patrick Kennedy directed things in East Boston; Joe O'Connell headed up Dorchester's sprawling Ward 20; and "Smiling Jim" Donovan controlled the immigrants living in the tenements and boarding houses of the South End's Ward 9. P. J. "Pea Jacket" Maguire was boss of Roxbury's Ward 17 until he was ousted by a young, up-and-coming politician by the name of James Michael Curley.

For many an Irish ward boss, however, politics was more than a chance to gain personal power or social advancement. It was also an invaluable opportunity to provide effective assistance to his own people at a time when they could not obtain many of the essentials of life from any other source. Their needs were largely basic but mostly unattainable—food and clothing, dentures and eyeglasses, jobs and pardons, medical care and legal advice—and the price of their political support was their ward boss's assurance that he would supply these needs.

John William Ward defined two major strains of thought in Boston's approach to political policy and public interest. The older strain, coming from traditional Puritan-Yankee-Brahmin sources, he called "rational politics." By this he meant a coherent system of bureaucratic politics designed to work in the "public interest" and tending toward a political leader who steadfastly pursued the "general good" and resisted selfish interests, pressure groups or single-issue constituencies. Such a system, Ward specified, appeals especially to administrators, corporate managers and salaried intellectuals. As the native Bostonian viewed public policy under this system, the function of government was to establish the rule of law for the community in a rational and equitable manner, to operate the financial system with honesty and frugality, and to insure that the political leaders of the city were gentlemen of background, education and experience.

The second strain—the newer strain in Boston history—Ward called "ethnic politics," a political culture that celebrates the personal, emphasizes family and friendship, and rejects the notion of affection earned only by achievement and performance. The emotional appeal of the ethnic politician, he said, is in a realm of "human values," with little or no legitimacy in the rational bureaucratic world. To point up the difference in these two value systems, Ward repeated a well-known anecdote about the proper Beacon Hill dowager who went ringing doorbells in South Boston on behalf of her candidate for the school committee.

At one house, an Irish housewife listened politely to the lady's appeal and then asked, "But doesn't he have a sister who works for the schools or has something to do with the school system in Boston?" The Boston lady drew herself up and said haughtily, "I assure you, madam, he's not the sort of man who would *ever* use his position to advance the interests of his sister!" Whereupon the South Boston lady responded, "Well, if the sonuvabitch won't help his own sister, then why should I vote for him?" and slammed the door.

To the newly arrived immigrant the major function of government was clear: to provide him and his family with safety and security, furnish them with the basic necessities of life, and offer them the practical opportunities for social and economic advancement. "I think that there's got to be in every ward somebody that any bloke can come to—no matter what he's done—and get help," Martin Lomasney is reported to have told the writer and social critic Lincoln Steffens. "Help, you understand; none of your law and justice, but help." Lomasney further philosophized: "The great mass of people are interested in only three things—food, clothing and shelter. A politician in a district such as mine sees to it that his people get these things. If he does, then he doesn't have to worry about their loyalty and support." It was as simple as that. Power and patronage went hand in hand in the Irish neighborhoods.

The Boston Irish used power and patronage to climb the political ladder in long and painful steps. In the early years after the Civil War, when the Democratic party was still tainted by the disgrace of secession and rebellion, Irish Democratic ward organizations were pitifully weak, displaying little unity, discipline or continuity. The only way local bosses could gain any political leverage at the city level was to throw their votes to entrenched Democratic politicians like Benjamin F. Butler, or to sympathetic and social-minded Yankees like Josiah Quincy III. The support of Irish voters was an important factor in the election of Butler as governor of Massachusetts in 1882, and most newcomers rejoiced when he appointed the first Irish-American to judicial office the following year. In 1884 the Irish provided further evidence of growing ethnic voting power when Irish-born Hugh O'Brien was elected mayor of Boston. He served four successive terms in that office, until the progressive Josiah Quincy took over the job in 1896. Quincy served until 1899, and after a single two-year term by Republican Thomas N. Hart, the bosses campaigned successfully for the election of Patrick A. Collins, the second Irish-born mayor in Boston's history.

With the election of Collins, South Boston just missed having a native
resident in the mayor's office. After his father died in 1847, Collins
emigrated with his mother to Boston, settled in Chelsea, and then moved
to Ohio when his mother remarried. In 1859 the family moved back
to Massachusetts, settling at 136 Silver Street in South Boston, where
young Collins worked at the upholsterer's trade while studying law.
In 1869 he entered the Harvard Law School, received his degree in
1871, and opened a law office on Washington Street. He became a
familiar figure in the neighborhood as he walked briskly every morning from his home in South Boston across the bridge to his office and
then back again every evening.

Collins moved steadily up the political ladder, serving two terms in
the Massachusetts House of Representatives before moving on to the
State Senate. After serving as chairman of both the Democratic City
Committee and the Democratic State Committee, in 1882 he became
the first Bostonian of Irish descent elected to the United States Congress. In his third term, however, Collins moved from South Boston
to Dorchester, not only to own a better house but also to prevent his
constituents from drafting him for a fourth term. Although lack of
finances would not permit him to accept cabinet positions offered to
him by President Grover Cleveland, Collins did accept the prestigious
and profitable post of consul general at London. When he returned to
Boston in 1897 to resume his private law practice, hard-pressed
Democratic leaders persuaded him to enter local politics again and run
for the office of mayor. In 1901, after a defeat two years earlier, Collins defeated Hart by the largest majority ever given a mayoral candidate, making it clear to all that the Irish were well on their way to
controlling Boston politics.

In most ways, the political organization of South Boston mirrored
that of Boston as a whole. With a population of over eighty thousand
people, the district was divided into three wards—Wards 13, 14 and
15. The lower end of South Boston constituted Ward 13, encompassing the main business and industrial area, from north and west of E
Street across to the Fort Point Channel and the area today occupied
by the Commonwealth Pier and the adjoining railroad yards. Still the
poorest section of South Boston, it had the largest population and the
highest proportion of immigrants. Because the large number of factories,
foundries, shops, stores and barrooms took up much of the limited space,
it was also the most densely settled section of the peninsula. Ward 15,
which ran south of East and West Ninth Streets on the south end of

Dorchester Street, was similar in many respects to Ward 13. It also possessed an industrial section along the lower end of Dorchester Avenue (the old Dorchester Turnpike), was thickly settled, and contained what by this time was the largest single Irish enclave in Boston—Washington Village, near Andrew Square. Yet Ward 15 was not as heavily congested as Ward 13, primarily because the industrial area was not as large. There was a good deal more room for private housing, most of which was made up of multiple-dwelling units.

The "upper end" of South Boston was Ward 14, fast becoming the most sought-after section of the peninsula. By far the most residential section of the district, it covered the large span of land from Broadway and Dorchester Street to City Point, including the entire beach area. Families usually "moved up" from the crowded confines of Ward 13 to the more spacious neighborhoods of Ward 14, with their wider streets, larger two-and three-family houses and delightful expanses of sandy beach. One area of Ward 14, however, adjacent to Ward 13 where Summer Street became L Street, was decidedly industrial, a continuation of the so-called Commonwealth Wharves, which included the Naval Annex. Since it included most of the City Point area, Ward 14 contained the remnants of the earlier Yankee population of South Boston. Though nearly as large as the other two wards, Ward 14 was much less densely settled. With more open space, a more financially secure population and with an important business and commercial district centered along Broadway and Dorchester Streets, it was regarded as a place where the "lace curtain Irish" lived before they were ready to move out of South Boston and into the more affluent suburbs of West Roxbury and Milton.

If the Irish were beginning to dominate politics in the city, this phenomenon was even more true in the peninsula district. By the early 1900s, the population of South Boston was overwhelmingly first- and second-generation Irish—and, therefore, largely Democratic, with political leadership and rank-and-file membership made up of people of Irish extraction. Not only were the Irish heavily involved in local political affairs, but no other major ethnic group offered a political counter-force in the area. There were significant numbers of Germans, Italians, Poles and Lithuanians living in South Boston by this time, but an extremely low percentage of them—not more than 10 percent—were registered voters. Undoubtedly most of these newcomers were intimidated by the impressive number of Irish living in the district and their control of the political apparatus from top to bottom. But other factors influenced their voting patterns. For one thing, as often happened with immigrants from western Europe, the more recent arrivals tended to join the Republican party in their zeal to demonstrate their loyalty to the U. S. Some associated the Democratic party with states' rights, secession, "bossism" and corrupt political practices. Others saw the Republican party as the party of Lincoln, the crusade against slavery and the preservation of the Union. In either case, they became members of a political party that was neither popular nor successful in South Boston. Furthermore, many Germans and Lithuanians were affiliated with the Socialist movement—something totally unacceptable to most traditionally conservative Irish Catholics. It is not clear whether these local groups were isolated or associated with national Socialist parties of the period, but they did make their views known through such publications as *Keleivis*, which started out as a socialist newspaper. These diverse political viewpoints did not allow these European groups to become integrated into the political mainstream of South Boston, or to challenge the prevailing hegemony of the Irish-Catholic majority.

South Boston's three wards, and its strong Irish representation, were a microcosm of Boston's complex structure of twenty-four wards. Each of the three wards had active political organizations, functioning ward committees, ambitious bosses, eager captains, obedient lieutenants and companies of ward-heelers and loyal workers. Like political networks everywhere at the time, most of these machines operated out of neighborhood clubs and associations. At first these were primarily social organizations, like the Red Berry Club, a fraternity of the older residents in the North End, or the Neptune Associates, one of the many boat clubs in the waterfront wards. These were chiefly recreational centers where members could meet to socialize and compare notes about the news of the district. "The club I knew best," one longtime resident recalled, "was the Tiger A. A.," located on the corner of Broadway and Dorchester Street. "A fine meeting place for fine fellows!"

During the 1880s, however, a new type of grassroots institution emerged, designed exclusively to engage in political activities in general and promote the political careers of their founders in particular. One of the earliest of the new political clubs was the Hendricks Club, organized by Martin Lomasney in 1885, through which he dominated West End politics for over a generation. Other chieftains followed Lomasney's example. In 1888 Thomas W. Flood organized the Somerset Associates in South Boston's Ward 14; in the early 1890s John F. Fitzgerald founded the Jefferson Club in the North End's Ward 6; and in 1901 the Tammany

Club of Roxbury's Ward 17 was established to promote the political career of James Michael Curley. With clubs such as the Somerset Associates, the Mitchell Club and the short-lived Samoset Club of Ward 15 available for planning and strategy, local ward leaders were able to get together to support some legislative measure of particular importance to South Boston, or to back a South Boston man for some statewide or federal office. Indeed, to stimulate further common efforts on behalf of the peninsula, several important ward bosses formed what they called the Harmony Board, a council of leaders from the three South Boston wards, very similar to the city's Democratic City Committee, which would plan strategy, support candidates and arrange alliances with other wards.

In one respect, however, South Boston was surprisingly different from many other neighborhoods. None of the district's three wards had a political leader with the kind of personal charisma or organizational talents of Lomasney in the West End or Fitzgerald in the North End. South Boston had not produced a real "boss"—a personality who could unify the three wards or act as unchallenged spokesman for the peninsula district as a whole. It still remains a puzzle why such an active political district failed to produce a single ward boss comparable to those in other neighborhoods. Perhaps it was because South Boston was a relative newcomer to the ward structure; perhaps intense rivalry and constant jealousy among local candidates prevented any one man from rising to the top for any length of time. Some have even suggested that a local tradition against keeping any man in public office too long— symbolized by the old saying, "One, two, up or out!"—might have been a factor. This saying meant that a local candidate was rarely defeated in his first or second try at public office, but by the third time he either moved up (to the State Senate, for example) or was expected to try his hand at some other type of work.

Joe Norton is a case in point. A career politician who had made his reputation as a leader in the city's Board of Aldermen, Norton presided over the Mitchell Club, "looked after the interests of his district," and was generally regarded as the obvious person to become permanent leader of Ward 14. But it never happened. Norton was constantly challenged within his own ward, and in 1909 he went down to defeat when his delegation to the state convention was defeated by a new coalition formed by such men as John E. Baldwin, Edward L. Logan and J. Frank O'Hare. This opposition left Norton "a small fish in a big pond," the *South Boston Inquirer* scoffed, "in fact, almost a minnow

in the political ocean.'' Norton remained in local politics but never
achieved the kind of prominence many people expected. A similar situation prevailed in Ward 15, where William S. McNary, former congressman and state representative, had been a leading figure for many
years. At what appeared to be the height of his political influence,
McNary suddenly lost a good deal of his power. McNary became so
involved in his numerous other interests (he was editing a business
newspaper and conducting insurance and real-estate activities) that he
allowed his Samoset Club to fold up and lost touch with his local constituents. He was also challenged by an effective coalition headed by
Representative James Lane and State Senator Patrick O'Connor, which
whittled away at his traditional base of support. Although McNary, too,
continued to remain an important force in Boston politics for many years,
his own hopes for a permanent political power base had been cut away.

About the closest thing South Boston produced to a ward boss like
Martin Lomasney was probably Jeremiah McNamara, a saloon-keeper
in the lower end's Ward 13. McNamara presided over a district largely composed of recent immigrants from Ireland. They were poor,
unemployed, depressed and desperately in need of food, shelter and
clothing—the very things upon which a successful ward boss built his
name and reputation. McNamara capitalized upon these assets, organized
his district, and ran into little opposition to his own political position
or to the election slates he put up at regular intervals. Although he maintained his one-man rule of Ward 13 for many years and continued to
be an important force in South Boston politics, there is evidence that
McNamara lacked the stamina and determination to rise to the top and
stay there. ''He gets discouraged when he has so many unemployed
people after him,'' the *South Boston Gazette* commented, ''and he is
unable to do anything for them.''

But solidarity in the South Boston wards was constantly threatened
not only by personal weaknesses; the political pressures of outside forces
threatened as well. Very often, the apparent unanimity of local political
leaders, expressed at sessions of the Harmony Board, fell apart under
the influences of other wards and other bosses. In 1909, for example,
Joe Norton defaulted on an agreement to support South Boston resident Edward P. Barry, a candidate for the post of Attorney General
of Massachusetts. Seriously indebted to Martin Lomasney for helping
him beat off the recent challenges of the Baldwin-Logan-O'Hare fac-
tion, Norton had to oppose Barry's nomination. His obligation to
Lomasney was more powerful than his commitment to his South

Boston colleagues. James Michael Curley also developed close connections with South Boston politicians, and in 1909 he expected the support of J. Frank O'Hare in his bid for chairmanship of the Board of Aldermen. Although O'Hare failed to come up with the votes Curley needed, the Ward 17 boss carried the South Boston wards the following year in the congressional elections. Such complex political relationships did a great deal to reduce the power and the solidarity of the South Boston vote before it could achieve desired results.

As time went on, South Boston residents began to resent this lack of personal influence and political representation, not only because of local pride and community status, but also because they saw their district losing its slice of the political pie to neighboring districts with more vocal, vigorous and visible representation at City Hall. South Boston saw itself as a loser in the Boston political game, and there was a growing feeling that South Boston was not getting the same degree of support for its local candidates or its special legislation that its citizens were supplying for candidates or legislation in other parts of the city. This sense of resentment and frustration created much interest and excitement when a South Boston native, Thomas J. Kenny, became a viable candidate for mayor of Boston in 1914. The thought that a South Boston man might finally take over the highest office in city government and be able to do constructive things for the peninsula district was exhilarating. It made the mayoralty election of 1914 one of the toughest and most exciting races in local political history.

The traditional dominance of old-time Yankees in the Boston political establishment had been most seriously threatened in 1905, when John F. Fitzgerald, boss of Ward 6, became the first American-born Irish Catholic to serve as mayor of Boston. Despite the subsequent complaints of such reformist organizations as the Good Government Association and the Citizens' Municipal League, despite the critical investigations of the newly-formed Finance Commission, and despite a new city charter that put city elections on a nonpartisan basis, Honey Fitz also defeated James Jackson Storrow in 1910 and returned to the mayor's office to enjoy the first four-year term in the city's history. Both the Yankee and the Democratic ward bosses wondered what would happen in 1914, when Fitzgerald would complete his term of office and move to newer pastures. Would the old Protestant establishment be able to name one of its own once again? Would it at least be able to choose an "acceptable" and respectable Irishman like Hugh O'Brien or Patrick Collins? Or would the local Democratic City Committee follow up on Fitzgerald's success and organize its collective support behind some other experienced political leader from one of the Irish neighborhoods?

It came as a great surprise to both factions, then, when thirty-nine-year-old James Michael Curley announced that his hat was in the ring. A former member of the state legislature and the city council, young Curley had served a single term in the United States Congress before deciding he preferred the more familiar climate of Boston politics. A charismatic personality and an imaginative campaigner, Curley presented a decided challenge to both the Yankee Republicans and the Irish Democratic ward bosses. He dismissed the members of the Good Government Association, an organization of business and civic leaders formed in 1903 to oversee the operations of city government, as simple-minded "Goo Goos." He characterized the Brahmin aristocracy as "clubs of female faddists, old gentlemen with disordered livers or pessimists croaking over imaginary good old days and ignoring the sunlit present." At the same time, he ridiculed the Irish ward bosses as a "collection of chowderheads," dismissing the influential Democratic City Committee as a pack of "empty eggshells" who were incapable of delivering the vote. He publicly rejected the support of both influential groups and appealed directly to the voters of the various ethnic neighborhoods on his own terms.

Curley, however, was far from the only contestant to come forward to claim the mayor's office. A surprising number of candidates rushed forward to file nomination papers, including John R. Murphy, a former state legislator from Charlestown and a protege of Martin Lomasney; John A. Kelliher, a former congressman from the South End; and Ernest Smith, a Progressive party city councillor running as an independent. Even Fitzgerald changed his mind and announced his intention to run for another term.

Finally, there was Kenny, the career Irish-Catholic politician from South Boston and the first resident of the district to make a serious run for the office of mayor. The son of immigrant parents, Kenny had graduated from the city's public schools, studied law while clerking for the law office of Marse, Loomis and Lane (a firm he later headed), and in 1912 received an honorary L.L.D. from Fordham University. Starting out as a member of the Democratic Ward Committee of Ward 15, Kenny moved into city politics first by becoming a member of the Boston Chamber of Commerce, and then by serving on the Boston School Committee from 1899 to 1907. In 1909, with the endorsement of the Good Government Association, Kenny was elected to the Boston City Council, where he rose to become president.

A rather dry and austere man, conservative and industrious, Thomas J. Kenny was reported to be a "demon for statistical details." He concerned himself mostly with budgetary matters and questions of public finance. During his term on the school committee, when he was chairman of the committee on supplies, Kenny established a reputation as a fiscal conservative by keeping down expenditures and purchasing "the best at the lowest cost in the best market." As a member of the city council Kenny continued his emphasis on fiscal issues. Even in working for improvements in his home district of South Boston, most of his efforts were confined to the area of public works, such as roping off the streets for the Evacuation Day parade, improving the grounds of South Boston High School, putting up new street lights, or appropriating funds for a new aquarium at City Point. Many people viewed Kenny as a "cold fish" or a tight-fisted "old lady." His critics recalled the time he delayed for a week the authorization of death benefits for a widow of a fireman killed in the line of duty, or the time he opposed an increase in pensions for retired city workers on the grounds that the new law would also apply to retired department heads as well. There were many other people, however, especially members of the Good Government Association, who commended Kenny for his honest, responsible and businesslike administration of city finances. They appreciated that Kenny was "not popular in some quarters" because he had been opposed to "spending money," but they regarded him as "a man of firm ideas." The reformers applauded his "intimate knowledge of the needs of the city" and his "commanding leadership in the city council."

In view of his rather lackluster appearance, his weakness as a campaigner and his popular parsimonious image, the fifty-year-old Kenny might not have been viewed as a serious challenger for the post of mayor in 1914 had it not been for an unexpected turn of events. With December 19, 1913, as the final deadline for filing nomination papers, the various candidates were preparing for some six weeks of active campaigning—from about December 1 to election day on January 13, 1914. On December 5, however, while watching firemen putting out a fire in the South End, Mayor Fitzgerald suddenly collapsed. Three days later he called upon all candidates to restrict their campaigning until after Christmas—presumably to give him time to get back on his feet and get his own organization started again—leaving only three weeks for active campaigning. In the interests of fair play, all the candidates agreed to comply with the mayor's request except James Michael Curley. Curley claimed Fitzgerald was faking, that he really delayed the race because he heard that Curley was about to give a series of public lectures. The first one, "Graft in Ancient Times and Modern," would call attention to nepotism in various departments of city government. The second lecture, "Great Lovers, from Cleopatra to Toodles," would obviously bring up Fitzgerald's well-known dalliance with a blond cigarette girl named "Toodles" Ryan, who worked at the Ferncroft Inn. According to Curley, Honey Fitz decided that discretion was the better part of valor, and claimed illness. Curley's claims widened considerably the already serious rift between the young Roxbury candidate and the Democratic ward leaders of the city. By Christmastime, the field had been whittled down drastically. Fitzgerald withdrew from the race by December 18; Murphy took himself out of the contest on December 22; Smith did not get enough signatures to be nominated; and Kelliher finally withdrew on December 31, when it became evident that he did not have a solid base of support. Only two candidates remained: James Michael Curley and Thomas J. Kenny.

Honey Fitz's withdrawal from the contest added to the bitterness of his personal feud with young Curley and created a serious problem within the Democratic party of Boston. The political leaders of the city "did not know where they stood," the *Journal* reported, describing rank-and-file voters as being "in a state of bewilderment." From the announcement of his candidacy, Curley had been formally opposed by nearly all the members of the powerful Democratic City Committee, who lined up behind Fitzgerald. Curley's refusal to observe the postponement in campaigning after Fitzgerald's collapse further enraged the old ward bosses. When Fitzgerald decided to retire from the race, the Democratic leaders were in no mood to accept Curley as Fitzgerald's successor. They regarded him as an impertinent upstart and a dangerous renegade who would build up a citywide political machine of his own and undercut the traditional role of the city bosses.

Yet it was by no means a foregone conclusion that the angry ward bosses would give their support to Kenny. Kenny seemed to personify the old-fashioned, subservient, compliant and "acceptable" Irishman the Yankees admired so much but which the Irish bosses had determined to reject. In the late nineteenth century the Yankee establishment had successfully delayed the coming of Irish supremacy by selecting such intelligent Irish-born leaders as Hugh O'Brien and Patrick Collins to serve as occasional representatives for their ethnic constituencies. As mayors of Boston both these men proved to be popular and efficient executives who managed the city in an orderly and conservative manner without indulging in "ethnic politics." All the time, however, they were properly deferential to the city's cultural traditions, and they never posed the threat of a larger takeover by a permanent Irish political apparatus. Fitzgerald's election demonstrated in dramatic fashion that if the ward bosses could get together and support a single candidate of their own, they could finally wrest political control of the city from the Yankees and establish a new power base in the Irish neighborhoods. Many of the bosses feared that election of Kenny, with his business support and his Good Government backing, might well mean a return to oldtime Yankee dominance.

When Fitzgerald withdrew from the contest, Kenny fully expected to get his personal support, as well as the official endorsement of the Democratic City Committee. No such endorsement was forthcoming, however. Fitzgerald announced that he was remaining "neutral" in this election, and the members of the Democratic City Committee split so badly over the race that they took no action at all. The *Record* reported that "a respectable portion of the committee" had already gone over to Curley, and that the Roxbury candidate now had at least nine ward chairmen, out of a possible twenty-six, supporting him. Although he was clearly disappointed, Kenny saw himself as a viable candidate. He still had the support of those disgruntled city regulars who feared Curley's personal ambition and his actions after Fitzgerald's collapse. Furthermore, Curley continued to emphasize that he was the underdog in the campaign, opposed by the "big bosses" and their political machines. He delighted in publicizing his opposition to such ward bosses as Diamond Jim Timilty and Jerry Watson, accusing them of being in league with the Good Government Association and the railroad companies. Many ward leaders resented this demagoguery and supported Kenny. More important, perhaps, was Kenny's official support from the Citizens' Municipal League, the political arm of the Good Government Association. Still embarrassed by the severe defeat Fitzgerald had inflicted four years earlier upon their own hand-picked candidate, James Jackson Storrow, and looking upon Curley as cast in the same political mold, members of the Good Government Association were determined to strike a blow for honest government. They came out clearly and publicly on behalf of Kenny's candidacy and took every opportunity to denounce his Roxbury opponent. Curley was "one of the chief exemplars in Boston of Tammany methods," they charged, whose election would mean "corruption in politics and business." "Mr. Curley's candidacy creates a crisis in city politics," the association stated. "We

strongly urge his defeat." In throwing their considerable support behind
an Irish-Catholic from South Boston, they assumed they would be able
to eliminate the issues of religion and ethnicity and force the voters to
concentrate on the merits of the two candidates. Finally, Kenny also
had the backing of the Republicans of the city, led by former governor
Curtis Guild. As a result, he received the public endorsement of nearly
every one of Boston's leading newspapers, including the *Post*, the
Transcript and the *Advertiser*. The whole race suggested that South
Boston might well have a native son in the mayor's office soon. Indeed, South Boston was seen increasingly as the "balance in the election" or, as Mayor Fitzgerald described it, "the determining factor in
the fight."

The campaigning in South Boston was a little slow getting started
because of the postponement. During these weeks, the Kenny campaign
made preliminary arrangements organizing committees, preparing
statements, printing pamphlets and drawing up plans for rallies and
parades. This campaign would focus less on pressing political issues—
reducing the tax rate, promoting new industries, raising employment
or providing better housing inspection—as on the overall moral and
ideological image each candidate projected of himself—and of his opponent. Voters were presented with a choice between good and evil,
honesty and corruption, rich and poor, immigrant and native, Irish ward
boss and State Street banker. Interest in the contest ran high, and in
wards where there were two "Democratic factions," people smoothed
over their old troubles and "united in their support for either Curley
or Kenny."

Since Curley had never agreed to abide by Fitzgerald's postponement,
he opened his campaign in South Boston on December 17, 1913—a good
two weeks before Kenny was ready to go into action. This decision was
something of a risk, because although Curley was a popular favorite
in many parts of South Boston, with his ready wit and his Galway charm,
he had also had some nasty tangles with rival politicians. Many people
recalled Curley's occasional failure to deliver the votes he had promised from Ward 17; that in the 1910 congressional elections he had opposed William S. McNary of South Boston; and that in the 1912 contest he had defeated another South Boston man for Congress, James
B. Connolly. Indeed, Kenny and others frequently reminded voters of
the district that in the 1910 election Curley had angrily denounced the
people of South Boston as "thugs, muckers, doormat thieves and milk-
bottle robbers." With a great show of confidence, however, Curley

moved into the peninsula district, reminding the voters that as a city councillor he had sponsored the enlargement of the L Street baths and other local improvements, and that as a congressman he had worked to increase employment by expanding the wharf district. He also pointed out that he had been responsible for bringing such a prominent national figure as Senator Champ Clark of Missouri to participate in the previous year's Evacuation Day parade. And to help property owners who complained of being overtaxed, Curley came up with a plan to renovate property and promote industrial development along Dorchester Avenue by having one thousand men contribute a thousand dollars each to a special fund. By December 22, Curley had already received the public endorsement of the Ward 14 Democratic Club of South Boston.

Although Kenny had agreed to delay the opening of his official campaign, his supporters had been hard at work behind the scenes. On December 22, 1913, his headquarters issued to the press a letter from Jeremiah McNamara, undisputed boss of Ward 13 and former president of the Democratic City Committee, announcing his support for Kenny. The jubilation of the Kenny supporters proved short-lived, however, when the following day McNamara denied that he had ever issued such a letter. The controversy was finally ironed out when, on December 24, after a conference with Kenny, McNamara announced that he was planning to support the South Boston candidate. The confusion, he explained, had occurred because of the release date of the letter, which was not to have been made public until after Christmas. With McNamara's endorsement finally clarified, Kenny pressed ahead with his efforts to gather neighborhood support, and by December 28 was able to make public a list of men who backed his candidacy and agreed to speak at his future rallies—highly respected personalities such as William C. Wall, former secretary to Mayor Fitzgerald and Kenny's South Boston manager; Francis J. W. Ford, well-known Harvard athlete and lawyer from South Boston; Arthur D. Cooper, newspaper reporter from the *South Boston Inquirer*; Herbert Callahan, lawyer and law partner in the firm of Creed, Costello and Callahan; and James B. Connolly, journalist and Curley's opponent in the 1912 congressional contest. Also on Kenny's bandwagon were John J. Lydon, editor and publisher of the *South Boston Inquirer*, and John H. Toomey, former editor of the local newspaper.

On December 30, 1913, Thomas J. Kenny formally opened his campaign with a series of personal appearances at which he called upon the voters of the district to "Make Kenny South Boston's First Mayor."

Reminding voters of his many services and achievements on behalf of the district, Kenny appealed to the residents as a neighbor and fellow South Bostonian and promised to bring to South Boston, at long last, its fair share of public funding. He pointed to his recent successes in the city council in getting allocations for a new courthouse, for an enlargement of the L Street bathhouses and for a new aquarium in Marine Park. He closed with a personal attack upon Curley that recalled his outburst against the people of South Boston as thieves and bottle-robbers. After a brief lull in the speechmaking, while the two candidates accused each other of fraudulent tactics with regard to signatures on their nomination papers, the campaign quickly heated up again.

It was a typical Boston political campaign of the period, with all the fixings. In those days before radio or television, open-air rallies were popular activities that drew thousands of participants in long lines of horse-drawn carts and wagons, automobiles and trucks, winding through the neighborhoods with horns blaring, trumpets blasting, whistles shrieking and red flares and torches lighting up the evening skies. Each candidate had his own large, flat-bed truck with a piano, a banjo player or an accordionist, a young Irish step-dancer, and a couple of song-and-dance men performing popular ragtime tunes for the crowds. Every now and then, the procession would stop at certain strategically located rally corners, where popular speakers like the retired light-heavyweight boxer "Hambone" Kelly would give an uproarious speech in favor of one of the candidates. Flood Square, at the corner of I Street and East Broadway, was a favorite rally corner; Perkins Square, at the intersection of Broadway and Dorchester Street, another; the corner of E and West Broadway was another favorite stop; and another was the intersection of Telegraph Street and Dorchester Street, just across from St. Augustine's Church. This last spot was especially important, because it was right on the boundary between Wards 13 and 15.

Having established a solid footing in the district, Curley now launched into a bold personal attack upon his opponent and his contact with the "vested interests" of downtown Boston. Accompanied by strolling musicians and singers, surrounded by cheering throngs as he spoke from the back of his automobile, the young candidate was both a lively entertainer and a stellar political attraction. The crowds responded with delight when he announced he would defeat Kenny "in his own precinct, in his own street, and if he lived in a six-tenement house, I'd beat him in his own house!" Playing on a theme that he would return to again and again throughout the campaign, Curley called upon Kenny to explain his connection with the New York, New Haven and Hartford Railroad. "I would like to know," he told the voters, "why the banking interests, the railroads, and the corporations are so anxious for Mr. Kenny's success in this campaign." Despite the fact that most of the city's ward leaders had already gone over to his camp, Curley continued to create the illusion that he was the helpless victim of the wrath of the city machine. "I *want* the opposition of the corrupt bosses and leaders, and I *want* the saleable and purchasable element to be opposed to me," he told the crowds with consummate political skill, "and then I will go in and beat them all!" Promising to operate the city administration according to the principles of sound business practice, Curley dismissed Kenny's political record as "weak" and "puny," and cleverly challenged him to a public debate—with the proceeds to go to the Carney Hospital in South Boston.

By this time Kenny was clearly on the defensive, even in his own home town. He responded angrily to Curley's allegations that he was in collusion with the New Haven Railroad. "In my entire career in public office," he declared indignantly, "I have never had any relations with the New Haven Railroad of any kind whatsoever!" He launched a series of personal counterattacks against Curley, accusing him of planting hecklers in the audience to shout down speakers and disrupt the proceedings at a series of rallies on January 5, and blaming him for organizing similar disruptions at a Kenny rally at Faneuil Hall a few nights earlier. If Curley were elected, he warned his listeners, he would develop a citywide political machine that would provide a never-ending source of patronage to the members of his Tammany Club in Roxbury.

But even Kenny himself must have seen that he was no match for Curley's personality or rhetoric. Even at this early stage, his attacks on Curley seemed shrill and defensive, his indignant arguments in his own defense questionable and insincere. Kenny saw he would have to rely much more upon careful organization and thoughtful planning to beat his opponent. Making every effort to line up more key political figures in the district who would pledge their support and provide the votes, Kenny reemphasized his role as South Boston's "native son," as the first great opportunity the district had to put one of their own into the mayor's office. Word quickly went about that it would be "political suicide" for any political figure who planned to remain "in the public life of South Boston" to oppose his candidacy.

Recognizing Kenny's tactics, Curley rounded up some additional political support of his own among a small group of influential lawyers

and key ward leaders in the district, including Representative James
J. Twohey of Ward 13; Representative John J. Murphy of Ward 14;
and John Creed, James Creed and Senator William P. Hickey of Ward
15. Perhaps his most useful endorsement came from Lieutenant Governor
Edward P. Barry, a popular native son, who had a great deal of influence in South Boston. Curley also had some strong support among
local businessmen. His largest contributor was Patrick Graham, a
manufacturer whose place of business was located in South Boston.

As the campaign entered its final week, the rallies increased steadily, and the pace of the contest grew in intensity. Despite all the support
he had gathered behind him in South Boston, it was evident from the
almost hysterical personal attacks he launched against his rival that Kenny
was becoming insecure and overwrought. On January 9, four days before
the election, Kenny issued a frenzied appeal to the voters of South Boston
on what he described as the "real issues" of the campaign. "Do you
want it understood all over the country," he asked, "that the city of
Boston has fallen into the hands of leadership which stands for everything
opposed to good government...which stands for the use of taxpayers'
money to build a personal political machine?" "I ask you," he repeated,
"do you want the city turned over to a gang of unscrupulous politicians?"

Curley, on the other hand, parried Kenny's attacks with easy grace,
using humor and sarcasm to blunt the effects of his opponent's frenzy.
In his closing rallies he produced gales of laughter by holding up his
hand, shaking his forefinger reprovingly, and clucking simply,
"Naughty, naughty, Tommy!" The constant taunt of "Naughty Tommy" followed Kenny for the rest of the campaign and made it more
difficult than ever for voters to take him seriously as a mayoral candidate. And all the while, Curley continued with his antibusiness tirades
against Lawrence Minot and the directors of the New Haven Railroad,
whom he accused of joining forces with the ward bosses of the city
in support of Kenny. On January 11, 1914, two days before the election, Curley conducted a series of whirlwind rallies in each of the
district's three wards. He called upon the crowds to give him their support as "South Boston's candidate," and he insisted that he was much
more entitled to their votes. "There never was a time when a South
Boston citizen came to me for assistance," he declared, "that didn't
find a true and sincere friend in James Michael Curley." During this
final swing an episode took place that would go down as a classic in
the popular folklore of the district. While speaking in Kenny's Ward
14, Curley decided to use the impressive backdrop of St. Augustine's

Church on Dorchester Street as an appropriate setting for a few remarks on the spiritual theme of forgiveness. "I am reminded by Brother Kenny," he intoned piously, "of those beautiful words in that beautiful prayer, Give us this day our daily bread and forgive us our trespasses ...." As he was speaking, out of the corner of his eye he caught sight of a bum lifting his new fur coat from his waiting automobile. "*Get that sonuvabitch, he's stealing my coat!*" he snapped at one of his lieutenants off to the side, and without breaking stride he continued to mesmerize the crowd with his golden voice: "...as we forgive those who trespass against us. And lead us not into temptation, but deliver us from evil, Amen." Some of the details change in the telling—the time, the place, the people and so on—but old-time political observers never fail to include this story as one of their favorite tales of "Young Jim" at the top of his form.

The momentum had clearly swung in Curley's direction, and from this point on the Kenny people simply went through the motions, holding final rallies and thanking their supporters for their hard work during the campaign. According to the newspapers, the Kenny organization had already given up the election as a "forlorn hope," placing any remaining hopes they had on a last-minute turnout of what they called the "silent vote." Even these hopes were dashed when a newspaper report on January 12, the day before the election, said that Martin Lomasney of Ward 8 had indicated his preference by putting a cross next to Curley's name on a sample ballot at the Hendricks Club.

The final results of the 1914 election came as no surprise. James Michael Curley became mayor of Boston by 5,740 votes and carried two out of South Boston's three wards. Despite subzero temperatures on election day, the turnout of voters was higher in South Boston than in most other parts of the city. Curley easily swept Ward 13, the lower end, with its large number of poor immigrants, gaining 1,272 votes to Kenny's 700 votes. Curley also took the City Point section of Ward 14 by a 119-vote margin. Although Kenny managed to carry his own home neighborhood of Ward 15, Curley made a remarkably strong showing in that district, losing by only 1,331 votes to Kenny's 1,479. Despite Curley's overall victory, the strategy of the Good Government Association in supporting an Irish-Catholic candidate showed productive results. Four years earlier its candidate in the 1910 election, James Jackson Storrow, had polled a mere 2,774 votes in the three South Boston wards, compared with Fitzgerald's 6,741—less than 35 percent of the total votes of the district. By contrast, Kenny received over 45 percent of the South

Boston vote, running up a total of 3,722 votes to Curley's 4,265—a far better showing than Storrow's, but not enough. South Boston voters had obviously decided that they would rely upon the young Roxbury candidate rather than one of "their own" to look after their political interests in the coming years.

Neighborhood politics was ethnic politics in those days, and vice versa. The city elections of 1914 were a colorful example of how an ethnic neighborhood like South Boston looked at city politics mainly in terms of the needs and desires of its own community. Curley had come to typify the social values and political ideals of the peninsula district much more closely and dramatically than the Good-Government-supported Mr. Kenny. In his charm, his wit, his appeals to Celtic origins and his outrageous assaults upon the old-time Brahmin establishment, Curley quickly became an "adopted son" of the neighborhood that never failed to give him its loyalty and its votes. Indeed, it often comes as a great surprise to many visitors—even to many native Bostonians—to learn that James Michael Curley was *not* a native of South Boston.

But while this decentralized political process may have been advantageous for the individual neighborhoods, as they used their blocs of ethnic votes as bargaining chips to put their own candidate into office and obtain a greater share of the municipal budget, that process did much to hamper the development of a coherent and comprehensive policy of city planning and municipal management well into the twentieth century. With the interests of the numerous separate neighborhoods constantly pitted against the needs of the downtown Boston area, it would become almost impossible for city leaders to formulate an overall long-range program encompassing the concerns of Boston as a whole. The image of Boston as a "city of neighborhoods" may have sounded warm, friendly and "comfortable," but it would go far toward preventing the development of a united and integrated municipality.

5

"MY HOME TOWN"

"THE CONCEPT OF NEIGHBORHOOD OFFERS TWO HUMANIZING characteristics to modern urban society," William C. McCready wrote in an essay on the Irish neighborhood. The first is the principle of "subsidiarity," the belief that nothing should be done by a larger organization if it can be done by a smaller one. The second characteristic is the principle of an "organic community"—a community in which members "trust each other, are vulnerable to each other, and have close social relationships." In such a neighborhood, according to McCready, people are allowed to feel that the community is theirs, and that what is most important in life happens at the local level. Although McCready draws heavily upon his own home neighborhood on the South Side of Chicago for his analysis of the ethnic neighborhood in America, much of what he says applies with equal validity to South Boston. As a predominantly Irish-Catholic neighborhood, it had clearly developed into an organic community, with the principle of subsidiarity drawing its members together into an extraordinarily close and vulnerable relationship.

The distinctive development of neighborhoods at the turn of the century grew out of the expansion and reshaping of the City of Boston after the Civil War. Between 1850 and 1873, almost every nearby city and town debated the relative advantages and disadvantages of annexation to Boston. Those in favor of annexation wanted to benefit from Boston's increasingly modern water and sewage services; those opposed did not want to lose their independence of action and their semirural way of

life. In 1868, however, Roxbury voted for annexation. Dorchester
followed in 1870; Charlestown, Brighton and West Roxbury joined the
others in 1873; and Hyde Park was added to Boston in 1912. This process increased the city's territory by 441 percent. Together with the
continued reclamation of land throughout the city (most notably in the
Back Bay), this territory created new havens for housing development,
speculation and middle- and upper-class migration. In this way, the city
became further segregated in its residential patterns—from the elegant
architecture of the Back Bay, to the middle-class "cottages" of West
Roxbury, to the tenements of the North End, to the double- and triple-
deckers of South Boston. By the beginning of the twentieth century,
the distinctive nature of the individual neighborhoods and the growing
differences between them made the people themselves sensitive to the
unique and special character of the place in which they lived.

Perhaps the most colorful and nostalgic period of South Boston's
history as a distinctive Irish-Catholic neighborhood took place during
the first quarter of the twentieth century—before the onslaught of the
Great Depression and the catastrophic effects of the Second World War.
Life in the peninsula district during that generation reflected the cultural
innocence and social naivete of small communities all over the nation.
Families still lived in the past—in an age of gaslights, cobblestones and
horse-drawn wagons—but modern industrial technology was also changing their lives dramatically and substantially. During this period of transition the people of South Boston created a highly idealized and decidedly
romanticized reputation of their district.

The intensified pride residents of South Boston felt in their
neighborhood was evident in a series of monuments and public buildings
that characterized the peninsula district as a place of special significance
and historic importance. In 1893, for example, the City of Boston
honored one of the leading heroes of the Civil War, erecting a statue
of the late Admiral David G. Farragut in the center of a circle at the
end of Broadway in South Boston's Marine Park, facing out toward
the waters of Pleasure Bay. In the decades after the Civil War, many
localities throughout the nation had honored such well-known military
figures as Ulysses S. Grant, William T. Sherman and Philip H. Sheridan,
but little or no recognition had been given to any naval hero of the conflict. Given the maritime character of South Boston, a monument
dedicated to the hero of Mobile Bay seemed most appropriate. The official unveiling of this statue on June 28, 1893, was the occasion of
a gala celebration in the district. The day was set aside as a holiday,

schools and offices were closed throughout the city, flags were displayed on City Hall and other public buildings, and residents of South Boston opened their homes to guests and visiting friends.

As large crowds looked on, an impressive parade stepped off about 2:30 and made its way along Broadway to the site of the unveiling. Leading off was a platoon of Boston's mounted police, followed by two companies of United States Marines from the Charlestown Navy Yard. After this contingent came battalions of sailors and naval cadets from several ships berthed in Boston harbor, various army and navy bands, the St. Augustine band and the St. Vincent drum corps. Organized groups of Civil War veterans and prominent political and military figures rode along in carriages, accompanied by several Russian naval officers, who attracted a great deal of attention. Twenty-five South Boston letter carriers waved to the crowds from a tally-ho coach drawn by six large horses, and behind them came a large float depicting the USS *Hartford*— Admiral Farragut's favorite ship.

After the parade reached the City Point site, the formal exercises began about three o'clock with the singing of the "American Hymn," an opening benediction, the reading of a special poem, the playing of music from Wagner's *Pilgrim Chorus* and an oration by former governor Alexander Rice. Little Annie E. Flood, daughter of Alderman Thomas W. Flood, did the actual unveiling. Dressed in a white sailor suit with darkblue piping, the young girl stepped forward and pulled the cord, unveiling Admiral Farragut. The statue quickly became a well-known landmark and still remains at its original location. A nearby artillery battery boomed out a noisy salute, promptly answered by the guns of warships anchored in the harbor. The festivities continued well into the evening until they were brought to what most residents felt was a fitting conclusion, a colorful display of fireworks lighting up the summer sky over City Point.

The dedication of the Farragut statue took place at a time when residents of South Boston were demanding a separate high school of their own, and in all probability the excitement of one event carried over to the success of the other. Although the grammar schools of the district had expanded at regular intervals to accommodate the growing population, young people had to travel considerable distances in all kinds of weather to attend one of the high schools in Boston. After six years of arguing and wrangling, however, South Boston residents finally obtained appropriation for the construction of their own high school. In 1895 they selected a site at the crest of G Street, on the top of Dorchester

Heights, where an old reservoir had once been located. Here they built a three-story high school of lightly mottled gray brick with limestone trimmings, designed along the lines of the executive mansion in Washington, D. C. Set well back from the street, sixteen granite steps led up to the central entrance, three doors that opened into a large vestibule finished in Knoxville marble. After a colorful dedication ceremony, at which Senator Henry Cabot Lodge delivered a moving oration, the high school was officially opened at the beginning of the school year in the fall of 1901. Boys and girls from South Boston who had been attending various schools in the city proper were now transferred to the new school in their neighborhood.

That year also saw the district's first official St. Patrick's Day parade. For many years the Boston Irish had held parades throughout the city in honor of St. Patrick, and in 1892 the city fathers authorized the closing of the Boston Public Library on March 17—much to the disgust of many native Bostonians. "Columbus didn't discover America; it was St. Patrick!" complained Thomas Bailey Aldrich, editor of the *Atlantic*, when he heard about the decision to close the library. Pressure continued to mount, however, and in 1901 the city authorized a parade in South Boston on March 17 under the guise of a public commemoration of the evacuation of Boston in 1776.

Because March 17 fell on a Sunday, observances were scheduled for Monday, March 18, 1901. The marching units assembled at Q Street (now Farragut Road), adjoining Marine Park. To provide shelter from the piercing March winds that came sweeping across City Point from Boston harbor, the Head House was heated for the occasion, providing welcome relief for the brass bands, the school cadets and the other shivering participants. Once under way, the parade marched the length of South Boston, across the bridge and into the city, with bands playing and marines and sailors from the USS *Hartford* and the USS *Lancaster* appearing as special guests. Political leaders in high silk hats, including Governor Crane, Mayor Thomas N. Hart and South Boston congressman Henry F. Naphen, rode along in an open horse-drawn barouche, standing up at intervals to acknowledge the cheers of the thousands of spectators who lined the march's route. The parade came to an end at historic Faneuil Hall in the heart of Boston, where the military and political dignitaries remained to be dined and feted. Back in South Boston, the South Boston Citizens' Association held a banquet at Gray's Hall on the corner of I and Emerson Streets, where Congressman Naphen delivered an address for the happy occasion.

This renewed interest in South Boston's history, especially its critical role in forcing the British to evacuate Boston, caused many residents to think about an appropriate memorial. Representative John J. Toomey took the lead in organizing local support for a monument to honor the great victory of George Washington and his troops at Dorchester Heights. At first, some residents feared that these new activities might interfere with ongoing efforts to build a new high school in the same general area. Gradually, however, city leaders like Josiah Quincy III came out in support of the project, and State Senator James A. Gallivan of South Boston secured passage of a bill authorizing the erection of a monument. In March 1899, Governor Roger Wolcott appointed a special committee to come up with an appropriate design. Peabody and Sterns won the public competition for the monument and erected a colonial Georgian-revival design executed in gleaming white Georgian marble. Rising from a mound ten feet high to a height of over a hundred feet, the monument overlooked the intersection of several walkways on top of Dorchester Heights.

The Dorchester Heights monument was completed in 1901 and officially dedicated on March 17, 1902, a day set aside for general celebration. Schools were closed, stores and businesses suspended operations, and people throughout the district decorated their homes for the occasion. Although it started out as a cloudy day, with a light rain lasting most of the morning, the weather cleared up in time for the parade at one o'clock. Headed by the Boston mounted police and the United States Marine Band, followed by contingents of soldiers and sailors as well as political dignitaries including Governor Winthrop Murray Crane and Mayor Patrick A. Collins, the parade made its way up and down the streets of the district until it finally arrived at the site of the new monument.

After the formal dedication, all sorts of games and athletic events occupied residents of South Boston for the remainder of the afternoon, and in the evening the South Boston Citizens' Association held an Evacuation Day banquet in Gray's Hall. Many families held open houses, various clubs and organizations conducted special programs, and the night finally came to a close with a series of band concerts and a rousing display of fireworks.

South Boston residents enjoyed these events to the fullest. With great pride in the distinctiveness of their neighborhood, they became more aware than ever of its historic importance. They saw the population of the district growing, its prosperity steadily increasing. Deeply conscious of the importance of social and economic mobility in the lives of their own families, they boasted of the great number of churches in their neighborhood, and the impressive private homes along East Broadway. These large two- and three-story brownstone mansions, with elaborate wrought-iron railings framing the outside steps and decorative wrought-iron fences running along the front, housed many of the district's most prominent business and professional leaders.

On the corner of Telegraph Street and Dorchester Street, across from St. Augustine's church, the triangular-shaped house of Dr. Frayer, the dentist, sat next to George Field's funeral home. At 204 and 206 Dorchester Street were two houses, joined together, where the lawyer Edward Creed lived alongside his brother Walter, a real estate broker. The popular John H. Toland, who represented Ward 15 in the state legislature for many years, lived at 196 Dorchester Street, next to a large house occupied by Edward Barry, former lieutenant governor of the Commonwealth. And in the next house lived two highly respected maiden ladies of the Protestant persuasion who found themselves, as one early resident put it, "adrift in a sea of Catholicism." Across Dorchester Street, on the corner of Seventh Street, was the substantial home of Judge Michael Creed. After the residences of Joseph O'Keefe, a prominent food distributor, and John McMorrow, a successful liquor dealer, came a cluster of physicians—Dr. Daly at 186; Dr. Bernard across the street; Dr. Hayes between Bowen and Fifth Streets. Beyond Gates Street, and only a short distance away from the Carney Hospital, was the huge private estate that eventually became John O'Brien's funeral home.

Moving up the hill across the intersection of Dorchester Street and Broadway, the list of well-known names continued, indicating the growing number of middle-class professionals making their homes in the area. Lawyers and politicians, merchants and manufacturers, coal and lumber dealers, real estate agents and insurance salesmen lived side by side along East Broadway, all the way from Dorchester Street to City Point. Some of the most impressive homes were atop Broadway Hill near M Street Park. On the corner of M Street itself was a magnificent residence that originally belonged to Otis D. Dana, founder of the Dana Hardware Corporation. Diagonally across the street, on the other corner of M Street, was the fine home of Joseph D. Fallon, judge of the South Boston Municipal Court. This residence, which had a spectacular view of Boston harbor, was later converted to a convent for the Sisters of Charity of Nazareth, who taught at the nearby St. Eulalia parochial school. Next door lived Dr. Michael F. Gavin, prominent physician and surgeon; and a few doors away was located the home of William Cains. Cains was the son of Thomas Cains, the original founder of the famous South Boston glassworks, and by this time the son was regarded fondly as the district's "grand old man."

As time went on, so many doctors and dentists established their practices along East Broadway between G Street and H Street that the section became a Doctor's Row, popularly known as Pill Hill. It was an especially attractive section of South Boston—a quiet, elm-shaded promenade—with fine residences and an obvious air of respectability. On the corner of G Street and Broadway, Dr. Redmond set up his practice; Dr. Charles Mackey became a popular general practitioner a short distance away; Dr. Edward Timmins served his South Boston patients in a fine house across the street; and Dr. Brunnick's office was located on East Broadway just before H Street.

This particular section of East Broadway attracted even more attention in 1913, when the large Municipal Building was constructed on the site originally occupied by the Mount Washington House Hotel. Constructed in the mid-1830s, the hotel served as the home for the Perkins Institute for the Blind from 1839 to 1912. The new Municipal Building was a large, red-brick, three-story structure built in what was called a "Renaissance Revival" style, with heavily framed arched windows ("arcaded fenestration") on the third floor. The work of Boston architect James E. McLaughlin, whose other works included the Boston Trade School, the new Boston Latin School, and the Commonwealth Armory, the building was a major example of early twentieth-century classical architecture. For over half a century the "Munie," as it was affectionately known, would serve the South Boston community as a kind of multi-purpose resource center, housing the South Boston District Court, a large assembly hall, a public gymnasium, facilities for public showers and the City Point branch of the Boston Public Library. With the other monuments, buildings, statues and churches, it was visible and tangible evidence that South Boston was not just another neighborhood, like Dorchester, Charlestown, East Boston or any other Irish-Catholic neighborhood surrounding the central city. South Boston was truly separate, distinctive and unique.

South Boston residents also took great pride in the natural beauty of their oceanside neighborhood, as well as the public works that made many of these natural resources available to their own people and to visitors from all over Greater Boston. Marine Park, looking out onto the Atlantic Ocean at the eastern tip of City Point, was the final link in Frederick Law Olmsted's famous string of public parks popularly known as the "Emerald Necklace." Constructed between 1878 and 1895, this was one of the most massive public projects ever undertaken by the city. Totaling over two thousand acres of open land, it extended from the Boston Common and the Public Garden down through the Fenway, out along the Jamaicaway past the Arboretum to Franklin Park, and then down Columbia Road and along the Strandway, until it ended with Marine Park in South Boston. Olmstead had also proposed building a causeway to link City Point with Castle Island, thus forming a protected bay (he planned to call it Pleasure Bay) for recreational boating and swimming, along with a pier for leisurely strolling and a playground for schoolchildren. Construction of the causeway was held up for many years, however, because even though the City of Boston owned City Point, the United States government had title to Castle Island and historic Fort Independence. But after Congress passed an act in 1890 granting Boston the use of Castle Island, a temporary wooden bridge was constructed connecting Marine Park with Castle Island, immediately attracting Sunday visitors, tourists and "promenaders" from all parts of the city. Many South Boston natives had serious reservations about the way in which the beauties of Marine Park were beginning to draw "rabble" and other undesirable elements from different parts of the city into their district. In 1892 a group of South Boston residents complained to the commissioners that Sunday arrests involved far too many "Cambridge people," and they expressed concern that the park was attracting "undesirable visitors" to their neighborhood. The federal government took back control of Castle Island during the First World War, and it was only in the 1920s that the temporary bridge was replaced by a permanent causeway connecting Castle Island with the mainland. The new walkway continued to attract couples, who strolled hand in hand along the strandway on a warm summer's night, stopped at Kelly's Landing or at the Head House for some fried clams and a cold drink, and then continued across the Causeway until they reached Castle Island. Every Thursday night, open-air dances under a covered pier festooned with colored lanterns reflected gaily in the waters below. Meanwhile, the Boston Society of Natural History requested space in Marine Park for what it called an "aquarial garden." Site plans for such a facility were prepared in 1889 and 1891, but it was not until after the turn of the century that the city began construction of a full-scale aquarium.

The ocean, of course, was a major source of refreshment and recreation for the residents of South Boston. With its unusually long shoreline and its splendid array of beaches, the district soon became popular. Now that streetcars had become electrified, the "Bay View" trolley would travel along Eighth Street alongside Dorchester Bay, turn up K Street, and then move along Sixth Street until it reached its terminus at City Point. During the hot summer months, visitors traveled in open-air trolleys with a top speed of six miles per hour and a fare of five cents a person. Thousands of families from all over the Boston area, loaded down with blankets, bathing suits and huge box lunches, enjoyed the beaches or held picnics on the grass at Marine Park. In the background loomed what had become the popular landmark of the City Point area— the restaurant and bathhouse known as the Head House, so called because it was at the head of the peninsula that jutted out into Boston harbor. An ornate, gingerbread structure, the Head House was designed in 1897 by city architect Edmund M. Wheelwright after a *rathaus* (municipal building) erected by the German government in Chicago at the 1893 Columbian Exposition.

The City Point area, too, offered great natural advantages for sailing, and as early as February 5, 1868, the first meeting of the South Boston Yacht Club took place in the boathouse belonging to Arthur Scott. The initial meeting of some fifty-nine yachting enthusiasts soon outgrew the small City Point location. On July 15, 1868, a new building was dedicated at the foot of K Street, and four years later, on April 2, 1877, an even larger building was constructed on East Sixth Street near P Street. On April 2, 1877, the South Boston Yacht Club was officially incorporated under Massachusetts Law, "for the purpose of encouraging yacht building and natural science," with the distinction of being the oldest chartered yacht club in the nation.

Even more popular than sailing, rowing and boating in the waters around South Boston was swimming, and one of the best-known swimming and bathing facilities in the district was the L Street Bathhouse. Interestingly enough, what ultimately became known as a major center of sport and recreation in the country actually started out as a serious effort to improve the health and welfare of the immigrant population of Boston. With the influx of Irish into the city in the mid-1840s, city officials had become gravely concerned about the lack of adequate sanitary facilities among the impoverished immigrants. In 1860 the Boston City Council appointed a special committee to look into the problems of public health. Among other things, this committee submitted recommendations for the immediate construction of a bathhouse. Convinced that moral purity and mental improvement were dependent on good public health, the committee maintained that a bathhouse would not only prove a beneficial health measure, but would also give poor people an "inducement to self-respect and refinement" and an "elevation in the scale of society."

The Civil War postponed further action on the bathhouse, but on March 5, 1865, only a month before the surrender of General Lee at Appomattox Courthouse, Mr. Israel S. Tafton submitted a report on public bathing that was immediately accepted by the Boston City Council. The council appointed a committee to determine appropriate sites for public bathhouses. The locations chosen were in the highly congested immigrant sections of town, where filth was widespread and sickness was rampant. The first six bathhouses, constructed with an initial allocation of ten thousand dollars, were placed at the following points: West Boston Bridge, near Charles Street; Warren Bridge, near the Fitchburg depot; East Boston, sectional dock at Border Street; Arch Wharf, Broad Street; South Boston, bottom of L Street; and Dover Street Bridge, South Pier. By June 1, 1865, three of the six bathhouses were ready for use, with the other three scheduled to open in three weeks. The experiment proved extraordinarily popular. The Dover Street Bathhouse, located close to the heavily populated, working-class Irish district in South Boston's lower end, served the largest number of people, with a summer attendance of 33,772—a high figure when the population of Boston was only 200,000. Although the L Street Bathhouse was fourth in attendance that first year, with a rather low seasonal attendance of 7,798, the figures rose each year as the Irish population of South Boston grew rapidly during the late nineteenth century. Most of the two- and three-decker houses in the district had running water but few bathtubs and practically no modern facilities for producing hot water. A bath was something reserved for one night a week—usually Saturday night—when enough water could be boiled in kettles on the black, cast-iron kitchen stove to fill a large galvanized washtub on the floor that eventually accommodated most members of the family. The chance for residents to be able to take a hot shower two or three times a week at a public bathhouse, using their own soap and paying only one cent for the use of a towel, was an opportunity working people quickly exploited. By 1900 the L Street Bathhouse had become such a popular and well-attended bath facility that a large new structure had to be built in the spring of 1901 to accommodate all those who wished to use it.

Humanitarian reformers and city leaders continued to hope that eliminating physical dirt would also eliminate moral dirt, that poor people would improve their habits once they were exposed to regular bathing and other forms of proper middle-class behavior. If everyone would only bathe daily, Mayor Josiah Quincy proclaimed, homes would be much cleaner, and men and boys who were now spending their time in saloons "might then find the home a fit place in which to spend an evening." Increasingly after 1900, however, the emphasis slowly shifted from cleanliness and godliness to exercise, physical fitness and recreation. As more and more new houses in the city were built with toilets, bathtubs, showers and modern plumbing, bathhouses were used less to bathe and shower, and more to swim and enjoy the warm sands of the beach. This certainly was true in the case of the L Street Bathhouse. Its new building was constructed in three separate sections—one for women and girls, one for men, and the third for boys—with each section separated from the other by a high wooden fence that extended out into Dorchester Bay. Regulations outlined acceptable behavior in facilities that provided over a thousand dressing rooms for many times that number of people. Superintendents monitored the rules, and police officers stood watch to insure order.

Until 1901 the original L Street Bathhouse opened its doors each day in accordance with the tides. Since the entire beach was covered by the ocean at high tide, bathers could use the beach only three hours before and three hours after high tide. With the construction of the new facility, however, this pattern changed. A wide channel enabled bathers to swim almost any time of the day. Because sunbathing at L Street was done in the nude or with a minimum of clothing, separate beaches were required. Males usually wore a small, three-cornered diaper called a "fig leaf," while the women commonly wore a brief, two-piece bathing suit. Those who came regularly to the L Street Bathhouse, summer and winter, rain and snow, became known as "Brownies" because of the deep, golden-brown tan they acquired from regular exposure to the wind and sun after salt-water swimming. Officially organized in 1902, the Brownies are perhaps most famous for their New Year's Day plunge into the ocean on days when the temperature is usually close to zero. Residents of South Boston insisted that swimming, bathing and tanning were excellent for the heart, blood, skin and circulation, and various stories made the rounds concerning the unusual, healthful properties of salt-water beaches. On July 7, 1910, for example, the *Boston Post* ran a story describing a woman who claimed to have experienced a

miraculous recovery from a nervous disorder by applying liberal amounts
of sand directly to her arms and legs. Having learned about this treatment in France, she announced her desire to introduce it to Boston.
While most of the residents probably took a dim view of this particular
treatment, devout Catholics in the district never failed to bathe in salt
water every August 15, the Feast of the Assumption, in accordance with
the widely held belief that the Blessed Mother had endowed the ocean
with special curative properties on that particular feast day.

The L Street Bathhouse provided a lifetime of healthful pleasure and
recreation for the families in South Boston, and it also initiated various
competitions in rowing and swimming—the most popular of which, as
well as the most demanding, was the Boston Lighthouse Marathon Swim.
A ten-mile race, popularly known as the "Boston Light," it was sponsored by the L Street swim club and drew thousands of enthusiastic
spectators each year. Swimmers began the race at the Charlestown
Bridge, swam east of Governor's Island, west of Long Island, west of
George's Island, and finally finished the grueling course at the Boston
lighthouse on Little Brewster Island, at the outer edge of Boston harbor, some ten miles from the city's waterfront.

The first person to attempt the Lighthouse Swim was Austrian-born
Alois Anderle, in August 1909. Although he managed to finish the
course, Anderle was disqualified because his navigator, George De Cost
of Dorchester, had steered the swimmer across Nix's Mate, which was
covered with water at the time, in an attempt to save time. Hitting his
arms on the bottom, Anderle had to walk six or seven steps to get across
the sandbar. The following year, eight contestants started the race at
the Charlestown Bridge, but only one finished—a fifteen-year-old Dorchester girl named Rose Pitonof. She was the only female in the race
and the youngest contestant. Navigated by her father and brother, she
completed the distance in six hours and fifty minutes. The irregular
course Pitonof followed, however, proved to be one of the longest ever
recorded for the race, as she stretched a ten-mile swim into a draining
twelve- or thirteen-mile ordeal. Swimming without goggles through what
the *Boston Post* described as "treacherous" waves and frigid waters
(at fifty-three degrees, it was the coldest harbor swimmers had experienced in months), Pitonof completed the course after exposure and
fatigue forced her opponents—all of them men—to drop out. Five hundred spectators watched the start of the race, and thousands gathered
along the route to cheer her on to the lighthouse.

Sam Richards came close to equalling Pitonof's popularity by completing the round-trip swim at least seven times between 1911 and 1930, but his greatest rival was a waiter at the old Westminster Hotel just off Copley Square—Bavarian-born Charlie Toth. Toth was at his peak just before and after World War I, breaking Pitonof's record in 1914 by swimming from the Charlestown Bridge to the Lighthouse in six hours and forty-eight minutes. The Lighthouse Swim continued to be an annual sporting event that attracted nationwide publicity until it was discontinued after World War II.

As rising birth rates and territorial annexation continued to increase the population of Boston's neighborhoods, an adequate supply of open space suitable for sport and recreation became more and more difficult to find. Advocates of public playgrounds became increasingly vocal about the pressing need for sports and organized recreation, which they saw as a more healthy outlet for the energies of young people than patronizing the pool hall, music hall or barroom. Under pressure from professional reformers, social workers, and a variety of neighborhood lobbying groups, the city government finally responded, and city appropriations for parks and playgrounds rose steadily and substantially in the course of the 1890s. By the turn of the century public and private forces had combined to establish for Boston one of the first comprehensive playground systems in the country. By 1915 the city was operating no less than forty playgrounds of various sizes and purposes. South Boston benefited from this development, with a large recreational area across from Carson Beach called McNary Park, in honor of a popular local congressman, William McNary (it would later be named Columbus Park); and another named the C. J. Lee Playground, better known as M Street Park because of its location on Broadway hill between M and N Streets.

Close to the immediate center of population, M Street Park was an instant success, drawing many residents to its sporting events despite the huge mounds of black anthracite in the coalyards directly behind the playing fields. During the twenties, former New England League pitcher Bill "Twilight" Kelly promoted semiprofessional baseball games at the park on Saturday and Sunday afternoons and during the weekday twilight hours of the late spring and summer months. Working men of the district could get home from work in the afternoon, gulp down a quick supper, and enjoy six or seven innings of a baseball game before darkness closed in. Not only did Twilight bring in some of the most popular semipro teams in the country—including the Harlem Colored

All Stars from New York and the heavily bearded House of David team from Salt Lake City—but he also fielded his own nine, Kelly's South Boston All Stars. Games between these local favorites and groups from other neighborhoods, such as the Town Team from Dorchester and the Cantabs from Cambridge, often attracted more fans to M Street Park than to Braves' Field or Fenway Park. And between innings Twilight Kelly would leave the pitcher's mound to make his lively way through the wooden bleachers with a big tin dipper, collecting enough nickels and dimes from the good-natured spectators to buy beer for the players when the game was over.

During the shorter afternoons of autumn, when the russet leaves fell from the trees and cold blasts of air swept across Broadway hill, the same crowds made their way to M Street Park to watch one of their local football teams in action. On many Sunday afternoons young South Boston athletes attending a nearby college or recent alumni keeping themselves in shape until they could get hired by a professional team played for these home teams. Many of these men, who soon became local sports heroes, are still remembered fondly by older members of the community. Tony Plansky, for example, a graduate of Georgetown University, played professional football for several years before becoming a successful track coach at Williams College. Joe Zapustas played pro baseball with the Philadelphia Athletics and football with the old Boston Shamrocks. George "Gigi" Keneally made his reputation as a football player at St. Bonaventure College before going on to become a coach with the Shamrocks. Herb Treat had been an All-American tackle at Princeton before marrying Madeline McMorrow and moving into a prominent South Boston family on Dorchester Street. And "Tubber" Cronin had been a successful football player at Boston College. Many old-timers still insist that Billy O'Leary, a speedy halfback for the Pere Marquette football team, was the best all-round athlete that South Boston ever produced. One of the more popular and successful local clubs was fielded by the Pere Marquette Council, Knights of Columbus, and was familiarly known as the "Peres"—always pronounced "Peeries." First coached by Leo Daly and managed by Mike King, the Peres usually went through their schedule undefeated, and at the end of each season they fought a classic contest with the Fitton Athletic Club from East Boston in a game that was usually played at Fenway Park to accommodate the great crowds that regularly came to cheer for their favorite team.

Perhaps the district's most famous athlete was James Brendan Connolly, who represented the Suffolk Athletic Club, a South Boston organization. After leaving Harvard College during his freshman year in 1896, Connolly borrowed money to pay his fare so that he could join the first American team going to the Olympic games in Athens, Greece. The young South Boston man became the first person to win an Olympic gold medal in modern times by winning the first event— the triple jump (then called the hop-step-and-jump), soaring forty-five feet to beat his nearest rival by three feet three inches. He went on to win the silver medal in the high jump and the bronze medal for the broad jump. Four years later Connolly won the silver medal in the triple jump at the Paris Olympics with a jump of forty-five feet ten inches. After trying his hand at local politics and running unsuccessfully for Congress as a Progressive candidate against James Michael Curley, he finally turned to writing books about Gloucester, fishermen, sailing ships and ocean travel.

Organized sport significantly intensified the feelings of unity and solidarity that had become a distinctive part of the spirit of the neighborhood. With their own beaches and bathhouses, playgrounds and parks, football and baseball teams, and a roster of legendary sports heroes, the people of South Boston could feel proud and comfortable in the insularity of their district and the fitness of their institutions. The expansive mood and militant spirit of the Roman Catholic Church in Boston during the 1920s and 1930s, under the vigorous leadership of William Cardinal O'Connell, strongly reinforced these sentiments.

Most of the familiar rituals and devotions of South Boston religious life during the late nineteenth century continued well into the twentieth with few significant changes. The people of South Boston, like residents of most Irish-Catholic neighborhoods in the Greater Boston area, joined in a calendar of popular Catholic religious devotions that strengthened their sense of solidarity. During Advent, in late November and early December, they prepared for the coming Christmas season by attending daily Mass and then enjoying the celebration of Midnight Mass on Christmas Eve, often followed by a festive early-morning breakfast of eggs, ham, bacon and sausages. During the cold, gray winter months of February and March, parishioners tramped through the snow and ice to daily Mass and conscientiously gave up candy, gum, cigarettes or liquor as personal acts of penance for the Lenten season. Their Lenten schedule usually included Wednesday-night services of the rosary, a sermon and benediction, as well as Friday-night services that featured the stations of the cross and benediction. One of the high spots at the close of the Lenten season came on Holy Thursday evening, when friends and neighbors crowded the streets of South Boston "making the seven churches," a pious custom that had no official church sanction but was a longtime part of local tradition. Catholics walked (driving a car was forbidden except in case of illness) to seven churches to visit the Blessed Sacrament, which was left exposed to public view after Holy Thursday services. By 1908, with the formal dedication of St. Eulalia's Church at the eastern end of the district, the people of South Boston could "make" the seven churches without even leaving the neighborhood. SS. Peter and Paul's, St. Vincent's, and the Holy Rosary Church had accommodated the Catholic population below Dorchester Street for many years, and St. Augustine's met the growing population in the Dorchester Street area. St. Monica's was originally established as a mission station for the people on lower Dorchester Street near Andrew Square, but in December 1907 it was made a separate parish, with Rev. Timothy J. Mahoney as its first pastor. The construction of the first Gate of Heaven Church between H and I Streets served the growing number of Catholics moving across Dorchester Street into the eastern half of the peninsula, and St. Eulalia's was formed at the corner of Broadway and O Street as a mission station for people moving into the City Point area. In May 1908, St. Eulalia's became a separate parish in its own right under Rev. Mortimer E. Twomey, and four years later Cardinal O'Connell formally dedicated the magnificent new Gate of Heaven Church after nearly seventeen years of construction. There were now seven separate parishes with seven major church structures serving the predominantly Roman Catholic population of South Boston. After the completion of Lent and the Eastertime festivities, the people usually considered their liturgical year at an end with the extremely popular "May Procession," a Sunday afternoon procession that started out from the church and wound through the streets of the parish. It featured the young children of the parish, dressed in white, escorting a litter that carried a large statue of the Blessed Virgin Mary. The procession would end up back at the church (at an outdoor shrine if the weather permitted) where a young girl would crown the statue with a small chaplet of flowers while parishioners sang favorite hymns to the Blessed Mother.

Within this broad pattern of devotional activity, many other practices intensified the strong religious bonds of the community. Parishioners accepted the custom of assigning specific aspects of faith and belief to individual months—March for St. Joseph, May for the Blessed Mother,

June for the Sacred Heart, July for the Precious Blood and October for the Rosary. Confessions were heard regularly on Saturday afternoons and evenings, and on Thursday evenings before the First Friday of every month. First Friday devotions to the Sacred Heart were very popular during this period, as were "Holy Hour" devotions, when parishioners spent an hour in church kneeling in adoration before the Blessed Sacrament on the altar. Novenas—nine consecutive days or weeks of prayer—were also expressions of religious piety, with parishioners attending their own parish or another parish that specialized in some particular devotion. Novenas to Our Lady of Perpetual Help were conducted at Roxbury's Mission Church; the Miraculous Medal Novena was held at St. Cecilia's Church in the Back Bay; and the Novena of Grace to St. Francis Xavier drew thousands to the Immaculate Conception Church in the South End. Every parish had its own cluster of devotional groups and associations, with Cardinal O'Connell assigning the Holy Name Society a special role as the leading male religious organization in the Boston diocese. Most parishes also had the Legion of Mary for women, different Third Order groups for lay people—of St. Francis, St. Dominic and Our Lady of Mount Carmel—and various sodalities for both married and single women. Every South Boston parish had a mission or retreat at least once a year, periods of intensive meditation, repentance and spiritual renewal directed by a vigorous orator from a religious order such as the Oblates, the Passionists or the Jesuits. A mission was customarily a two-week affair, with men attending one week and women the next. A retreat, by contrast, was usually a single week, with men and women mixed.

This strikingly devout spirit of Catholicism was also accompanied by the expansion of the parochial school system under the personal direction of William Henry O'Connell, who succeeded the aged and infirm John J. Williams in 1907 as Archbishop of Boston. Still not fifty years old, the new and dynamic young prelate was determined to liberate the Catholic Church in Boston from what he regarded as the dominance of Protestant Yankees. With the election of a Boston-born Irish Catholic, John F. Fitzgerald, as mayor of Boston in 1906, and with David I. Walsh becoming the Commonwealth's first Irish-Catholic governor in 1914, O'Connell saw the Irish moving into positions of considerable political power and wanted them to achieve positions of prestige and influence in social and cultural affairs as well. With his unusual capacity for administration, he set about organizing the parochial school system with the same enthusiasm he displayed in centralizing every other aspect of diocesan affairs. On numerous occasions, he reaffirmed his view that Catholic education was indispensable to a proper moral and religious life. "There is, as you know, just one point of view," he declared in 1930, "and that is, Catholic children should attend Catholic schools."

The number of parochial schools grew substantially during the O'Connell years, and several South Boston parishes participated in the movement to provide Catholic education for as many children as possible. The Sisters of Notre Dame operated grammar schools for both boys and girls at SS. Peter and Paul's parish and St. Augustine's parish, with enrollments of over one thousand pupils at each school; the Sisters of St. Joseph staffed a grammar school at the Gate of Heaven parish, with an enrollment of over one thousand boys and girls; and the Sisters of Charity of Nazareth staffed a similar school at St. Eulalia's parish with some nine hundred students. The Polish church, Our Lady of Czestochowa, operated a school with an attendance of about five hundred boys and girls, with the Felician Sisters providing instruction in Polish language and history in addition to the regular curriculum.

None of the four smaller parishes—St. Vincent's, the Holy Rosary, St. Monica's or St. Peter's, the Lithuanian church—had the financial resources to support a parochial school, a subtle but significant demonstration of the peninsula's slow division between lower-income, blue-collar families in the lower end of the district, below Dorchester Street, and the growing middle-class families who were moving across Dorchester Street toward City Point. Most families in the lower end, crowded together on narrow streets and living in small wooden houses and tenements, could not afford the nominal tuition and school supplies required in the parochial schools. Most of these families continued to send their children to the public schools—or "Protestant" schools as the parochial-school children used to call them. Many families living in the City Point area, while hardly well-to-do or even comfortable, were nevertheless able to provide a little extra money to give their children what they regarded as the benefits of a Catholic education. Of the nine Catholic churches officially listed for South Boston, the five which maintained successful, full-time parochial grammar schools during the 1920s and 1930s were located east of Dorchester Street. This percentage of 55.5 percent compared more than favorably with the overall diocesan average which had risen from 35.9 percent in 1908 to only 48.6 percent at the time of O'Connell's death in 1944.

These parochial schools probably never enrolled more than a total of five thousand boys and girls in any one year—a very small portion of South Boston's large grammar-school population. And they had very little impact on the district's high-school population, since only St. Augustine's successfully maintained a high school for girls over a significant period of time. Nevertheless, they did reinforce the value system of that community, solidifying its proud parochial spirit. Taught almost entirely by nuns in traditional black habits and starched white wimples, the pupils spent their school days in a deeply religious atmosphere. Surrounded by statues, holy pictures and inspirational sayings, they supplemented their regular studies with lessons on the catechism, stories from the Bible and classes on Christian values. In most South Boston schools, there was also a special emphasis on the social and cultural heritage of the Irish race. Irish songs and stories were an integral part of the instructional program; Irish saints and Irish feast days were usually celebrated with extra enthusiasm; and at St. Augustine's school romantic scenes from the Irish countryside were painted on the walls of the auditorium. All these things helped reinforce the stories and reminiscences of the "old country" many of the children were hearing from their parents and grandparents at home.

The parochial schools also promoted a definite spirit of patriotism. With the slogan "For God and Country" emblazoned over the front doorway of the building, and with morning prayers followed by the pledge of allegiance to the flag, the schools made every effort to promote the virtues of civic pride and to demonstrate in a positive way that Catholicism was compatible with democracy. Through lectures, classroom discussions, essay contests and textbooks especially designed for a Catholic audience, the schools attempted to introduce pupils to the "Catholic side" of history by emphasizing the role of Catholic men and women in the discovery and exploration of the country in early days, and in the more recent fight to maintain the constitutional form of government.

But the spirit of patriotism was by no means restricted to the curriculum of neighborhood schools; it was also carried over into other activities in many of the parishes. St. Vincent's parish organized an impressive regiment of marching cadets and a fife and drum corps that quickly became a popular feature of the annual St. Patrick's Day parade. Dressed in blue Civil War-type jackets, black-visored Civil War caps and white duck pants, the St. Vincent's Boys' Regiment was drilled by Fr. Francis McNeill himself, who personally went around to local businessmen and shopkeepers for contributions to keep the regiment going. St. Augustine's parish also produced a smart cadet corps, which

paraded in handsome gray uniforms; and the Gate of Heaven parish
turned out a uniformed marching band that took part in many local
parades. These activities coincided with similar efforts by Cardinal
O'Connell, who frequently organized colorful parades, massive
assemblies, outdoor rallies and public demonstrations of all kinds to
display the patriotic loyalty of the Catholic people. Angered by the Ku
Klux Klan's program of anti-Catholic bigotry during the 1920s and the
scurrilous attacks on the Catholic Democratic candidate Al Smith during the Presidential campaign of 1928, Catholics were particularly determined to leave no doubt about their loyalty and dependability as
American citizens.

South Boston sustained itself as a unique and comprehensive community partly because its residents also shared the same social activities
and popular amusements. Gunther Barth, in his recent study, *City People:
The Rise of Modern City Culture in Nineteenth-Century America*, has
examined the influence of such things as apartment houses, the local
press, the department store, the ballpark and the vaudeville house on
the life of the community. He argues that these local institutions help
create a distinctive "city culture." In South Boston, for example, the
people of the neighborhood shared a common historical tradition, enjoyed the same environmental advantages, participated in the same
recreational activities, learned the same songs, memorized the same
stories, and generally enjoyed a common social and political culture.

But even within the neighborhood society, smaller groups shared
mutual concerns and pursuits. Almost every ethnic group had its own
particular club, hall, meetingplace or association. The Irish penchant
for music, laughter and storytelling, brought people of Irish extraction
to the by this time mostly private clubs of the Ancient Order of Hibernians, where, in the words of one resident, "one could buy beer on
Sunday at reasonable prices." By the early 1900s there were eleven
divisions of the AOH meeting in South Boston. The halls most frequently
used were on West Broadway; at the Clan-na-Gael Hall on D Street;
on National Street near the Carney Hospital; and at Gray's Hall at Emerson and I Streets. Other Irish social clubs at the turn of the century included the Irish-American Club; the Wolfe Tone Club; the Celtic
Association; and Clan-na-Gael, founded in 1867 as a successor to the
Fenian movement. Some of these clubs promoted Irish culture—music,
dancing, history and literature. Others tried to strengthen the nationalist
movement for a British-free, united Ireland. And still others served simply as social centers where friends and neighbors could relax among their

own people, talk over old times, and exchange the latest news and gossip.

Other ethnic groups in South Boston also had their halls and clubhouses where they met regularly to socialize and reinforce their national and cultural heritage. German residents gathered at the German-American club the night before each national holiday, feasting on sauerkraut, pig's knuckles, potato salad, rye bread and huge steins of beer, singing and dancing to the music of a German band until two in the morning. The Polish-American club on Dorchester Avenue, founded about 1900, was a popular place for newly arrived Polish immigrants to socialize and learn about the habits and customs of their adopted country. Not too far away, Lithuanian immigrants established their own clubs, not only to meet their friends and neighbors, but also to preserve their ancient language and distinctive culture. At the South Boston Lithuanian Citizens' Association on West Broadway (popularly known as the "Lith Club"), or at the Lithuanian Nationalist Association on East Fourth Street, immigrants got together, had a drink or played chess, and then went upstairs for a concert of classical music, a scholarly lecture or a display of oil paintings. The Czech club on Columbia Road not only provided the usual social facilities for its small number of members but also served as a place where the Czechoslovakian Constitution of 1918 was partially composed. One local resident recalls Jan Mazaryk, soon to be the first president of the post-World War I Republic of Czechoslovakia, discussing with her father and his friends the exact wording of the new document which they based upon the Constitution of the United States.

By the first quarter of the twentieth century, therefore, South Boston displayed all the outward signs and symbols of what sociologists later categorized an "ethnic community." Modern social scientists differ considerably in their definitions of the term "ethnic community." Some scholars feel that ethnicity is something inherited from an Old-World country; others see it as something developed in the New-World environment. Some writers question whether factors of race and religion should be included in an examination of class and ethnicity or considered as distinctive phenomena. Still other authorities wonder whether the whole concept of community is the result of the subjective views of native insiders or an artificial definition imposed by outside observers. Whatever the nature of the academic controversy, South Boston appears to have taken on such a distinctive and easily recognizable personality that it would have to qualify as an ethnic community under any definition. Over the course of its long history, the locality had succeeded in combining such an unusually large number of distinctive social, religious, cultural and political characteristics that it could no longer be regarded either as just one more projection along a jagged coastline, or as a carbon copy of similar ethnic neighborhoods in Boston. South Boston was a separate and unique community in its own right.

The very geographical location of the district contibuted directly to its separateness. Residents of the isolated peninsula had always felt themselves part of a unique settlement, a place set apart, where they would have to live and work together in the face of what they often saw as the neglect and disdain of other parts of the city. Protestant Yankees demonstrated this commonality of interests when they sent their angry memorial to the city authorities in 1847, complaining about the lack of municipal services. As the number of Irish Catholics rapidly increased they also came to look upon themselves as a proud and embattled part of a separate community that did not always receive respect or recognition from the rest of the city.

The resident's pride also included the natural features of South Boston. People regarded the salt water, fresh air, grassy parks and sandy beaches as special gifts from God. They took full advantage of these natural resources, becoming extremely proud of their physical prowess and athletic ability, which they attributed to their superior toughness and the benefits of their natural environment.

Certainly, the extraordinary series of patriotic events at the turn of the century, linking South Boston with the patriotic heritage of America itself, did much to create what Talcott Parsons has called a form of "cultural history." The erection of the Farragut statue, the construction of the Dorchester Heights monument, the building of South Boston High School and the public observance of Evacuation Day as part of the district's private and traditional observance of St. Patrick's Day, contributed to the patriotic spirit of the people of South Boston and their shared sense of community. That few, if any, residents could trace their ancestry back to Revolutionary days (or even to Civil War days) did not really matter. This "shared sense of history," Parsons wrote, "applies to those who themselves or whose immediate forebears have joined the community long after certain other crucial events took place." These public celebrations gave residents one more reason for the pride they shared with their friends and conveyed to their children.

By the turn of the century, although there were some doctors, dentists, pharmacists, lawyers and real estate agents in the City Point area, most people in South Boston could be classified as "working class" people, and a definite class conciousness contributed to their perception of themselves. The lower end had many day laborers, longshoremen, tavern-keepers, grocers, industrial workers and bricklayers, while east of Dorchester Street lived carpenters, plumbers, electricians streetcar conductors, policemen, firemen and letter carriers. Whatever their occupation, parents worked hard, took pride in their jobs and raised their children to admire the working-class values of hard work and determination despite their modest homes and meager incomes. Schoolteachers commonly reminded children that while it was acceptable to come to class wearing clothing that was sewn or patched, it was expected that the garments would be washed and ironed.

No matter what their socioeconomic level, most people in South Boston lived on close and sometimes intimate terms with their neighbors. Their two- and three-decker houses were not only an efficient form of immigrant architecture, allowing a maximum amount of living space on a minimum amount of land, but they also brought three or four families together into one extended household. These families exchanged clothes, shared food, loaned each other money, cared for each others' children, nursed the sick and buried the dead in a pattern of communal life that could be found all through the district. Although their wants were simple and their luxuries few, these same people reacted strongly when the phrase "working class" or "lower-income" was interpreted to mean poor, impoverished or lazy. They refused to admit they were "poor"; they denied they lived in "slums"; they objected to outsiders describing their houses as "shacks" or "tenements." They took pride in their personal independence and deeply resented any suggestion that they were "on the dole" or dependent upon any other form of welfare or public charity. These resentments continued through the years and flared up again during the school desegregation controversy of the 1970s, when supposedly sophisticated social workers, magazine writers and television reporters from other parts of the country invariably described South Boston as a slum area and its people as the poverty-stricken victims of urban blight. Above all, they were acutely conscious that many people in other parts of the Bay State regarded them as low-class "shanty Irish," and their district as the roughest, toughest neighborhood in the city, a "spawning ground of politicians and prize-fighters, policemen and plug-uglies." Such discriminatory views only served to draw the families of South Boston even closer together into a solid working-class community determined to hold onto its own distinctive beliefs and values in the face of growing outside disapproval.

Finally, there was the Church, which acted in conjunction with social, cultural and ethnic factors to weld the people of South Boston into an even more homogeneous community. There might be a variety of ethnic groups in the district—Irish, Italians, Poles and Lithuanians—but in one form or another they were warmly and intimately associated with their respective parishes. All people in South Boston automatically identified themselves with a particular parish. "It was as if your church, your parish church, was your extended family," one nun recalled, "and the priest was the father, with all the patriarchal connotations."

This communal association took place during the prescribed prayers and formal rituals of Sundays and Holy Days of Obligation, but it also extended seven days a week during the school hours, the working days, the periods of play, the times of recreation, the joys of festive parades and the solemnities of funeral processions. Day in and day out, from one season of the year to the next, the Church was a constant force in the lives and loves of the people of South Boston, from the youngest to the oldest, providing a deep spiritual foundation for their already strong sense of community.

By the turn of the century, then, South Boston had become totally and self-consciously solidified into what sociologists would view as a classic example of an ethnic neighborhood. Ethnic groups, according to Peter Rose, are frequently identified by distinctive patterns of family life, language, recreation, religion and other characteristics that differentiate them from others. "Above all," he concludes, "members of such groups feel a sense of identity and an 'interdependence of fate' with those who share the customs of the ethnic tradition."

These people were also of the same social class, with similar interests and tastes, a common educational background and occupations that brought them into touch with one another and involved common types of experiences. Such people, Milton M. Gordon observes in *Assimilation in American Life*, inevitably feel "comfortable" with one another. The people of South Boston were certainly "comfortable" with one another, and "comfortable" with the distinctive type of ethnic neighborhood they had developed over the years. It was a warm, friendly, comfortable community where everyone knew one another, shared the same customs and enjoyed the same pastimes. Its people were safe from outside contacts, and its values were protected from alien influences. Residents were happy to have it that way—they wanted it that way—and they were instinctively hostile to anyone who would think of changing it.

And that was exactly the point—there were few signs that anybody wanted to change the character and structure of *any* of Boston's ethnic neighborhoods. Native Brahmins looked upon the exodus of the Irish, and of later ethnic groups, into the outlying neighborhoods as nothing less than a godsend. Neighborhoods like South Boston, Charlestown, East Boston, Dorchester and Roxbury were safety valves that kept the poorest of the immigrants from moving out of their squalid shacks along the waterfront and into the heart of old Boston. The neighborhoods siphoned newcomers off from the inner city at regular intervals and provided places where different nationalities could hold their church services, sing their rowdy songs, play their outlandish games and practice their ethnic customs without disturbing the peace and quiet of Beacon Hill.

Writers have frequently alluded to the clannishness of the immigrants, their refusal to participate in the affairs of the city and their reluctance to give up their traditional ways in favor of the social and cultural ethos of their new home. "Unable to participate in the normal associational affairs of the community," Oscar Handlin wrote in *Boston's Immigrants*, "the Irish felt obliged to erect a society within a society, to act together in their own way. In every contact therefore the group, apart from other sections of the community, became intensely aware of its peculiar and exclusive identity."

Handlin's observation is certainly true, but it does not mention that these attitudes were encouraged by native Bostonians, who agreed that the people in the neighborhoods *would* do best to lead their own lives, go their own ways, do their own things, and stay with "their own kind." In many ways, the urban neighborhoods are as much of an invention of downtown Boston as they were the product of the various nationalities themselves. Ethnic neighborhoods became not merely temporary institutions, taking care of the dispossessed newcomers until they could make the gradual transition into the mainstream of American life, but permanent and essentially stagnating urban institutions in which most of the immigrants and generations of their children would remain for the rest of their lives.

Well into the twentieth century, people in neighborhoods such as South Boston grew up with the knowledge and the reassurance that this was the way it *ought* to be—the way that was natural to Boston's "city of neighborhoods." They would live in separate neighborhoods designed for different people, different nationalities, different races, different religions—all living together happily, peacefully and harmoniously— but always separately.

PHOTOGRAPHS

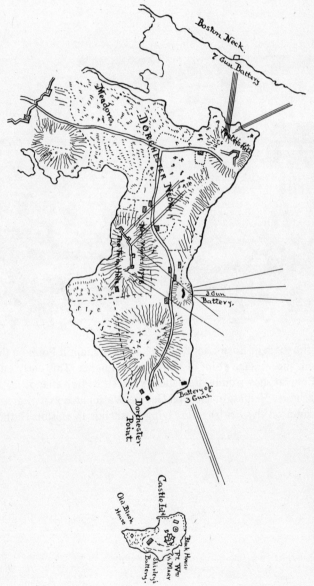

An early sketch of Dorchester Neck in 1777, believed adapted from the map drawn by Henry Pelham in 1775 for the use of the British occupation forces in Boston.

A view of the town of Boston in the 1830s, with Windmill Point on the right, as seen from the vantage point of Dorchester Heights. This early engraving by W. J. Bennett shows quite dramatically the strategic value of the occupation of Dorchester Heights by General George Washington as a means of training his cannon on the British ships lying at anchor in Boston Harbor.

South Boston Branch Library

An early horse-drawn coach makes its leisurely way past the South Baptist Church on the corner of C Street and Broadway.

South Boston Historical Society

A native of County Cavan, Ireland, Andrew Carney came to Boston in 1814, began work as a tailor, and later became a partner in a successful clothing firm. A dedicated philanthropist, his gift of seventy-five thousand dollars established the Carney Hospital in the heart of South Boston to serve the needs of poor immigrants.

Carney Hospital

A common stereotype of immigrants depicted them as drunkards and wastrels. This cartoon of the Know-Nothing era shows a whiskey-drinking Irishman and a beer-sodden German stealing the ballot box in some large American city.

In the wake of the Great Famine, nativists feared Irish immigrants bringing their Roman Catholic religion with them to America. These fears are reflected in this cartoon of the 1850s, with the names of prominent Irish counties providing the stepping stones for the "fiery" clerical invasion of the New World—here personified by Paul Cullen, Archbishop of Armagh.

Boston's second Irish-Catholic mayor was Patrick A. Collins, a native of Fermoy, County Cork. Although forced to leave school to work at menial jobs, he eventually graduated from the Harvard Law School, became a member of the state legislature, was elected to Congress, and was later named consul general in London. A monument to Collins on Commonwealth Avenue describes him as "a talented, honest, generous, serviceable man."

The Perkins Institute for the Blind a short time after it took over the Mt. Washington Hotel on Broadway and H Street in South Boston in May 1839. Under the direction of Dr. Samuel Gridley Howe, the Perkins Institute became famous throughout the world for its progressive experimentation in the care and treatment of the blind.

Courtesy of the Boston Public Library, Print Department

South Boston became famous for heavy industries that provided employment for unskilled labor unavailable in other parts of Boston. Chemical works, glass factories and shipyards made up a major portion of the district's industrial output, while iron factories such as the Bay State Iron Company produced plate iron, ship plates, armor plates and railroad iron vital to the Union war effort during the Civil War.

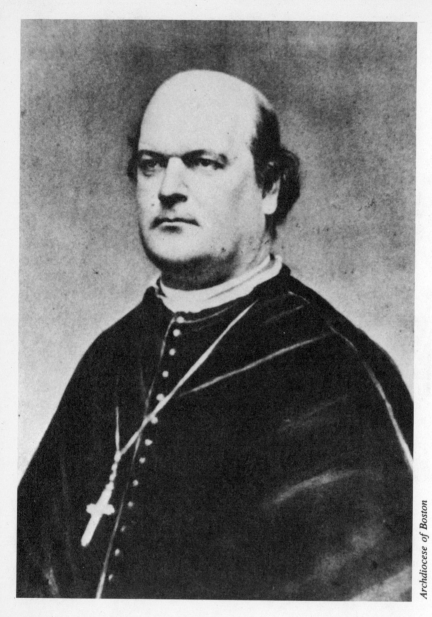

Archdiocese of Boston

A Bostonian by birth, John Bernard Fitzpatrick was the third Bishop of Boston (1846-1866) and the first Catholic bishop granted an honorary degree by Harvard University. His mother and father are buried in St. Augustine's Cemetery, and he himself was interred there until his remains were later moved to the new Holy Cross Cathedral.

A bronze statue of Admiral David Glasgow Farragut was commissioned by the city of Boston and placed in Marine Park on petition of the South Boston Citizens Association. The work of English-born sculptor Henry Hudson Kitson, it was dedicated on June 28, 1893, with an elaborate parade and patriotic ceremonies.

St. Augustine's Church Archives

The oldest Gothic-style building in New England, St. Augustine Chapel on the corner of Dorchester Street and Sixth Street is one of the major historical monuments in South Boston.

Courtesy of the family of Francis Birmingham

Having a son serving as an altar boy was a cherished hope of every South Boston family at a time when the Catholic Church was an intimate part of the neighborhood's social and religious life. Here, a group of altar boys pose for a formal picture at St. Vincent's Church in 1901, dressed in their cassocks and surplices.

Modeled after a municipal building erected by the German government at the 1893 Columbian Exposition, the Head House was an ornate gingerbread structure that became one of the most famous landmarks in the City Point area. Located at the head of the peninsula where it jutted out into Boston Harbor, the structure had a bathhouse and a restaurant, and on Sunday afternoons during the summer a German band serenaded listeners from the large restaurant balcony. On December 5, 1942, the famous structure was destroyed by fire.

South Boston Historical Society

Castle Island dates back to 1634, when Governor Dudley selected the strategic island for the sea defense of Boston. Over the decades the British developed the fortifications until they were driven out in 1776 when they were forced to turn the island over to the colonists. In 1789 Massachusetts ceded Castle Island to the United States, and in 1799 President John Adams came to dedicate the fort as "Fort Independence." Colonel Sylvanus Thayer, "the Father of West Point," reconstructed the present fort on Castle Island, retaining the five-bastion concept developed by earlier commanders.

South Boston Historical Society

Fort Independence was closed as an active commissioned defense works in 1879, and in 1888 the City of Boston made plans to place the island under the jurisdiction of the Park Department. Congressman Patrick Collins from South Boston passed a resolution allowing the city to construct a causeway to the island, but President Grover Cleveland vetoed the idea. Three years later, however, because of continuing pressure from residents, the Government agreed that Boston taxpayers could build a causeway from Marine Park to Castle Island. Here are Bostonians making their way out to the island on opening day, July 29, 1892.

To commemorate the crucial role of South Boston in forcing the British to
evacuate Boston in March 1776, residents pressed for a historical monument.
After a public competition, the city chose a design executed in white Georgian
marble. In 1978 the National Parks and Recreation Act authorized the City
of Boston to transfer the five-acre Dorchester Heights site to the National Park
Service.

Courtesy of the family of Francis Birmingham

Grammar school graduation was always a gala event, especially for pupils who would go no further than the sixth grade. Here the students of the Bigelow School, class of 1899, line up for a graduation picture in their best suits, hair carefully combed, with many of them wearing the boutonierres furnished by their proud families for the occasion.

Looking down West Broadway towards F Street at the turn of the century, with the viewer standing at Perkins Square where Broadway intersects with Dorchester Street.

A view of South Boston during the 1930s, looking west along Broadway from L Street. The streetcar tracks were still in place, bringing the streetcars along Broadway to Dorchester Street, where they would branch off to go either further along Broadway to Broadway Station, or along Dorchester Street to Andrew Square.

During World War I residents of South Boston followed with great interest the exploits of the Twenty-Sixth Division—the Yankee Division—which had been formed from New England national guard units. Here, Boston mayor Andrew J. Peters greets the division commander, General Clarence Edwards, at the mustering out parade of the Yankee Division in April 1919.

Striking Boston policemen leave the station house in civilian clothes, with their uniforms over their arms. Sparked by the discharge of nineteen policemen for joining a union, the Boston police strike lasted less than a week, early in September 1919. The lack of a uniformed presence threw the city into a frightening period of anarchy and violence with consequences that lasted for many years.

Courtesy of the Boston Public Library, Print Department

A group of young women engage in group calesthenics under the summer sun at Carson Beach.

South Boston Historical Society

A football game between the Pere Marquette Council, Knights of Columbus, and the Weymouth Athletic Club, on November 15, 1925, at the C. J. Lee Playground—M Street Park—with the smokestacks of the Edison Plant on First Street in the background.

Courtesy of the Boston Public Library, Print Department

Popularly known as "Honey Fitz," Mayor John F. Fitzgerald was an energetic individual who demonstrated his talents for politics at social functions and athletic events. Here he tosses out the first ball on the opening day of the local baseball season. Fitzgerald was the first Boston-born Irish Catholic to become mayor of Boston, demonstrating that the ethnic voters of the city were moving into positions of greater power and influence.

An inveterate campaigner, James Michael Curley was a charismatic figure with a golden speaking voice and biting wit. For nearly forty years he dominated the Boston political scene, appealing to ethnic voters in the various neighborhoods with his continuous flair for the unexpected and the dramatic.

Born in the Andrew Square section of South Boston, John W. McCormack dropped out of school in the eighth grade to become the breadwinner of the family when his father died. After passing the bar examination in 1913, he served a brief stint in the army and then began a distinguished career in politics. Eventually he rose to become one of the most powerful men in the country as Speaker of the United States House of Representatives. Known for his sense of compassion and his dedication to the cause of social justice, McCormack brought quiet dignity to a lifetime of public service.

Courtesy of the Boston Public Library, Print Department

A graduate of the Oliver Hazard Perry School in the City Point section of South Boston, Richard J. Cushing became Archbishop of Boston in 1945, and was elevated to the rank of Cardinal in 1958. Especially dedicated to the concept of service, he brought the solace of religion to the aged, the infirm, and the disadvantaged. Here he is shown serving a meal on the Feast of St. Joseph at a home for the aged conducted by the Little Sisters of the Poor.

Once characterized as "South Boston personified," John E. Powers was a lifelong resident of South Boston who rose through the political ranks to become president of the Massachusetts Senate. A well-known figure in every part of the city, "Johnny" was frequently called upon by people who needed personal assistance and political advice. Here he and his wife accompany Governor and Mrs. Endicott ("Chub") Peabody as Powers receives a tremendous reception in his home wards on his retirement from the Massachusetts Senate in 1964.

Courtesy of the Boston Public Library, Print Department

In 1961, Louise Day Hicks won a seat on the Boston School Committee, where she became a vocal critic of plans to desegregate the school system. She won widespread acclaim in the ethnic communities for her support of neighborhood schools and her opposition to what she regarded as misguided social experiments. Her cry, "You know were I stand!" brought roars of approval from her South Boston followers who applauded her stand against court-ordered busing.

Associated Press

Yellow school buses became a familiar sight as they carried students through
the streets of South Boston in the mornings and the afternoons. Here a convoy
of motorcycle police escorts buses as they leave the Gavin School at the close
of school on the third day of court-ordered busing designed to integrate the
Boston schools. Police also lined both sides of the street to keep control of
onlookers while the buses were traveling through.

Courtesy of the Boston Public Library, Print Department

One of the most colorful and controversial figures in Massachusetts politics is South Boston native William M. Bulger. A graduate of Boston College High School, Boston College, and Boston College Law School, Bulger moved steadily up the echelons of state office until he finally became president of the Massachusetts Senate. A witty and articulate public speaker whose annual St. Patrick's Day roasts have become nationally famous, Bulger was a prominent opponent of court-ordered busing and an eloquent defender of the rights of parents to determine the education of their children.

Mayor Raymond L. Flynn, his wife Cathy and members of his family march
along Broadway in the annual St. Patrick's Day parade. A graduate of South
Boston High School, Flynn graduated from Providence College on a basketball scholarship and then entered local politics. An outspoken opponent of court-
ordered busing during the turbulent seventies, Flynn was equally opposed to
violence in any form. He was elected mayor of Boston by a substantial margin
in 1983 and won re-election in a landslide victory in 1987.

6

CHANGING TIMES

W ORLD WAR I INTERRUPTED THE RELATIVELY UNEVENTFUL
routine of life in early twentieth century South Boston. But
though the outbreak of war in August 1914 and the German
invasion of neutral Belgium sent shock waves around the world, most
Americans followed President Woodrow Wilson's advice to remain
neutral "in thought as well as in action." Many ethnic groups, particularly, argued that Americans should stay apart from Europe's problems and allow Great Britain to pull its own "chestnuts" out of the
fire. During 1914 and 1915, Irish-Americans closely followed the activities of Patrick Pearse, Thomas MacDonagh, Joseph Plunkett and
other members of the Irish Republican Brotherhood as they mobilized
to overthrow British rule in Ireland. British brutality in putting down
Dublin's abortive Easter Week rebellion in April 1916, especially the
execution of the leaders before firing squads, inflamed old hatreds and
confirmed the belief of many South Bostonians that the British were
every bit as savage as the Germans and should get no aid from the
American people.

As time went on, however, sentiment gradually swung in favor of
the British and against the Germans. The startling announcement by
the German government that after February 1, 1917, its submarines
would follow a "sink on sight" policy made hostilities almost inevitable
as a series of unarmed American merchant vessels were sent to the bottom the following month. On the evening of April 2, 1917, President
Wilson went before a joint session of Congress, reviewed the hostile

actions of the German government, and asked for a declaration of war. Within the week, both the Senate and the House of Representatives had voted overwhelmingly in favor of war with Germany.

In short order Boston became a patriotic city where the word "slacker" was used to characterize any young man who did not rush off immediately to put on the khaki and sail off to France to make the world safe for democracy. Recruiting tents went up on Lafayette Mall, Liberty Bond drives were launched all over the city, and thousands of young draftees received their basic training at Camp Devens in Ayer. According to the *Boston Globe*, the rush to enlist broke a thirty-five-year-old record for recruiting. Those who stayed home worked with the Red Cross, the YMCA, the YWCA, the National Catholic War Council, the Jewish Welfare Board, the Salvation Army or the Knights of Columbus. Pupils at South Boston High School raised money to send "comfort kits" to graduates of the high school serving in the armed forces. "Victory boys" tended victory gardens, turning over the money they earned to their teachers as contributions to service agencies. Members of the women's local Nev-a-tel Club held a large dance at the newly constructed Municipal Building on East Broadway to supply surgical dressings for the South Boston Red Cross. Food and fuel shortages affected most families, who put up with "wheatless Mondays," "meatless Tuesdays" and "porkless Saturdays." Lack of coal closed the Capen School, sending students to afternoon sessions at the Benjamin Dean School at the corner of H and Sixth streets.

With the construction of a huge army supply base in South Boston at an estimated cost of $75 million, Boston became the military and naval headquarters of New England and the principal war shipping port to Europe. Boston harbor was mined, and a wire net was stretched across the channels to keep out German submarines. In July 1918 the United States Army notified the Park Department that it intended to install antiaircraft guns on the "old fort" at Castle Island. Although the island continued to remain open to the public, as it had been since 1909, military guards were posted at the entrance and within the fort itself. A garrison was stationed in the fort, and a concrete foundation for an antiaircraft emplacement was poured on Adams Bastion, although the weapon itself was never installed.

The people of Boston followed the news of the fighting overseas very closely, paying particular attention to reports of the Twenty-Sixth Division, the "Yankee Division," which had been formed from the national guard of New England in the late summer of 1917 and included the best known of Boston Irish-American regiments, the old "Fighting Ninth" of Civil War fame, which had been incorporated into the 101st Regiment of Infantry and commanded by Edward L. Logan, a South Boston native. A graduate of the Harvard Law School, Logan had fought with the Ninth Massachusetts Infantry in the Spanish-American War and later represented Ward 14 in Boston's Common Council. One of the first four American divisions to arrive in France, the Twenty-Sixth was the first actually to go into the trenches. Under Commander Clarence R. Edwards it saw action in the front lines for 210 days and took part in most of the major engagements in that period—at Belleau Wood, Chateau Thierry, St. Mihiel and the Argonne Forest. Residents of South Boston were especially proud to learn that one of their own "boys," twenty-six-year-old Michael J. Perkins, a graduate of the Bigelow School, had been awarded the Congressional Medal of Honor for his "conspicuous gallantry and intrepidity, above and beyond the call of duty." As the 101st Infantry advanced through the tangled underbrush in the Belleu Bois on October 17, 1918, the Americans came under heavy fire from a large German machine-gun nest. Crawling forward to the pill box, Private Perkins blew the door open with a grenade, drew his trench knife, and then rushed into the emplacement. In hand-to-hand combat he killed or wounded several of the Germans, silenced seven machine guns, and marched out with twenty-five prisoners. He became a local hero, and in later years the district named its American Legion post in memory of Michael J. Perkins.

The exciting news of the exploits of the Yankee Division during the spring of 1918, the progress of the doughboys smashing against the Hindenburg Line, and the even more exciting rumors of a possible German collapse by the end of the summer were overshadowed, however, by the frightening specter of illness and disease at home. What the strange malady was, where it had come from, how it was transmitted, how long it would last, no one really knew. People first learned about the disease late in August, when the *Boston Herald* reported that thirty sailors had come down with what was called "Spanish influenza." Taken off their training ships at Commonwealth Pier, the men were kept in hospital tents on Brookline's Corey Hill. By September 3 the number of cases had gone up to 119. About the same time, thousands of young soldiers stationed at Camp Devens were hospitalized, stricken with influenza or pneumonia. They were part of General Henry McCain's Twelfth Infantry Division, which was in the last stages of its training before embarkation to France. By the middle of September, the camp hospital, which normally accommodated only two thousand soldiers, was treating eight thousand, part of a worldwide epidemic that was raging throughout Europe, China, India and most of Asia.

Influenza took a terrible toll all over the country, from Boston to Seattle, Philadelphia to San Francisco. New York City recorded over three thousand new cases in a single twenty-four-hour period; and on October 10, Philadelphia listed an all-time high of 528 deaths in one day. In Boston health officials did not know how to deal effectively with what was obviously becoming a full-scale epidemic. Recommending fresh air and sunshine as the best preventative measures, army and navy doctors urged people to avoid crowds. Bostonians, however, insisted on holding mass rallies in support of the current Liberty Loan drive, and jammed into Fenway Park in record numbers on September 11 to watch the Red Sox defeat the Chicago Cubs and win the World Series. Conditions went from bad to worse. By the end of the month, influenza was racing through the city, and the death rate was accelerating at an alarming pace. On October 1, the epidemic reached its frightening peak as the *Boston Globe* reported the death of 206 people. "In the last week of October 1918," one modern historian has said, "2,700 Americans died 'over there' in the battle against the kaiser's army. The same week, twenty-one thousand Americans died of influenza in the United States."

Theaters, clubs, lodges and other gathering places were shut down, and at the end of the first week in October all the Boston schools were ordered closed until further notice. A great many Protestant churches suspended their services, and Catholic churches held only low masses to keep their services as brief as possible. Deaths were happening so fast, and gravediggers were so scarce, that secondhand circus tents were used to cover stacks of coffins in local graveyards until proper arrangements could be made. In order to relieve the congestion in regular hospitals, Cardinal O'Connell offered the facilities of St. John's Seminary to the Massachusetts Emergency Public Health Committee as a home for convalescents. Doctors and nurses worked overtime during the crisis, while priests made their tragic rounds visiting the sick, giving the Last Rites and burying the dead. Nearly a thousand Catholic nuns of the diocese, representing twenty different sisterhoods and ninety convents, went from house to house caring for families, preparing meals, washing clothes, dispensing medicines and mothering bereaved children.

For people in South Boston the influenza epidemic seemed especially disastrous. Mrs. Nina Hayes, a lifelong South Boston resident, recalls the sad story of her husband's grandmother, Mrs. Feeney, who lived on the first floor of a two-decker with her husband and nine children. During the epidemic a Mr. Mcglone living on the second floor caught the flu. With Mrs. Mcglone pregnant at the time, Mrs. Feeney went upstairs and cared for the sick man herself. "Mr. Mcglone died," said Mrs. Hayes, "and so did Mrs. Feeney—leaving nine kids!" Whether it was because the impact of multiple deaths seemed so much greater in such a closely knit community, whether it was because this particular strain of the virus took a heavier toll of young fathers and mothers, or whether (as many residents believed) there was something in the "Irish blood" that made them more susceptible to the disease, the residents of the peninsula district felt that they were particularly hard hit by the strange malady. "We used to call it 'galloping pneumonia,' " recalled John W. McCormack, the future Speaker of the House of Representatives. Just when everyone thought that things would be much better as the war was drawing to a close, the terrible disease struck. "You couldn't walk down any street in South Boston," he remarked, "without seeing the black mourning wreath on every door...it was horrible." Older residents can still remember scenes of the horse-drawn wagon moving slowly along the street, stopping before the houses to take out the bodies of those who had died during the night. One local doctor complained that he could not walk down any street in the district without people rushing out, clutching wildly at his clothing, trying to drag him into their homes to tend to the sick members of their families.

South Boston's Carney Hospital cared for at least four hundred victims of the disease in its building atop Dorchester Heights. Three of the four doctors who regularly treated these victims caught the disease themselves, and one died. Because of the ravages of the epidemic, and the large numbers of doctors who left to enter military service, the Carney had to close down its out-patient department for the first time in its history. But if the patients could not come to the hospital, members of the hospital were determined to bring whatever care they could to the people. The Daughters of Charity, who staffed the hospital, became a familiar sight, their distinctive headdresses like great white wings as they traveled about the neighborhood bringing medicines to the sick and small baskets of food to the destitute. One nun described the desperate circumstances of one family she visited: "The mother had just died, and there were four sick children in two rooms. The man was fighting with his mother-in-law and throwing a pitcher at her head." At the end of the year Mayor Andrew J. Peters wrote a letter express-

ing his personal gratitude "for the valuable services rendered to the
City of Boston by the Carney Hospital during the influenza epidemic."

Although people continued to suffer for months to come from the
effects of influenza and pneumonia, by November 1918 the worst effects began to diminish. Schools reopened on October 21, boxing
matches started up again at various clubs around town, schoolboy football
games resumed, and saloons, billiard halls and soda fountains were
allowed to open their doors to customers. People felt free to come out
on the streets on November 11 to celebrate the long-awaited news of
the armistice as whistles shrieked and church bells pealed. That same
evening, hundreds flocked to the Cathedral of the Holy Cross in Boston's
South End to attend a special Mass of Thanksgiving and hear Cardinal
O'Connell sing a joyous *Te Deum* heralding the end of the fighting.
The following evening, hundreds more crowded into Symphony Hall
to enjoy a gala victory celebration organized by city officials. People
from the neighborhoods obviously felt it was safe enough to travel into
the city on November 27 to attend the large public reception at the State
House in honor of General Clarence Edwards, popular commander of
the Yankee Division, who had just arrived home from Europe. On April
25, 1919, in spite of unseasonal thirty-seven-degree weather, citizens
from all over Greater Boston lined the streets of the city to greet the
returning veterans of the Yankee Division as they marched triumphantly
to the blare of brass bands and the cheers of the crowds.

Certain disturbing omens, however, suggested that the postwar years
were not going to be quite as cheerful as the end-of-the-war celebrations indicated. Only two weeks into the new year a terrifying molasses
explosion rocked Boston's North End. In 1915 the Purity Distilling Company had built a giant molasses storage tank on the water side of Commercial Street, opposite Copp's Hill. A short time after noon on January
15, 1919, the great tank exploded, sending some fourteen thousand tons
of molasses flowing down the streets of the North End. Altogether,
twenty-one people lost their lives, and more than 150 were injured.
Horses were swallowed up, houses destroyed, stores crumpled and
warehouses smashed to pieces before the huge wave subsided to a depth
of two or three feet. Firemen cleaned up the sticky mess by hosing down
the area with salt water and covering the streets with sand, but the
memory of the event lingered on. For many years to come the residents
of South Boston could smell the sweet odor of molasses on hot summer
days when the wind came across the channel in the right direction.

People were also finding it more difficult to keep up with the rapidly
rising cost of living. After the war prices continued to go up—food costs
by 84 percent; clothing by 114 percent. Working-class people all over
America found their fixed incomes quickly falling behind, with the cost
of living in 1919 double what it had been five years earlier. Conscious
of the great profits that banks, industries and public utilities had made
during the war years, workers released their frustration in a series of
protests and public demonstrations. During the year 1919 alone there
were 3,600 strikes involving some four million workers. Early in January
New York harbor workers walked off the job, and two weeks later about
3,500 dress- and waist-makers struck for a forty-four-hour work week
and a 15 percent pay raise. In Seattle thirty-five thousand shipworkers
conducted a work stoppage to dramatize their demands for higher wages
and shorter hours, sparking a general strike that brought the entire city
to a standstill.

Boston also felt the impact of postwar industrial warfare. As early
as July 4, 1918, even while the fighting was still going on in Europe,
five thousand New England fishermen began a strike that lasted more
than a month and involved a variety of maritime workers. Nine days
later the elevated railroad workers went out on strike and forced Bostonians to walk to work for four days during a summer heat wave. Once
the armistice had been signed, labor troubles became more frequent.
In April 1919 Julia O'Connor led the Boston Telephone Operators out
on strike to press their demands for better hours and an increase in wages
from sixteen to nineteen dollars per week. The women were supported
by the members of the International Brotherhood of Electrical Workers,
who helped tie up telephone service throughout New England. On
September 2, 1919, six Boston theaters closed their doors as the result
of a strike by the Actors' Association, and local newspapers gave front-
page coverage to the big Labor Day parade through the city of eight
thousand marchers from the ranks of the metalworkers from the arsenal
and the shipyards.

Labor Day also brought discussion of the ongoing problems of the
city's police department. On August 1, 1919, over nine hundred Boston
policemen had voted to join the American Federation of Labor in an
attempt to raise their wages and improve their working conditions. A
patrolman on the Boston Police Department received $1,200 a year—
about twenty-three dollars a week—according to a salary schedule that
had been adopted in 1898. In 1913 living costs had already risen 37
percent over 1898 figures, and by 1919 the cost of living had gone up

another 79 percent. The wartime boom had produced substantial wage increases for many Boston-area workers—steelworkers, shipriggers, pipefitters, carpenters and mechanics of all sorts. But the policemen still worked for the same meager salary. Furthermore, for that salary patrolmen had to work seven days a week, with only one day off in fifteen. They also had to spend one night a week on reserve in dilapidated station houses that were old, bug-infested and overcrowded. Affiliating with the AFL was the only way that many policemen felt they could bring enough pressure to bear on city officials to produce substantial changes.

Police Commissioner Edwin Upton Curtis, furious over policemen joining the AFL, promptly dismissed nineteen patrolmen he considered responsible for organizing the union. Policemen, he stated, were not employees, they were state officers. Affiliating with any outside organization such as a labor union, he insisted, would compromise a policeman's sworn duty to carry out impartial law enforcement. On Tuesday, September 9, 1919, the policemen responded with a strike vote that was overwhelming: 1,134 men voted to strike; only two were opposed.

Once word of the strike vote got around, groups of people collected in the afternoon at police stations throughout the city—at Station 10 at Roxbury Crossing, Station 11 at Fields Corner, Station 13 at Jamaica Plain, Station 14 at Brighton, Station 19 at Mattapan. Near the corner of East Fourth Street and K Street in South Boston, over a thousand people gathered in front of Station 12. A few were sympathetic friends and relatives who had come to applaud the strikers and demonstrate against those who remained on duty, but most were there to vent their anger and resentment against local patrolmen who no longer had the protection of uniform or badge. The Gustin Gang came up from their hangouts on lower Dorchester Street between Eighth and Ninth Streets to join in the excitement. Deriving its name from the leader, "Stevie" Gustin, this gang, from the vicinity of St. Augustine's Church, was reputed to be the toughest street gang in Boston. As soon as the striking patrolmen appeared in the doorway of the station house and began walking down the long flight of steps, they became the targets of a barrage of mud, stones, bottles, eggs and ripe tomatoes as the crowd hooted and hollered at their victims.

An even larger crowd gathered in front of Station 6 on D Street, just off West Broadway in South Boston's lower end, waiting for the striking policemen to leave the afternoon shift. A loud roar went up as the door opened and the patrolmen began to exit. Some still wore their uniforms, minus the badges; others had changed into civilian clothes and carried their uniforms over their arms. They were forced to run a gauntlet of jeers and catcalls while being pelted with rotten eggs and ripe tomatoes and subjected to angry jabs and wild punches.

As darkness settled over the city, the crowds of people indulged in vandalism and destruction. The trouble started downtown, where mobs smashed windows, looted clothing stores and broke into jewelry shops along Washington, Tremont and Boylston Streets. Quickly the violence spread to almost every neighborhood, where troublemakers, especially teenagers and unemployed young people, took advantage of the police absence. In Roxbury a gang stole a buggy and set it afire in front of the Roxbury Crossing police station. In Dorchester another gang built bonfires on the car tracks and smashed the windows of the streetcars forced to come to a stop.

In South Boston looters and pillagers were out in force. Rampaging up and down the lower end of West Broadway below Dorchester Street, they smashed windows, ransacked grocery stores and flung sugar, flour, eggs, fruits and vegetables into the middle of the street. Gangs of youngsters brought streetcars to a stop by yanking the trolley cords. Then they broke the windows and threw stones at the passengers as they tried to get out. At the height of the rioting, ten thousand people reportedly milled up and down Broadway. The Mohican Market, Wallenheim's Bakery, the Budnick Creamery, Connors' and O'Keefe's grocery stores, bicycle shops, tailor shops, fruit stores, clothing stores and liquor stores along Broadway from Dorchester Avenue to City Point had their fronts smashed and their windows demolished. It was nearly one o'clock in the morning before Police Superintendent Michael Crowley could bring in small groups of policemen to break up the crowds and send the rioters off to their their homes. Bob Toland remembers being hustled upstairs to bed by his mother as one part of the noisy mob made its way down the middle of Dorchester Street on the way to Andrew Square, while his father closed all the blinds and remained on guard downstairs with a revolver in his lap and a water glass half-filled with bullets on a small table beside him.

To prevent another day of violence, the following morning, Wednesday, September 10, Mayor Peters called out the state guard within the Boston area—the Tenth Regiment, under the command of Colonel Thomas Sullivan, the First Cavalry Troop, the First Motor Corps and the Ambulance Corps. Peters was already being assisted by a makeshift

volunteer militia of prominent Back Bay Brahmins, old-time Beacon
Hill residents and about fifty Harvard underclassmen, but he felt the
time had come for more professional military discipline. Later that afternoon, Governor Calvin Coolidge responded to Mayor Peters's request
for additional troops. He called up the Eleventh, Twelfth and Fifteenth
regiments of the national guard and ordered them to duty in Boston.

For most of the day the city slowly pulled itself together. The streets
were swept of debris, broken windows were boarded up, and long strands
of barbed wire were strung across smashed doors and damaged en-
trances. Hundreds of bankers, stockbrokers, insurance agents, store-
owners and shop proprietors from the downtown business district lined
up at police headquarters to get licenses to carry pistols. At the nearby
municipal court at Pemberton Square, fifty rioters who had been taken
into custody on charges of breaking, entering and larceny were having
their cases heard. And at the South Boston District Court Judge Edward Logan, former commander of the Yankee Division's 101st Infantry, handed out stiff sentences of six months in the house of correction to rioters arrested the night before.

For a while it looked as though the city might escape another night
of rioting. The incidents that occurred—handbags snatched, pockets
picked, petty acts of thievery—were regarded as relatively minor. To
contain such incidents and prevent them from mushrooming into another
full-scale riot, former lieutenant governor Edward Barry of South Boston
brought together a number of law-abiding residents of the district to
form the South Boston Vigilance Committee. Together with his neighbors
along Dorchester Street—Doctor Daly, John Toland, Eddie Creed and
George Fields—they had acquired several revolvers and enough ammunition to defend their homes and present a united front. They hoped
that this would be enough to maintain the momentary calm and
discourage any further outbreaks of violence.

But it did not work. As the afternoon wore on, young boys roamed
the streets of South Boston looking for trouble, and another crowd
gathered in front of Station 6 on D Street. The news had gone around
that volunteers from Harvard had been assigned to patrol the South
Boston area, and angry residents showed their displeasure by pelting
the station house with rocks, tin cans and bottles. Captain Daniel Murphy decided to keep his thirty Harvard "subs" inside the station house
for the night rather than have them risk the anger of the mob outside.

By late afternoon state guard regiments had begun to converge on
Boston from all points of the compass. The first to arrive and occupy

the East Armory was the Tenth Regiment, whose units were located in such Boston neighborhoods as Roxbury, Dorchester, Roslindale and Brighton. From Newton, Framingham, Lowell and Lawrence came the Eleventh Regiment, while the Twelfth Regiment represented Cambridge, Arlington, Medford and Stoneham. From Quincy and the South Shore towns came the Fourteenth Regiment, while the Fifteenth Regiment brought in troops from Salem, Gloucester and other North Shore towns. The Twentieth Regiment, arriving from the Springfield area, did not pull into Boston until nearly midnight.

The guard units arrived none too soon; the city's downtown area had once again become the scene of a violent clash between a mob of troublemakers and advance units of police volunteers and helmeted militia units. Not until about ten o'clock at night was Scollay Square finally cleared of civilians, as national guard reinforcements marched up Washington Street with fixed bayonets and set up an armed barricade around the entire area.

Earlier that same evening, army trucks rolled up lower Broadway in South Boston, carrying 350 national guardsmen of the Tenth Regiment. After the troops dismounted they were greeted with taunts and jeers and showered with stones, sticks, vegetables and tin cans. Gradually, however, as the uniformed soldiers with rifles and bayonets took up positions along Broadway, the crowd slowly drifted toward Station 6. The rioters suddenly came to life again just after eight o'clock, when they spied three off-duty volunteers walk out of the station house and head for the streetcar stop on Broadway. With loud shouts of "strikebreakers!" the mob chased the volunteers down the street and surrounded them. Monsignor George Patterson, pastor of St. Vincent's Church, rushed to the scene and thrust himself between the screaming rioters and their terrified victims, but his pleas were completely ignored. The volunteers were rescued only when a group of armed guardsmen broke through the crowd and led the volunteers back to safety of the station house.

By the time Superintendent Crowley drove up Broadway on a tour of inspection about ten-thirty that night, he found that the Tenth Regiment had things pretty well in hand. Small bands of young people had been busy smashing windows and stoning passing cars, but there had been nothing like the previous night's general devastation. About eleven o'clock, however, just when authorities concluded that the excitement was over for the night, trouble broke out on West Broadway near E Street. A gang of local youths, some rumored to have pistols, had

collected around an isolated squad of national guardsmen lined up in
front of O'Keefe's grocery store, the A&P market and Shea the Hat-
ter's haberdashery shop. The gang members pressed forward, taunted
the guardsmen, pelted them with mud and stones and dared them to
"make something of it." One of the guardsmen managed to get to Station 6, a block away, and call for help. Captain Thomas Hadley immediately called out the Tenth Regiment's Company G and marched
the unit up the hill in close-order formation with bayonets fixed and
riot guns at the ready. The rioters pulled back temporarily, but soon
moved back to confront the guardsmen as they arranged themselves
across Broadway in a skirmish line.

The confrontation between the rioters and the guardsmen worsened
by the minute. Even when the beleagured soldiers fired a warning volley
the crowd refused to be intimidated. They continued to taunt the troopers
and shower them with more stones and tin cans. When Captain Hadley
stepped forward and called upon the rioters to disperse, a rock in the
forehead sent him staggering backwards. Recovering his balance, he
called out "make ready!" When his men had reloaded their weapons
he gave the command "aim!" Suddenly there was a burst of rifle shot
as the guardsmen fired into the mob at point-blank range. Cries of terror went up, panic swept through the crowd, and people trampled all
over each other in a frantic effort to get away. When the smoke finally
cleared, Anthony Czar of Broadway, sixteen-year-old Robert Sheehan
of L Street, and twenty-one-year-old Robert Lallie were lying on the
ground with fatal wounds. Thomas Flaherty was wounded in the leg,
Helen Keeley received buckshot in the head, and eight more people
were treated for less serious wounds, including Vinnie Plansky of Bowen
Street, a popular local athlete who had been a three-letter man at South
Boston High School and who had just come off a winning season on
the Pere Marquette baseball team.

Like the clash at Lexington Green, the Boston Massacre or the shooting
at Kent State during the Vietnam War demonstrations, no one could
later recall whether there had been any order given to fire, who had
fired the first shot, or what had been the immediate provocation for
the deadly volley. But whatever the unaswered questions, the shooting
ended all disturbances in South Boston and took away any further ap-
petite for rioting. STATE GUARDS' RIFLE FIRE KILLS TWO, the
Globe headline read the next morning, LIVELY SKIRMISH IN SOUTH
BOSTON. There was an air of finality about the headlines, as there
was about the official response to the bloody skirmish. "The firing,"

Adjutant General Jesse F. Stevens reported, "had a salutary effect; it cowed the mob." And indeed, except for sporadic incidents troubles in other parts of the city also quickly diminished. The prompt response and massive military retaliation did much to cut the troubles short, but most of the rioting burned itself out rather quickly. Without leaders, direction or purpose, vandals and hooligans had instinctively taken advantage of a momentary vacuum of power to wreak as much havoc as possible just for the perverse fun of it. Confronted by harsh military force and denunciation by members of the clergy and other members of the established community, the troublemakers quickly disappeared. By Thursday morning the state guard was in unchallenged control of the city, and the police strike was definitely over. On December 21, 1919, the last units of the state guard were finally relieved of their patrol duties, and a new Boston police force, recruited in large part from young men recently discharged from military service, was in operation.

Although the worst effects of the strike lasted no more than two or three days, it would be a great many years before the people of South Boston recovered from its bitter aftereffects. Many family men from the district—fathers, brothers, uncles, cousins, nephews—lost their jobs as policemen and were never allowed back on the force. But the whole episode also reminded people that great differences still separated the Irish-Catholic population of South Boston from the political and financial leaders of Boston society. Governor Coolidge, Mayor Peters, Police Commissioner Curtis, local political leaders and most commanders of the national guard were old-line Protestant Yankees residents of South Boston associated with the traditional, upper-class establishment of the city. Local politicians, businessmen, lawyers, postal-workers, foremen, city-workers, laborers, longshoremen—whether lower-income people or middle-class professionals—felt themselves tarred with the same brush for what a small band of hooligans had done. This general reinforcement of social distinction suppressed some of the obvious class distinctions between the poorer people of the lower end of the district and their more well-to-do neighbors east of Dorchester Street. The "us versus them" attitude toward in-town Bostonians helped bind the residents together in a common cause, despite the growing economic differences that might otherwise have created more substantial class divisions within the community itself. The refusal of leaders to respond to the grievances of the patrolmen or to support their efforts to raise wages and improve working conditions came across as a complete lack of sympathy and understanding. Some old-time residents still harbor resentment against those Harvard students who offered their services as scabs and strikebreakers, a dramatization in their eyes of the gap between the workers and the owners, between the people and the princes.

The police strike also raised the old specter of religion. Many Irish Catholics saw the crisis of early September as evidence that the old religious bigotry of Know-Nothing days still lay disturbingly close to the surface. Conservative reaction against the leaders of the police strike and the union organizers who encouraged it seemed to follow President Harding's nostalgic call for a return to "normalcy." Clearly in line with the general postwar reaction against all things foreign, this reaction was in keeping with the isolationist emphasis on loyalty, conformity and "100 percent Americanism." No doubt recalling the role of Irish immigrants in the Draft Riot of 1863, a number of Bostonians saw the police strike as a lawless outbreak of anarchy that could be attributed to the unstable nature and untrustworthy character of Irish Catholics. The latest event simply confirmed what many local Bostonians already suspected—there were "too many Irishmen" on the police force, and they should be replaced them by more "husky Yankee boys," more "full-blooded Americans" to instil more "Americanism" into the force. "Good Americans and Yankees," they declared, "do not strike!" The people of South Boston viewed these outspoken sentiments as proof that old-time Bostonians continued to regard them as an inferior race still not fully assimilated into the Boston community. In the face of a growing paranoia during the 1920s against Reds, radicals, bolsheviks and socialists, buttressed by a distinct national prejudice against Roman Catholics, Jews, blacks and ethnic groups of all sorts, most Irish Catholics pulled back even more deeply into groups of their own religious and national backgrounds, within the safety and security of their own ethnic neighborhoods.

More than ever before, separateness became almost an unwritten law in South Boston. Young and old held firmly to the conviction that South Boston could maintain its distinctiveness as an unusually friendly, orderly and tolerant community as long as "outsiders" stayed away and local people stayed with their "own kind." Extremely proud of the variety of ethnic and national groups in their district—Irish, Germans, Italians, Poles, Lithuanians, Czechs, Armenians, Albanians—residents nevertheless developed a clear (though unwritten) understanding of the proper relationships among these different groups. At work, in political affairs, and in community activities, they were all expected to meet together, associate on an equal and democratic basis, and work together

for the common good. In personal and private affairs, however, each
group was expected to stay with its "own kind." Young people were
encouraged to "keep company" with members of their own national-
ity and their own religion in order to avoid embarrassing consequences.
The prospect of a marriage between an Irish boy and an Italian girl in
those days, for example, was apt to create as violent an explosion among
members of both families as the shocking and unthinkable prospects
of a "mixed marriage" between a Catholic and a Protestant. Always
allowing for individual exceptions, there were clearly drawn lines that
defined where most of the Polish people lived (in the Andrew Square
section), where the Lithuanians lived (between C and E Streets on the
west side of Dorchester Street), and where the Italians made their homes
(along Third Street between H and L Streets). A number of Jewish merchants came into South Boston every morning to open up their clothing
shops, variety stores and meat markets along Broadway—Gorin's
Department Store, Saphir's, Segal's, and Pober's clothing stores,
Slocum's Toy Store, Bennie's Meat Market—and did a thriving business
with their South Boston customers. But every evening they closed their
stores and returned to their homes in the Jewish district of the city along
Blue Hill Avenue. It was understood that Jews did business in South
Boston but did not live there. The same was even more true of black
people, most of whom lived at this time in the South End of Boston,
in the vicinity of Massachusetts and Columbus Avenues. Since blacks
had neither business nor commercial interests in South Boston, there
was little reason for their coming into the peninsula, except for an occasional visit to the beach at City Point or a picnic at Marine Park.
As a result, many South Boston whites grew to maturity without ever
having seen or spoken with a black person. The only significant exception was the high school student who traveled into Boston to attend
Boston English, Boston Latin, Boston Trade or the High School of Commerce. In most cases, however, a young white person had little occasion to leave South Boston for any appreciable length of time, and there
was little incentive for a young black person to spend much time in
this totally white neighborhood across the channel. There were no laws,
rules or regulations concerning this matter—it had simply always been
that way. Even in the late forties this working relationship was still very
much in effect, and members of the various national groups still seemed to believe that the system provided assurance of freedom and protection for all groups. "I never had any problems," Dhmitri Nikolla,
who had emigrated from Albania and moved to South Boston in the

1950s, insisted. "Everybody keeps to themselves. Lithuanians keep with Lithuanians; Italians keep with Italians; the Irish keep with the Irish," he recalled. "We have our customs, they have their customs. We have our church, they have their church. But there's no conflict whatsoever."

In setting up these clearly defined dividing lines, the Irish Catholics imposed equally vigorous restrictions within their own ranks. The sense of privacy, of space, of what would later be characterized as "turf," was extremely important to people in South Boston—as it was to most other ethnic groups living in the crowded confines of an urban metropolis. Most immigrant people had gone so long without freedom, land, property or any sense of permanence or security that when they finally found some little corner of the world to truly call their own, they determined to hold on to it forever. It became *their* piece of turf; it belonged to no one else. They would never give it up, and they would never let anyone take it away from them. This defensive (and usually unconscious) spirit of possessiveness could be seen in the way families spread their blankets and opened their folding chairs on the beaches of South Boston at a very precise spot—"at the foot of I Street," "at the foot of K Street," "at the foot of M Street," and so on—day after day, week after week, all summer long. Children invariably followed the practices of their parents, and many years later it would be possible to identify longtime South Boston families from their location on the beach.

Many second- and third-generation Irish-Catholic families, those born in the late teens and early twenties, lived in the same two- and three-decker as their parents and grandparents, including many who had actually made the journey across the Atlantic from the old country. The pattern of large, interdependent families continued to be the rule rather than the exception. "The presence of unmarried sisters, brothers, aunts, uncles, and cousins made the Irish-American social fabric unique," Hasia Diner wrote in her study of Irish immigrant women. "Unmarried women and men dotted the Irish-American landscape, clearly and unabashedly." Indeed, researchers surveying social life in South Boston in 1907 discovered that in keeping with the old-country customs, many Irish sons between the ages of twenty and forty-five still lived at home with their families and were still unmarried. At a time before social security, unemployment insurance, retirement benefits, or old-age homes, it was also customary for young couples to take in grandfathers, grandmothers, maiden aunts, spinster sisters, widowed sisters-in-law and separated brothers-in-law (no one was over "divorced" in South Boston in those days; occasionally a couple was said to be "legally separated"). As the years went by, however, the peninsula began to show more tangible evidence of a changing socioeconomic structure. Families gradually moved up from the lower end toward the City Point area. The most prized districts were nearest the beaches, and most residents regarded streets running parallel to the strandway, such as Marine Road and Columbia Road, as prime real estate property. In a very short time, houses became identified with the families which had occupied them for several generations, and residents could usually name the families on a street-by-street basis.

During the 1920s and 1930s the main shopping center along West Broadway, between F Street and Dorchester Street, was still a bustling district, a prosperous bridge between the older and newer sections of the commuity. The substantial Ellis building, just below F Street, housed a popular and well-patronized furniture store, while Carey's furniture store on the nearby corner of F Street and Broadway offered competition among some of the older residents. Side by side, on either side of F Street, the Five-and-Ten and Kresge's both did a thriving business despite their proximity. And all the way up to Dorchester Street a variety of department stores, clothing shops, shoe stores, stationery shops, appliance outlets and fruit stores attracted customers from all parts of the district.

Increasingly, however, as residents with better jobs, higher incomes and loftier expectations moved across Dorchester Street into the City Point area, that part of the district below F Street—the lower end—was slowly becoming older, shabbier and less desirable as a place to live. A number of old South Boston families continued to live in large and comfortable two- and three-story homes between B and C Streets. Newer families with marginal incomes occupied the rundown double- and triple-deckers between D and E Streets. Working men, widowers and newly arrived immigrants, whose prospects for employment were dim and whose incomes were always unpredictable, settled into the numerous tenements, rooming houses and cold-water flats interspersed among the small barbershops, cobbler shops, grocery stores, corner variety stores and barrooms. Many of the local churches—St. Vincent's, SS. Peter and Paul's, the Holy Rosary—were nearly a hundred years old and poorly maintained. Even the newer buildings were badly in need of repair. Most toilets were still in unfinished cellars with dirt floors, and plumbing was old and decrepit. In many locations electricity had not yet fully replaced the original gas fixtures. Wooden clapboards were hanging loose; the paint was peeling and flaking; wooden steps were worn and splintered. Pubs that had once been the meeting places of hard-working laborers, teamsters and longshoremen, who dropped by each night for one or two beers and an hour's gossip before going home to a hot supper, had now become neighborhood taverns, where working men spent the entire night and where unemployed workers spent most of the day bemoaning their fate and sharing their melancholy stories with friends in similar straits. Brawls were frequent, gambling became routine, and the violence in the lower end took on more sinister and dangerous characteristics.

Young people, too, marked out their "turf" and left no doubts about their territorial imperative. Teenagers "hung out" regularly on the street corners of their respective "blocks," a natural and routine method of peer socialization and a way of making sure that groups from other blocks did not cross the invisible line between neighborhoods. Most of these street corner groups soon formed into "gangs," complete with colorful jackets and valiant names—the Cougars, the Tigers, the Eagles—and engaged in almost continuous controversy. Occasionally, several local gangs formed a temporary alliance against an invasion by a similar group from Dorchester, Roxbury or East Boston, but generally they spent their time jousting with each other. Most of the time these confrontations (always called "gang fights") were demonstrative—more like ancient tribal rituals, they broke up after a complicated series of warlike postures, shouts and exaggerated martial gestures. Often enough, however, clashes became violent, ending in bloody noses, broken heads, fractured arms and sometimes worse. Most of the fighting was done with fists, though fighters sometimes resorted to clubs, baseball bats, bricks and beer bottles. Firearms, considered the weapons of professional criminals, were generally unavailable and rarely used in gang fights. The gangs also frowned on knives, daggers and stilettos, and many Irish regarded those who used such weapons as sneaks and cowards. A typical tough South Boston lad felt that a "real man" needed nothing more than hard fists and bare knuckles to assert his manhood, something William F. Whyte observed in his study of conflicts between Irish and Italian youths in Boston's North End. For Irish boys, the purpose of the sport was to "beat up" their opponents, wrote Whyte, and while they legitimately dealt out bruises and welts of all kinds, it was "against the rules" to kill or seriously injure an opponent. Under these circumstances, he continued, it was natural that the Irish were shocked when an Italian defended himself with a knife. In some cases when this happened, "they gave him a more serious beating than he would otherwise have received." Though modern readers may assume such local brawls were peculiar to the immigrant experience, during the seventeenth and eighteenth centuries young men from the North End and the South End customarily engaged in public free-for-alls that often resulted in broken heads and bloody noses. As late as 1800, according to Dr. Edward Reynolds, the "old feud" between South Enders and North Enders was still the occasion of a "regular battle" every Thursday and Saturday afternoon, "not unfrequently [sic] the occasion of very serious injury to wind and limb." The question of "turf," therefore, seems to have been a sensitive issue in the Boston area long before the immigrants arrived—but it was one the newcomers adopted with gusto. Members of these youthful gangs often maintained close association with one another over the years, like members of an alumni association or veterans of a combat regiment. Dr. William J. Reid, former headmaster of South Boston High School, recalls a man who donated a large sum of money for a new scholarship. When asked in whose name the scholarship was to be established, the man thought for a moment and said: "Make it the gang on the corner of Old Harbor and Eighth Street."

Invariably, most residents of South Boston still answer to a nickname carried forward from their youth. In *The Last Hurrah* Edwin O'Connor's practiced ear picked up nicknames unique to Boston political circles when he created Ditto Boland, Cuke Gillen, Nutsy McGrath, Footsie McEntee and the late Knocko Minihan, whose hilarious wake became a classic of modern ethnic fiction. But O'Connor only scratched the surface of a phenomenon that was an integral part of life in South Boston. Tagged with a nickname at an early age, a youngster carried it with him to his grave. One observer has suggested that the practice stemmed, at least in part, from the common Irish use of nicknames not only as an outlet for their irrepressible humor, but also as a practical means of identification. Parishes in Ireland usually had many families with the same surname—Ryan, Flaherty, Kelly, Sullivan, Murphy and so on. As a practical means of distinguishing between the individuals, the Irish became adept at supplying nicknames that described the person and suggested some measure of local opinion. Liberally applied throughout South Boston, such nicknames are still used today to identify popular residents. Some are fairly flattering (Basher Connolly, Jabber Joyce, Tuffy O'Hare, Packy O'Toole); some are basically descriptive (Fingers Farrell, Giggles Flaherty, Peanuts McGrath, Shinner Sullivan);

some have a malicious humor about them (Bugs Ahearn, Pickles Foley, Hambone Kelly, Onions O'Neil); and a few are downright insulting (Wacko Hurley, Dumbo McElroy, Sniffer Shea). In one way or another, nicknames served as a permanent bond among young men of the district and helped to solidify further the feeling of comradeship over the years.

While there were many differences separating the people of South Boston—ethnic, social and economic differences, differences in age and background, differences between those who lived in the lower end and those in the City Point area—the quality and variety of entertainment throughout the district encompassed all social and ethnic groups and provided a definite stimulus to the spirit and vigor of the community as a whole. Without going outside the confines of their own neighborhood, the people themselves combined to provide a wealth of clean, wholesome and constructive entertainment for the entire peninsula. On warm summer nights it was customary for families to congregate on their own front steps, talking, greeting the passers-by, and joining together in singing favorite tunes. "Every Saturday or Sunday night in my house people would come to sing and talk," Bob Toland recalled. "My uncle Charlie played the accordian and the piano—and we had *two* pianos, believe it or not, one on the first floor and one on the second floor—and that was a weekly event, another melting pot, if you will, where people from all walks of life and from all parts of South Boston came to enjoy themselves." Conscious of the old-country traditions of music, dancing, storytelling and speechmaking, South Boston families encouraged the young people of the district to develop their native talents. Parents dug into their meager savings to give their sons and daughters dancing lessons, music lessons (the piano was a particular favorite), singing lessons and instruction in public speaking—popularly known as "elocution." Local churches of all denominations, as well as neighborhood groups and associations, continued to sponsor shows, plays, musical comedies, operettas and minstrel shows.

Over the years, especially as it became easier to identify talented young people with fine singing voices and acting ability, the shows became more elaborate, more sophisticated and more professional. The minstrel show, particularly, became one of the district's favorite musical productions, and parishes vied with one another to put on the most elaborate show, with blackface performers, dynamic end-men, tambourine players, cake-walk specialists, tap dancers and the kind of minstrel music made popular by Al Jolson. "No immigrant group had produced so many minstrel stars as the Irish," J. Anthony Lukas wrote in his Pulitzer prize-winning book *Common Ground*, "and well into the twentieth century, minstrel shows remained a fixture of Boston's Irish neighborhoods." It is difficult to measure how much the blackface minstrel show contributed to negative racial attitudes among the white population of South Boston. Certainly the minstrel show confirmed, in a musical setting, the common stereotype of the lazy, shiftless and simple Negro ("Mistuh Bones") reflected at this same time by characters like "Amos and Andy" on the radio and Steppin Fetchitt in the movies, and by a vaudeville and burlesque tradition that capitalized upon racial slurs and ethnic insults. But written reports and oral interviews seem to make clear that most residents viewed the minstrel show—like jazz music itself—as an indigenous and delightful American art form that they thoroughly enjoyed for its own sake. Whatever ugly forms of racism the blackface idiom provoked appear to have been latent at the time.

The coming of the motion picture during the early 1900s provided a new and breathtaking form of entertainment and furnished another public location where friends and neighbors of all ages and walks of life could get together. Before the show started patrons chatted about local news, and they patronized one of the local hangouts when the movie was over. Joe's Spa, on the corner of Broadway and Dorchester Street, was a popular location, and Stahl's Ice Cream Parlor, on Broadway near Flood Square, attracted a smaller clientele from the City Point section with its delicious ice cream and homemade candy. During the twenties the first silent movies were shown at several makeshift theaters, rather clumsily converted from halls originally constructed for other purposes: on Broadway near D Street was Congress Hall, a virtual wooden matchbox; farther up on West Broadway, near F Street, was the Olympia Theater; and in Flood Square, on the corner of Broadway and I Street, was the Imperial Theater (the "Impy"), another firetrap, on the second floor of Gray's Hall. Children would stand in line on Saturday afternoons clutching their nickels tightly in their hands, waiting to go in and thrill to the latest adventures of Tom Mix, Pearl White or Douglas Fairbanks, or roar with laughter at the antics of Charlie Chaplin or Buster Keaton. The matronly piano player would be given a thunderous round of applause when she walked down the center aisle to take her seat at the piano, and it would usually take fifteen or twenty minutes of community singing (with the lyrics of the latest hits flashed on the screen) before the youngsters had quieted down enough for them to enjoy the next two hours of comedy, drama or adventure. Since the early two-reelers did not run very long, the first movie shows were often prolonged by vaudeville acts—especially at the Saturday matinees and the evening shows. Singers, acrobats, magicians, jugglers, bicyclists, clowns and slapstick comedians of all sorts were a regular part of the bill—often supplemented by local favorites who regularly performed at talent shows and amateur hours.

During the winter of 1914 a young man using the stage name of Freddy James and billing himself as "The World's Worst Juggler" performed his act at the Imperial Theater and developed a line of patter that would eventually make him one of the country's most famous comedians under the name of Fred Allen. Out of this era, too, another local performer, Bennie Drohan, who started his vaudeville career at the Imperial, created the song that was destined to become world famous as the anthem of the South Boston community—"Southie Is My Home Town." While outsiders have tended to trivialize this simple ditty or exaggerate the shortcomings of its nostalgic lyrics ("Born down on A Street, Brought up on B Street...") they have often overlooked its role as an authentic piece of local folk music that glamorized and epitomized the values— pride, strength, loyalty and unity—that residents believed made South Boston such an extraordinary and memorable neighborhood. The lyrics called attention to the district's widespread notoriety and popularity ("There's something about it, /Permit me to shout it, /It's known for miles around..."); they reminded listeners of its diverse population ("It has lawyers and preachers, /Doctors and teachers, /Men from the Old County Down..."); and they emphasized the distinctive character of the neighborhood ("It will make you or break you, /But never forsake you, /Southie is my home town"). Simple to sing and easy to remember, this song grew in popularity until it eventually brought the name and reputation of South Boston all over the country.

As "talkies" and full-length features appeared, and the motion pic-ture industry emerged as a permanent and significant part of the na-tional economy, motion picture theaters began to be designed as a separate and often exotic form of American architecture. Soon South Boston had its own theaters dedicated to this new art form. In the early 1920s the Broadway Theater went up near F Street, just across from the Five-and-Ten. With an orchestra, a loges and a balcony, the Broad-way (or the "Newie," as some people called it) was a good example of the new trend in architecture, with its ornate decorations and elaborate wall hangings. A few years later the Strand, a smaller and less ornate theater, was constructed on Broadway between K and L Streets, open-ing with Lon Chaney starring in *Tell It to the Marines*. As Hollywood production grew, these theaters showed double features, short subjects, Movietone News, coming attractions and short serials, which would end with a chapter each week on a highly suspenseful note. The growth of the movies gradually eliminated vaudeville and live performances generally. A delightful and nostalgic period, it seemed at the time that it would go on forever.

But the good times did not last. In October 1929, the stock market collapsed, and the resulting financial catastrophe quickly spread its crippling effects to every other phase of the nation's econmy. Over five thousand banks were forced to close their doors during the first three years of America's Great Depression, undermining the financial operations of businesses and wiping out the savings of hundreds of thousands of people. Factories either cut their production to a minimum or shut down operations completely. By the end of 1930 about 6,500,000 Americans were out of work, and by 1932 this figure had more than doubled. Every city in the country saw the advent of bread lines and soup kitchens to meet the desperate needs of despondent men, anxious women, and hungry children.

The City of Boston and its surrounding neighborhoods also felt the full force of the Great Depression. Half a dozen bankers collapsed on the floor of the Boston Corn Exchange and had to be carried off to local hospitals, according to the *Boston Globe*. The most "pathetic scenes" occurred in the customers' room of the brokerage houses, where ruined speculators often "broke down and wept." Other brokers and investors congregated in small groups, "stunned by the misfortune that had overtaken them." In communities like South Boston, working-class families were especially hard hit by the loss of jobs and the impact of deflation. Small savings, painfully accumulated over the years, quickly disappeared. Mortgages on homes and small rental properties—two-, three- and four-family tenement houses—were foreclosed. Husbands and wives surrendered their insurance policies for their cash value; customers pleaded with grocery store owners for further extensions of credit; families had to return appliances they had recently purchased on the installment plan. "Those are not happy memories," Arthur Gulinello recalled. "We were getting thirteen dollars a week, and we were paying $23 a month for rent. We were so poor we couldn't even afford a radio. But my mother went down to McShane's—I think it was sixteen dollars for an Emerson radio and that, to me, was pure happiness." Stores closed for lack of customers; hospitals ran short of patients; old theaters went out of business; the new theaters attracted customers by running two major features, a variety of cartoons, serials and newsreels, and by offering free sets of dinnerware.

Despite an impassioned attempt by the Good Government Association to "stamp out Curley and Curleyism," James Michael Curley was elected to a third term as mayor of Boston in 1929, with South Boston coming in decisively on his behalf. On taking the oath of office at Symphony Hall on January 6, 1930, Curley promised to furnish "work and wages" for those who were in need of "sustenance and employment." He called for an ambitious Fifty-Year Plan to develop industry, commerce and municipal construction. Emphasizing long-range economic planning and city-financed construction, he promised to put the city's jobless to work on new libraries, health units and recreational facilities.

A contract for $117,288 to build a concrete walk to Castle Island furnished temporary work for a number of South Boston residents. Working along the beach through the cold winter months, many with insufficient clothing and most without gloves, the men wrestled huge rocks into place to protect the banks along the harbor side of the walk from erosion by waves and the wash from passing ships. The roadway—Castle Island Boulevard—was finally completed in 1932. Projects such as these were hard to come by, however, and despite his ambitious promises the new mayor was unable to get the large federal appropriations he wanted to expand his patronage system through an extensive program of public works. He resorted to stopgap measures—hiring snow shovelers at five dollars a day to clean the streets for the city's upcoming 1930 tercentenary celebration, for example—but these steps fell far short of meeting the crisis. By the spring of 1930 at least forty thousand workers were jobless, with some estimates putting the figure as high as 100,000. As patronage dried up and local relief systems broke down, panhandlers roamed the streets, idle workers waited for boats to come into the Fish Pier with unsaleable scraps of codfish, and the jobless curled up on park benches or huddled in the doorways of public buildings. South Boston saw its own version of "Hooverville" go up on the sprawling dump just beyond Columbia Circle off the old Mile Road leading to Dorchester, where destitute vagrants tried to find shelter in flimsy cardboard packing crates or makeshift shanties pieced together out of abandoned sheets of corrugated tin.

Conditions became even worse as many of the local factories and industries shut down. In the early part of the nineteenth century, South Boston had been the center of much heavy industry, and its blast furnaces and iron foundries turned out cannon, shells, bridges, iron-clad ships and locomotives for the Union army during the Civil War. By the turn of the century, however, most of the large glassworks and iron foundries had moved out of state or gone out of business completely. In their place a number of smaller enterprises offering full-time and part-time jobs to the residents of the district had sprung up. There were, of course, two or three industries that dominated the local economy and offered a lion's share of the jobs. The Walworth Manufacturing Company, for example, on East First Street between M and N Streets, employed nearly 1,500 workers. Established in 1842, it had developed into one of the largest manufacturers in the world of pipes, valves and fittings used in lighting, heating and ventilation. Close by was the Metropolitan Coal Company, where huge mountains of soft anthracite coal piled up and regularly sent showers of black cinders to blanket the playgrounds of M Street Park. Some distance away, in the lower end of South Boston close to the Fort Point Channel, the Domino Sugar Company operated day and night and employed nearly 1,500 workers. The plant produced about one thousand barrels a day of fine granulated sugar out of the beet and raw cane sugar brought in by large vessels from Cuba and the various islands of the Caribbean. The Gillette Razor Company, a relative newcomer to South Boston but one which was fast becoming one of the district's largest employers, had started out in 1901 as a small shop over a local hardware store. Wisconsin native King Camp Gillette persuaded some friends to invest five thousand dollars in a company to manufacture a safety razor he had invented. Because he had come up with an early example of planned obsolesence—a product people would use, throw away and then buy again—Gillette's company prospered and expanded in a very short time.

In addition to these local giants, scores of other business and manufacturing enterprises were scattered throughout the peninsula. Many of the older companies were clustered around A, B and C Streets in the vicinity of West First and Second Streets. The Boston Asphalt Company, the Chapman Valve Company, the American Brass and Copper Company, the Diamond Match Company and the Bay State Belting Company were typical of the small industries located in the lower end. The Estabrook Company turned out boilers, castings and plumbing supplies, and the Hersey Manufacturing Company designed machinery for all kinds of industrial purposes. The United Carr Fastener Company at 1230 Columbia Road, popularly referred to as the "Button Factory," employed over 100 local residents making buttons, zippers and clasps of all kinds. Farther up on East Fourth Street, between G and H Streets, was a large red-brick factory, the L. B. Smith Company, known as the Silversmiths, where the manufacturing, plating and cleaning of silver products were carried on. As the population of the district moved along into the City Point area, industries quickly followed. Along First Street a string of concerns did a thriving business, hired neighborhood people and contributed to the local economy. Linde Air Products specialized in compressed air; the Clifford Manufacturing Company produced thermostatic controls; and the Stetson Fuel Company provided coal and oil for the district. The Za-Rex Company, which manufactured jellies and fruit syrups, was only one of a number of small industries located in a complex near the junction of L and Summer Streets, across from the huge Edison Electric Plant. The Suffolk Brewery, on the corner of Eighth and G Streets, Lynch's Barrel Factory, the Boston Molasses Company and the Raincoat Factory on the corner of Sixth and N Streets, had all provided opportunities for steady employment or part-time work for local men and women. At N and Seventh Streets, the New England Confectionery Company hired many local women as candy-packers, turning out rolls of popular sugar candies known as "Necco wafers."

With the onset of the Great Depression, however, most of these employment outlets disappeared. "As long as the Button Factory was making all kinds of noises with its belts and whatever kinds of machinery they had in there, we knew that times were good and that a lot of people were employed," one resident recalled. "But when we didn't hear any noises coming from the Button Factory, then we knew that times were bad." As banks failed, businesses collapsed, and the American export trade fell off, the resulting drop in factory production meant the widespread loss of jobs throughout the community. From July 1931 to December 1932, unemployment in all trades in Boston averaged 29.72 percent, very close to the 30.17 rate reported by twenty-three other large American cities. A few factories shut down completely; most cut back their hours, spread the work around and tried to stay in operation with skeleton crews and piecework. South Boston workers were also affected by the serious changes taking place in other aspects of the New England economy. Textile factories were beginning to move into southern states in search of cheaper labor and more available raw materials. Central heating in homes and businesses killed the market for woolen underwear and heavy wool suits, and young women showed a decided preference for the new lightweight fabrics made of silk and rayon. The collapse of the local textile market and the decline of the boot and shoe industry caused severe cutbacks in employment in the numerous wool and leather

houses along Summer Street. At the same time, Boston also declined
as a port city. The volume of cargo and the value of goods shipped
through the port of Boston dropped steadily from 1925 to 1930, and
small gains in passenger traffic failed to compensate for these losses.
The jobs that had been available to South Boston residents at the docks
and on the piers disappeared along with the other opportunities for work
throughout the city.

South Boston survived the worst effects of the Depression, to a great
degree because of the interconnected family network that was still the
hallmark of the community. Those who still had jobs parceled out their
meager incomes to friends and neighbors who were out of work. Families
shared their butter, eggs and sugar with one another, exchanged shoes
and clothing for the children and opened their homes to relatives who
needed a place to live. In the closely knit parish system of the day, officers and members of the various St. Vincent de Paul societies worked
overtime helping the needy in days when there were no public social
or economic benefits available to ease their plight. According to Bob
Toland, whose father was the head of the St. Vincent de Paul Society
in St. Augustine's parish, those who rang the doorbell of his house to
obtain food checks were invariably women. "A male was a rarity."
Most men were embarrassed to be seen walking up the steps of Mr.
Toland's house on Dorchester Street, so they sent their wives—and very
often they sent them at night so they wouldn't be noticed. "They were
proud and they were independent," Toland said, "but alas, they were
ashamed." Although they managed to keep themselves together, these
people were at a loss to explain what had happened, how it had happened, and who was responsible for it all. Most working-class Irish-
Americans had been totally committed to the vision of upward
mobility—the Great American Dream. If they worked hard, remained
sober, obeyed the law, saved their money, sent their children to good
schools and remained true to their religion, then their future would be
bright and their horizons unlimited. But the Great Depression put an
end to that dream. "The economic collapse of 1929 and the twelve years
of depression that followed," William Shannon wrote, "ended a world
for the American Irish." The unprecedented disaster that destroyed the
nation's economic system, he said, "broke the rationale they had lived
by."

The appealing voice of a Catholic priest from the Midwest, Father
Charles E. Coughlin, captured the attention of "shocked and disoriented
millions" of middle-class and working-class Irish Catholics and was

probably the first to persuade them to accept the notion of a more positive
role for the national government in the lives of the American people.
When Fr. Coughlin began broadcasting in the fall of 1930, he attacked
traditional laissez-faire economics and called for a positive program of
government action to bring justice and charity into the industrial system.
Early in 1931 he further appealed to the isolationist mood of ethnic
groups by denouncing the Versailles Treaty, blaming the Depression
on the greed of international bankers and warning that Europeans were
trying to drag the United States into another war. Throughout the spring
and fall of 1931, he spoke out boldly against President Hoover and the
free-enterprise policies of the Republican party.

Fr. Coughlin quickly became a favorite among Irish-Catholic families,
who gathered in front of their radios every Sunday afternoon at four
o'clock and listened to his broadcasts with an almost religious devotion. First of all, the Irish believed in him because he was a priest who
spoke out boldly on general moral and ethical principles the way they
thought a priest should. Secondly, he identified the enemy—J. P.
Morgan, Bernard Baruch, the House of Rothschild and other international bankers—playing subtly but effectively upon the anti-Semitism
among some Irish Catholics, who feared the unseen power of Jewish
financiers. Third, and perhaps most important, Fr. Coughlin provided
a strong religious justification for loyal and obedient Irish Catholics
to become openly critical of their political leaders. The priest himself
led the way in February 1932 with a public assault on President Hoover,
whom he labeled "the banker's friend, the Holy Ghost of the rich, the
protective angel of Wall Street." Fr. Coughlin called for Christian principles to be injected into the modern economic structure in keeping with
the social ideals of such papal encyclicals as *Rerum Novarum* and
Quadragesimo Anno. "Drive the money-changers from the temple!"
he cried as he pointed to the "New Deal" being offered by the
Democratic candidate as a place where Christian teachings could be
found. "It is Roosevelt or ruin!" he exclaimed to his radio listeners
in the autumn of 1932. "The New Deal is Christ's Deal!"

The people of South Boston joined with voters throughout the nation
in contributing to the landslide victory of Franklin D. Roosevelt in
November 1932. Hopefully, almost desperately, they looked forward
to his inauguration the following March as the entire American banking system seemed to be crumbling about them. Public confidence in
the banks was quickly ebbing, despositors were withdrawing their money
in panic, and one bank after another was closing its doors and declar-

ing bankruptcy. Before heading back to Boston after attending the inauguration of President Roosevelt on March 4, 1933, Governor Joseph B. Ely proclaimed the closing of all Massachusetts banks, and at 4:00 P.M. the following day Roosevelt himself ordered a national banking holiday. Even as Governor Ely was telling the people of the Commonwealth that "it is a patriotic obligation to remain calm," Boston policemen were taking elaborate precautions to protect every financial house in the city against possible attacks by irate investors.

During the emergency Bostonians pulled together. Catholic churches offered special prayers for the welfare of the new President and the safety of the nation, while a corporate communion was held throughout the Episcopal Diocese of Massachusetts at the direction of the Reverend Henry Knox Sherrill. On Sunday night, March 12, residents of South Boston gathered around their radios, along with families everywhere in the country, to listen to FDR's first "fireside chat" and to hear the soothing voice of the President assure them that the worst of the crisis had passed, that it was now safer for them to put their money in one of the reopened banks than to keep it "under the mattress." When, on March 13, all banks in the City of Boston received permission from the federal government to reopen their doors, the President's hearty words of reassurance seemed to have come true. As deposits exceeded withdrawals, praise was lavished upon the new President from every quarter. James Michael Curley extolled the "courage and vision" that had saved the nation from bankruptcy, and the Boston City Council passed a resolution praising the "summary, intelligent and courageous action taken by President Roosevelt and Governor Ely."

Despite the strong and enthusiastic support of the Irish for FDR and his New Deal programs, a combination of factors prevented Boston from getting the amount of money it should have received for a city of its size and importance. For one thing, administration leaders in Washington had a deep distrust of James Michael Curley and other influential political figures in Boston; they feared that government appropriations would be wasted, mismanaged or stolen. For another, political feuding, neighborhood rivalries and conflicts among various ethnic groups added to the national perception that Boston was not a city that could handle large sums of money honestly, equitably or responsibly. As a result, public funds for early emergency projects under the Federal Emergency Relief Administration (FERA) and the Civil Works Administration (CWA), as well as the later and more extensive programs under the Public Works Administration (PWA) in 1934 and the Works Progress

Administration (WPA) in 1935, never reached the levels of other American cities.

Of the funds that did come into the Boston area, however, much was carefully funneled by Colonel Thomas Sullivan, head of the city's relief headquarters, to the residents of South Boston. Statistics show that the South Boston Irish were proportionately more strongly represented on the work rolls than North End Italians and West End Jews. Italo-Americans in the North End, for example, received less than half the number of WPA openings to which their rate of joblessness entitled them, while people in South Boston got 14 percent more than should have been the case. As one disgruntled North Ender put it, the Irish "gouged" people who "can't speak good English." One federal official was struck by the numerous ways in which blue-collar classes in Boston were divided by the kind of harsh ethnic competition in which "each group felt victimized." Old-line Yankees regarded all but their own "breed" with suspicion, he observed, while the Irish looked down on the Italians, and so on, in order of immigration, "to an extent that really colors all thought." And yet there were times when the clannish spirit of South Boston took precedence over even ethnic differences. "I can remember being on the WPA, which was controlled mostly by the Irish," recalled John DeCosta who was of Portuguese descent. "I was working at the Fairview Cemetery, and I was treated coolly until they found out that I came from South Boston. One or two guys from Southie who were working there knew me and said, 'Oh, he's all right!' "

Despite the jobs and meager welfare checks provided by New Deal programs, there were those who criticized Roosevelt for not providing enough assistance to the poor, disabled and elderly, and who listened to the promises of colorful public figures for more elaborate schemes of social welfare. Senator Huey Long of Louisiana came out with a highly publicized "Share the Wealth" program; Dr. Francis Townsend of California offered a plan to provide people over sixty with an income of two hundred dollars a month; and Fr. Coughlin organized a new political movement—the National Union for Social Justice—to press for more decisive action by the federal government. In 1936 the priest began publishing a newspaper called *Social Justice*, which almost immediately became required reading in ethnic neighborhoods. Every Sunday morning hundreds of South Boston parishioners eagerly snatched up their copy of *Social Justice*, piled up alongside stacks of the Sunday editions of the *Globe*, *Herald* and *Post* outside St. Augustine's, the Gate of Heaven, St. Eulalia's and the other Catholic churches in the district.

These working-class people clearly felt that the priest from Michigan was fighting as their champion in the struggle between the rich and poor, the haves and have-nots.

Encouraged by his devoted followers, Coughlin came out publicly against Roosevelt and organized his own political convention in Cleveland in August 1936. Declaring that the choice between the other two parties was the difference between "carbolic acid and rat poison," the convention nominated Republican William Lemke of North Dakota for President and Thomas C. O'Brien, a Boston Democrat who had been district attorney for Suffolk County, for Vice President. Despite his boast that he could deliver at least nine million votes, Coughlin's bid for political power proved an embarrassing failure. Not only did the lackluster Lemke poll fewer than a million votes, but Coughlin himself lost a good deal of popular support. Undaunted, the Radio Priest returned to the airwaves in 1937, stepping up his violent attacks against FDR and the New Deal and launching into a campaign against Jews in America. Caught up in the Spanish Civil War, he encouraged the formation of quasimilitary organizations under the name of the "Christian Front." Increasingly certain that Roosevelt was leading the nation into war, he supported the campaign against the cash-and-carry program in the fall of 1939, denounced FDR's plans for a peacetime draft in 1940, and early in 1941 joined in the assault against the Lend Lease bill.

In the face of world conditions, support for Fr. Coughlin and his staunchly isolationist position slowly but steadily weakened in neighborhoods like South Boston. His Irish-Catholic supporters had always applauded his attacks on Herbert Hoover and laissez-faire economic policies to the point where James Michael Curley referred to Boston as "the most Coughlinite city in the United States." When the priest visited the city in 1935, he was given a triumphal welcome by the City Council and the Massachusetts legislature. He was at the peak of his power then, and South Boston was the "prime bastion" of his support. But the elections of 1936 were a turning point in the relationship of the Michigan priest and his East Coast followers. Most Boston Catholics had serious reservations about any priest getting directly involved in partisan politics, and many of them were shocked by the increasing stridency of Couglin's anti-Semitic remarks. Though Lemke and O'Brien ran stronger in Boston than in any other major American city, polling over 11 percent of the popular vote in working-class districts like South Boston, where support for President Roosevelt dropped off in 1936, this was a far cry from the sweeping victory that Coughlin had predicted.

Congressman John McCormack pointed out the softening of the South Boston vote in 1936 to President Roosevelt, warning him that the "sullen, discontented and bitter" people who had gone out of their way to support Fr. Coughlin's sticker candidates were obviously in need of greater federal assistance. After 1936 South Boston residents achieved an even more substantial lead in their percentage of federal jobs. While other parts of the city waited in vain for public housing to be constructed, South Boston proudly witnessed the completion of Old Harbor Village, which was, according to Charles Trout, "the single completed example of what a handsomely designed federal housing project could be." And it seemed to produce the desired political results. The "rank and file" of the crowds in South Boston simply "loved" Franklin D. Roosevelt, Clem Norton told James Roosevelt as they traveled over to attend the dedication ceremonies for the project. Two years later the election returns showed a definite increase in favor of New Deal candidates, and by 1940 more South Boston voters supported FDR than had backed Al Smith in 1928.

While many older residents continued to support Fr. Coughlin and the America First Committee in their efforts during 1939 and 1940 to prevent passage of the Lend Lease program, younger members of the district were becoming more reconciled to the need for greater national defense. The German invasion of Poland in 1939, the collapse of France in 1940 and the successful movement of Japanese forces into French Indochina and other parts of Southeast Asia emphasized the growing danger of a new world conflict that would certainly involve the United States. Already many familiar faces were no longer seen around the neighborhood as a number of young men enlisted in the armed services, anticipating a war that would eventually call them to the colors. Mothers and fathers read the daily newspapers with increasing apprehension during the summer and fall of 1941 as the clash of American naval vessels and German submarines in the North Atlantic seemed to make a full-scale conflict inevitable. When President Roosevelt issued a "shoot-on-sight" order after several U. S. destroyers were torpedoed in waters off Iceland in September and October, most people felt that a formal declaration of war with Nazi Germany was close.

But when war did come, it came from a different point in the compass. Early Sunday morning, December 7, 1941, waves of Japanese fighters, dive-bombers and torpedo planes roared across the Hawaiian island of Oahu, toward the American naval base at Pearl Harbor, where ninety-six ships of the Pacific Fleet lay at anchor. Within less than two hours nineteen American ships were sunk or disabled; 188 airplanes destroyed; about 2,400 soldiers, sailors and civilians killed; more than 1,100 people wounded. The attack on Pearl Harbor sent shock waves across America. Hundreds of residents of South Boston had already returned from Mass and were getting ready to sit down to Sunday dinner when the startling news of the naval disaster broke into their regularly scheduled radio programs. Still in a state of shock and disbelief, they joined millions of other Americans around their radios the next day to listen to President Roosevelt's six-minute address to the Congress: "Yesterday, December 7, 1941, a date which will live in infamy, the United States was suddenly and deliberately attacked by naval and air forces of the Empire of Japan." Less than an hour later Congress, with one dissenting vote, approved the declaration of war against Japan. Three days later Germany and Italy officially joined their Japanese ally and declared war on the United States. That same afternoon Congress responded in kind without a single dissenting vote, and the United States was fully involved in the Second World War.

The torpedoes that sank the American battleships at Pearl Harbor, as one historian put it, also sank "America Firstism" and put an end to any further thoughts of negotiated settlements. "The only thing now to do," conceded isolationist Senator Burton K. Wheeler, "is to lick hell out of them," and the people of South Boston wholeheartedly agreed. "The Nation is at War," announced the *South Boston Gazette*; "Let Us have no Peace." Like so many communities all over the United States, South Boston quickly took on a military air. A war of this magnitude brought an end to more than a decade of depression and unemployment, and soon local men and women were hard at work in war plants, factories and shipyards. The Walworth Manufacturing Company, the United Carr Fastener, the Linde Air Products and numerous other local industries geared up for wartime demands. The Commercial Filters Corporation on the corner of A and West Third Streets operated a special "Victory Shift" in order to further increase production. This was a four-hour shift, usually from 6 P.M. to 10 P.M., which attracted grocers, garage mechanics, railroad workers, salesmen and businessmen who wished to make a contribution to the war effort after their regular working hours. Commercial Filters turned out valuable filters that were used in airplanes, ships, submarines, tractors, hospital sterilizers—and at the end of the war were also used in the construction of the atomic bomb.

Because supplies of many materials were cut off by the war or assigned to military uses, the government began rationing certain scarce commodities, issuing books of ration stamps to families for such things as sugar, coffee, butter, cheese, gasoline and fuel oil. Individuals, civic groups and youth organizations in the district tried to help the cause of victory by turning in heaps of scrap metal to be recycled or collecting old automobile tires in well-publicized scrap-rubber drives. The war spirit soon affected many otherwise normal aspects of life in South Boston. The Carney Hospital, for example, took special precautions to provide "every possible protection" for the patients in the event of blackouts and air raids. Fears of espionage and fifth-column activities caused Castle Island to be closed to the public by order of the War Department, which now reclaimed the property from the city under the war emergency. Army guards stationed in a small guardhouse at the beginning of the causeway turned back anyone who did not have proper identification. At night additional guards took up positions along the causeway itself, at intervals of about two hundred yards, so that they could challenge visitors driving out to the island.

Throughout the district the local draft boards were busier than usual, as over four thousand men aged twenty to forty registered for military service. Young men and women who had rarely, if ever, been out of Massachusetts were now sent out to all parts of the United States for basic training—Fort Myers, Virginia; Camp LeJeune, North Carolina; Fort Benning, Georgia; Maxwell Field, Alabama; Camp Shelby, Mississippi; Fort Leonard Wood, Missouri; Fort Sill, Oklahoma; Fort Lewis, Washington; and Camp Pendleton, California. After basic training they went to ports of embarkation and then all over the world. Some went to the Pacific Theater of Operations, where they took part in the fighting on Guadalcanal, at Midway and the Coral Sea, and in the jungles of the Philippine Islands. Others traveled across the Atlantic to the European Theater of Operations, where they saw action in North Africa, on the beachheads of Anzio and Normandy, and in the frozen terrain of the Battle of the Bulge.

Small red-white-and-blue service flags hung outside the white-lace curtains of two- and three-decker houses, reminding friends and neighbors how many members of the family were serving in the armed forces—a blue star for every one still on active service; a gold star for every one who had been killed in action. But in their own way, those little flags also served as silent signals that a unique period in South Boston's history had come to an end. A more simple time had come and gone in the life of this neighborhood. Old-time "Southie" would never be the same.

But the community prided itself on having withstood the demoralizing impact of the Great Depression, adjusted to the considerable social and political changes of the New Deal, and survived the terrible ordeal of World War II. It had come out of it all intact, even more unified as a neighborhood than ever before. Indeed, it was during this period of global warfare that the name and fame of South Boston was spread throughout all parts of the United States and to many parts of the world— at least according to the reports of veterans who recall hearing rollicking choruses of "Southie Is My Home Town" sung at army posts, naval depots, PX's and barrooms from South Carolina to Georgia, Texas to California. By the time the war had ended South Boston, for better or worse, had become the only one of the city's two dozen neighborhoods to epitomize the "Boston Irish" at their open-hearted, ebullient best, or their brooding, belligerent worst.

The general public tends to seize upon certain signs and symbols to personify and even stereotype various social, racial and ethnic groups. Certainly the single image of "Beacon Hill" comes close to encapsulating the notions of the Yankee heritage, the Brahmin influence and the conservative Protestant tradition of Boston. In much the same way, "South Boston" had come close to symbolizing, in a single community, the "other" Boston—the immigrant spirit, the Irish character and the Catholic influence in the city. How long it could sustain that image in the face of the enormous changes that were about to overtake the city of Boston, however, was difficult to determine as the war came to an end, and the young veterans came marching home.

7

UNDER SIEGE

WITH AN EARTH-SHATTERING BLAST OF ATOMIC POWER, World War II finally came to an end. Admitting defeat on August 14, 1945, the Japanese signed the formal surrender terms aboard the battleship *Missouri* anchored in Tokyo Bay on September 2. Like the rest of the nation, Boston returned to some semblance of normal life—as returning veterans discovered when they found the Red Sox winding up the baseball season in seventh place.

But Boston was losing more than ballgames. In 1945 the future of the city was very bleak. Years of neglect, a decade of depression and a generation of political feuding between natives and newcomers had taken a toll. By the time the war was over the city was in terrible condition. The *Boston Globe* called Boston "a hopeless backwater, a tumbled-down has-been among cities." John Collins, a future mayor, said that there was a kind of "malaise of spirit." "We were all kind of ashamed," he recalled. Even the fashionable Back Bay had lost its old elegance. "Commonwealth Avenue is a beautiful street in many ways," the *Back Bay Ledger* observed, "but it looks like a deserted village in many block lengths, where house after house has been boarded up, and the one-time residents gone." City income was going down, city taxes were going up, and established businesses were abandoning Boston every day to relocate in cities with lower taxes, cheaper labor, better benefits and a more congenial political climate.

With other local neighborhoods South Boston experienced significant changes in its traditional patterns of life and society during the postwar

years. A number of old and familiar institutions that had bound the people
of South Boston together now began to weaken. Some even disappeared
completely. Families were increasingly smaller in size as the number
of children steadily declined and older relatives were placed in
sanitariums or convalescent homes instead of being kept at home. Even
the century-old Carney Hospital was forced to leave its familiar location atop Thomas Park and Old Harbor Street and move to a larger site
in Dorchester in 1945, when Archbishop Cushing decided that more
modern facilities were needed. The Catholic Church itself, while still
an important force, no longer had the all-pervasive influence it once
had before the war, and the break-up of the parochial school system
reflected the shakiness of the archdiocesan financial structure. "When
I was a youngster," Bob Toland recalled, "we would have a mission
or a retreat, and you couldn't find standing room in the church or in
the choir loft. Today, churches in South Boston are notorious for their
empty benches. Young people have far different standards, different
ethical criteria from what we had when I was a kid. I'm not saying that
we were right in many ways. We lived in a very rigid society, with
a lot of rules—particularly with the strong religious influence. A great
deal of that has left South Boston. In some ways that's good," he mused,
"but in some ways that's bad." With radio and television bringing a
whole new galaxy of stars in baseball, football, hockey and basketball
into the home, local sports heroes were all but forgotten. Instead of
heading for the M Street Playground or McNary Park, younger fans
flocked to Fenway Park, Braves Field or the Boston Garden for big-
time sports events. People lost interest in amateur theatricals, local
operettas and parish minstrel shows now that they could stay home and
watch professional extravaganzas on television. Young men who had
graduated from college were no longer interested in playing cards and
drinking beer with old men at the clubs, councils and lodges. With
automobiles, good salaries and a wide circle of friends outside the Boston
area, they had new priorities and different social outlets.

World War II had had a profound effect on the relationship of the
younger generation and their old neighborhood. The government had
taken thousands of young men and women from working-class families,
most of whom had seldom been outside of New England, and sent them
all over the world to fight for their country. As they traveled from the
Atlantic to the Pacific, from Europe to Asia, these young people experienced a culture shock of enormous proportions. Unlike the disruption of life during World War I, this dislocation was not for a few months

or a year; it was for three or four years—or even, in the case of many who had anticipated the war and joined one of the services in 1939 or 1940, for as many as five or six. For many of these young men and women, nothing was ever quite the same after 1945. The old links had been severed; the old attachments had been broken. Better educated, more experienced, less parochial, more casual about their ethnic roots and less defensive about their religious views, they packed up and left the old three-deckers and moved out to new split-level ranch houses that sprang up in the suburbs during the 1950s. Indeed, during the postwar years the deep pride most early inhabitants had always taken in their Irish heritage too often seemed to take on the kind of cheap and superficial characteristics that became especially noticeable during the district's annual St. Patrick's Day parade. Green derbies, make-believe shamrocks, plastic shillelaghs, Tin-Pan Alley songs and over-sized lapel-buttons proclaiming "Kiss Me, I'm Irish!" made their appearance, and old-time residents complained about young people of every ethnic background from many different communities flocking into South Boston to drink, fight and turn a traditional neighborhood festivity into a blatant excuse for an ugly and embarrassing brawl.

The whole character of the district seemed to be changing. "South Boston is no longer strictly Irish," commented John Joyce, operator of Joyce Brothers Service Station at the intersection of Old Colony and Dorchester Avenues. "Every year the Irish population has grown smaller. There are many fine Polish and Lithuanian families now. There's a Puerto Rican colony on D Street. Also a number of Cubans. Times have changed." Even those veterans who wanted to remain in South Boston were discouraged by the policy of Boston banks that classified South Boston as a "blighted" or "depressed" area and refused to grant mortgages or assign home-improvement loans in that neighborhood. As a result of this policy of "redlining," most young families were forced to purchase houses in suburban areas where the mortgage rates were lower and the banking policies more encouraging. In a short time, older parts of the neighborhood began to show signs of the blight and decay predicted by the banks. Maintenance and repairs became prohibitive, homes fell into serious disrepair, streets were no longer cleaned, parks and playgrounds were soon neglected, and vandalism became commonplace. Whether they were leaving by choice or by default, the wholesale departure of young veterans and their families was reflected in a sharp drop in the neighborhood's population figures. Just before World War I South Boston's population had risen to an all-time high of nearly eighty thousand people. After that, however, the figure went steadily downward. In the twenty years between 1950 and 1970 almost twenty thousand of these former residents moved out of the district or died, bringing the population down to about thirty-eight thousand—and it continued to decline.

Public housing also did much to transform the character of South Boston, a transformation that started during the depression years when the PWA Housing Division was authorized to undertake a program of slum clearance and to construct public housing for low-income working families at rents they could afford. Eventually the federal Housing Division built some fifty-one housing projects, and as one of the favored cities Boston was singled out for a pilot project as early as 1933. As the result of a complicated series of political delays, real estate fights and bureaucratic postponements, however, it was another five years before all the arrangements could be worked out. The PWA construction contract was finally awarded to one of Mayor Curley's "pet" contractors, and the site chosen was located in Congressman John W. McCormack's home district. In 1938 South Boston's Old Harbor Village—with three-story, plain brick buildings set around square courtyards, described by one modern historian as "by far the best-designed, best-built project the city was to see in the next thirty years"—was finally ready to open its doors. But those doors would not open to anyone on municipal welfare. The rentals of Old Harbor Village (later renamed the Mary Ellen McCormack Project, after Congressman McCormack's mother) were set at $22.15 per month for three rooms, and $31.90 for five. This was a far cry from truly "low-cost housing" and much too expensive for anyone without a full-time job and a regular income— definitely not a "happy hunting ground for the poor," as Councilor R. Gardiner Wilson, Jr., of Dorchester expressed it.

The following year, a second housing project was begun in South Boston, this time under the auspices of the Boston Housing Authority, which had been established by the City of Boston in 1935. Staking out some sixteen acres in the general vicinity of St. Augustine's church, an area bounded by Columbia Road, Old Harbor, East Eighth and Dorchester Streets, and Old Colony Avenue, the BHA started work in 1939 on a low-income complex of three-story brick buildings, 873 units in all, that would become known as the Old Colony Project. To qualify for admission a family must have resided in Boston for at least a year before filing, its income could not exceed six times the rent, and it must have been living under substandard conditions "detrimental to health, safety and morals." South Boston residents were notified that preference would be given to families whose homes had been demolished to make way for the new project.

Although some old-time residents looked at the Old Harbor and the Old Colony projects as rather alien intrusions in the neighborhood, the fact that they were on the outskirts of the district and generally occupied by familiar friends and relatives allowed them to be gradually accepted as part of the community. But the same could not be said of the D Street Project. In 1941 the construction of an even more extensive housing project in the lower end of South Boston—in the general vicinity of SS. Peter and Paul's church, running from Dorchester Avenue across to Broadway, from A Street up to D Street—forced the demolition of entire blocks of old wooden houses in the heart of the lower end and wiped out an entire Catholic parish—the Holy Rosary Parish—including the small church itself. "After the last Mass on Sunday, February 6, 1942," the *South Boston Gazette* reported with an air of sad finality, "there will be no parish of the Church of Our Lady of the Rosary." "And do you know how we moved?" asked Jack Reid, whose family was among those displaced by the incoming D Street project. "With our bathtub in a horse and wagon, and the front door. It was a beautiful front door that we had just bought," he recalled, "and my mother was very proud of it."

The Old Harbor and Old Colony projects in South Boston maintained a remarkable degree of homogeneity as older, white, Irish-Catholic residents practically bequeathed their well-maintained rentals to close friends and relatives with the sympathetic cooperation of local managers. The D Street project, on the other hand—delayed by World War II and finally opened in 1949—deteriorated quickly. For one thing its 676 apartment units in the lower end were isolated economically and socially from the rest of South Boston. During the 1960s especially, with the extensive redevelopment of neighborhoods throughout the city, thousands of displaced residents were dumped into public housing simply because there was no place else for them to go. For the first time in twenty-five years, public housing turned from being low-income housing for working-class families to being permanent homes for the poor, disadvantaged and dispossessed. With the courts imposing stricter limits on the power of project managers to screen out potential troublemakers or to evict those classified as undesirable, many managers and their staffs simply gave up. Supervision and maintenance in projects across the city fell off sharply. Trees and shrubs were uprooted, benches and playground equipment destroyed, door locks broken, windows smashed, hallways unlighted, basements scarred by vandals and walls defaced by spray-paint and graffiti. The population of the projects changed markedly, too. An increasing percentage of the new families were without fathers, and an even larger percentage was on some form of public welfare. Now, more than ever, "the project" was regarded by longtime residents as something completely separate and distinct from the community.

Opposition to the tenants in the D Street Project was not necessarily directed at the seventy-one black families who made their homes there before the busing crisis; indeed, one former resident recalls that the people "seemed more frightened of the Puerto Rican families than the blacks" because of their foreign language and strange customs. The resentment seemed directed at the newcomers more because they were poor, dirty and slovenly. Families from Dorchester, Roxbury and the West End were "riffraff" or "project rats." They were never regarded as "true" residents of South Boston. Natives of South Boston always considered themselves blue collar—indeed, this was a proud part of their rough-and-ready exteriors. But they had always protested vehemently against the tendency of outsiders to categorize them as "poor," "disreputable" or "disadvantaged." Part of their reaction against the newcomers was their instinctive fear that these people would eventually burden the old neighborhood with just such labels. "Public housing in South Boston has been a disaster," one South Boston woman commented, reflecting the generally held views of the older inhabitants. "People who can't afford to live anywhere else wind up there." "They are uneducated. They don't know how to keep a hall clean; they don't know how to cook a meal; they don't know how to plan a budget. They get money from welfare, and they don't know how to manage it. The kids are spending it on cookies and Coca Cola instead of getting a good well-balanced meal." "I'm not down on all welfare people—don't misunderstand me," the woman added hastily. "But this is what you see in those public housing places. It goes down the tubes, and we end up with D Street." Indeed, among South Boston natives, the expression "D Street" became the local term for the worst type of lower-class welfare housing—the kind to be avoided.

In addition to the impact of housing developments, changes in the city's traditional political structure added even further to the breakdown of the neighborhoods after World War II. Roosevelt's New Deal programs had produced a vast network of federal agencies that replaced neighborhood politicians and big-city bosses. In the past the lifeblood of South Boston's political system had been the ability of popular and colorful politicians like "Edso" Carroll, "Billso" Hickey, Martin Touhig, "Sonny" McDonough, Jimmy Condon and Johnny Powers to deliver the greatest amount of services—jobs, favors, housing, medical care, legal assistance—in the shortest amount of time, to as many friends as possible. With the passage of such New Deal legislation as social security, unemployment insurance and workmen's compensation, followed after World War II by the wide-ranging veterans' benefits contained in the G.I. Bill of Rights covering housing loans, professional training and college education, there was much less reason for anyone to go to the local ward boss for help when Uncle Sam could provide bigger and better benefits. And with more federal offices, court houses, post offices, banks and veterans' bureaus appearing on the scene, civil-service appointments provided numerous jobs far beyond the jurisdiction of local politicians.

It was at this point that men like Congressman John W. McCormack and other federal officials became much more influential contacts for favors and positions. Born in 1891 on Vinton Street in the Andrew Square section of South Boston, John McCormack attended the John Andrew Grammar School on Dorchester Street but was forced to drop out of school in the eighth grade when his father died. The breadwinner of the family at thirteen, he sold newspapers and did odd jobs until he got work as an office boy in a downtown law office. Although he never attended law school, he "read for the law" on his own and passed the Massachusetts bar examination in 1913 at the age of twenty-one. After a brief stint in the army during World War I, McCormack was elected as a state representative, and after two years he moved on to the Massachusetts Senate, where he spent four years. Unsuccessful in his bid for Congressman James A. Gallivan's seat in the United States House of Representatives in 1926, the young man got his opportunity with the death of Gallivan two years later. McCormack took the Twelfth Massachusetts Congressional seat in the House—a seat to which he would be reelected twenty times, serving a total of forty-two years. As McCormack grew in power and influence in Washington he became an irresistible magnet for residents of South Boston whenever they needed help. A call to "Gene" Kinnally, McCormack's faithful and industrious secretary, would almost inevitably bring personal assurances from "Uncle John" himself that the problem would be taken care of. While McCormack continued to maintain a warm and highly personal touch in dealing with these requests, it was clear that the new largesse was coming from an expanding federal bureaucracy, not local coffers.

The availability of federal funds on an unprecedented scale made it possible for the new mayor of Boston, John B. Hynes, after defeating James Michael Curley in 1949 and again in 1951, to launch his ambitious multi-million-dollar program of urban renewal. Conveying an air of quiet confidence, administrative ability and personal integrity— in sharp contrast to the image of his roguish and unpredictable predecessor—Hynes pulled together a working coalition of the two most hostile elements of Boston politics. Protestant-Brahmin-Republicans extended to Hynes both the political legitimacy and the financial cooperation they had so long denied Curley. Irish-Catholic-Democratic leaders, in turn, worked with the Yankee establishment on the basis of equality and respect.

Certainly an important but subtle factor in improving the political atmosphere in the city at this time was the emergence in 1945 of Archbishop Richard J. Cushing as the spiritual leader of Boston's Catholic population. The son of a blacksmith from Cork and a housemaid from Waterford, Cushing was born in 1895 at 808 East Third Street, in a South Boston that still based its values on family, friendship and religion. "They were good years," he recalled of those days of his youth at the Benjamin Pope Primary School at the corner of O and East Fifth Streets. "We were ordinary people, poor but comfortable...South Boston folks are still a laboring people, born and brought up in an area which has contributed greatly to America's way of life." Little concerned with elaborate rituals or complex theology, Cushing was more interested in updating the Church and making it more relevant to the everyday needs of "ordinary" people. To dramatize what he regarded as the direct and personal role of the Church, he said Midnight Mass at Christmastime for the inmates of the Walpole State Prison; he administered First Holy Communion and Confirmation to retarded children at Hanover; and he sliced turkey at his annual Thanksgiving Day dinner for elderly people at Blinstrub's Village in South Boston. By the time he was appointed Cardinal in 1958, Cushing was already preaching in Protestant churches, speaking in Jewish synagogues and generally promoting a feeling of fellowship and goodwill among the various ethnic and religious groups in the Greater Boston area.

Taking advantage of this new spirit of brotherhood and cooperation, Mayor Hynes worked with Boston banks and a variety of federal funding agencies during the prosperous years of the Eisenhower administration—those "affluent" years—to begin renewing the face of a badly scarred city. After establishing the Auditorium Commission to undertake the design of a multipurpose auditorium in a part of the city occupied only by abandoned railroad tracks, he created the Government Center Commission to plan an expansive area for municipal offices in the shabby, rundown section of Scollay Square. He also launched a program of slum clearance, starting in Dorchester in 1956, moving into the South End in 1957, and then turning the attention of his Redevelopment Authority to the narrow streets and crowded tenements of the West End. Claiming that the old area was "so clearly substandard" that the only way it could be saved was by "sweeping clearance of buildings," he had the wrecking crews soon at work demolishing houses, bulldozing entire city blocks and displacing residents for whom no adequate provisions had been made. The ruthlessness of the demolition program produced such a wave of horrified reaction that the future of urban renewal became very much in doubt. "The experience of the West End," Walter Muir Whitehill observed, "created a widespread conviction that if urban renewal were necessary in Boston, some less drastic form must be devised."

When Hynes announced he would not run for a third term as mayor of Boston, residents of South Boston were extremely optimistic about the chances of one of their own popular leaders taking over the office, slowing down urban renewal in the downtown area and paying more attention to the everyday needs of the neighborhoods. Senator John E. Powers was a politician whom one writer classified as "South Boston personified." Born in South Boston in 1910, Powers was only eight years old when his father, a streetcar motorman, was killed in an accident. He grew up in an atmosphere of poverty and hard work intensified by the impact of the Great Depression. In 1938 he ran successfully for state representative, and until 1955 he was never defeated for public office.

During his career Powers became a well-known figure in every part of the city. In the neighborhoods people frequently called on him for personal assistance and political advice. In the state legislature he built a reputation as a friend of organized labor and an expert parliamentarian. After moving up steadily in the ranks of the House leadership, in 1946 he was elected to the State Senate. In 1949 he became Democratic floor leader in the Senate, and in 1959 he was elected its president. In 1955 Powers made an unsuccessful attempt to unseat John B. Hynes, attacking the incumbent for being too friendly to the landlords and real estate interests of the city. In 1959 Powers made a second attempt to capture the mayor's office after Hynes announced he would not run again. After a preliminary in September whittled down a field of four to two finalists, Powers and Register of Probate John F. Collins, most observers felt that with his many years of political experience, the support of organized labor and the backing of most local newspapers Powers would win an easy victory in November.

However, several factors operated in Collins's favor. First, there is little doubt that his courageous comeback from a crippling bout with polio, much in the tradition of F.D.R., created sympathy and respect that worked to his political advantage. Second, at a time when television was just becoming an influential factor in American politics (the famous Kennedy-Nixon television debates were less than a year away), Collins conveyed an honest, clean-cut, wholesome image to Boston voters, while Powers came across as a tough, arrogant, old-time politician. Collins and his campaign managers capitalized on this unsavory image, attacking Powers as a "little Napoleon" with close ties to Boston's criminal society. On Friday, October 30, only four days before the election, internal revenue agents raided several "bookie" joints in East Boston, one of which belonged to a former boxer named Salvatore Bartolo. That same evening, on the eleven-o'clock news, John Collins displayed photographs of Bartolo's Ringside Cafe in East Boston with a large "Powers for Mayor" sign over it, as well as pictures of Powers (and several other people) standing alongside Bartolo himself. These pictures were also printed in large front-page ads in newspapers the day before the election with the heading: "Stop Power Politics!" It was a skillful, eleventh-hour maneuver, and it produced results. In perhaps the biggest upset in Boston's political history, Collins defeated Powers for mayor of Boston by twenty-four thousand votes. Although "Johnny" swept Wards 6 and 7 in South Boston by 60 and 70 percent, all the other wards of the city tipped in favor of Collins and left the Powers supporters stunned and bitter. Their best chance of getting a South Boston man into the mayor's office since 1914 had been stolen, they complained, by a "dirty trick."

Once he took office, Mayor John F. Collins did, in fact, try to placate the neighborhoods and ease anxieties about urban renewal by practicing it in a much "less drastic" form. In 1960 he selected the experienced and much-heralded Edward J. Logue to head up the Boston Redevelopment Authority in an attempt to demonstrate that the program would now have professional direction. And his appointment of the highly respected Monsignor Francis J. Lally, former editor of the *Boston Pilot*, as Chairman of the BRA was a move calculated to guarantee residents of the various communities that urban renewal would now take on a more humane and enlightened character. But residents of the neighborhoods were not convinced. Frightened at what had happened to the poor people of the West End, they refused to be taken in by cosmetic changes with little future protection. They were determined to prevent bureaucrats, bankers and out-of-state real estate developers from moving into their neighborhoods, taking over their property and destroying their communities. The expansion of Logan Airport in East Boston, the spread of the Harvard Medical School complex into the Mission Hill area and the impact of the Tufts-New England Medical Center on the Boston Chinatown district were only a few examples of the type of encroachment every neighborhood feared.

Indeed, the BRA actually drafted plans for reversing the structural decline of the aging South Boston neighborhood under the heading of a "General Neighborhood Renewal Plan." Estimating that some 47 percent of the district's housing stock was badly in need of repair or demolition, especially in the lower end, the plan called for 22 percent of the housing stock to be torn down, some new housing constructed, and the remaining dwelling units rehabilitated. The BRA was especially critical of the fourteen public school buildings in South Boston, most of which had been constructed before 1900. It scheduled six of the schools for demolition almost immediately, and most of the others for substantial repairs and improvements. In addition to assistance for commercial enterprises and private home-owners, the BRA also called for a "Special Development District" for industry, with better zoning, safer streets and more effective access roads. The 1965 BHA plan was scheduled to begin in 1969 at an estimated cost of over $30 million, to be completed by 1972. The united resistance of angry South Boston residents, who feared that these ambitious plans would destroy the family character of their community and displace old-time residents as they had seen happen in the West End, stopped the BRA plans cold.

Hardly had the residents dealt with the BRA when they found themselves faced with another scheme—this time from entrepreneurs, urban planners and city officials—calling for the site of a 1976 World's Fair to be located on nearby Columbia Point, with serious ramifications for South Boston. According to elaborate projections, temporary and permanent housing would be created in the neighborhood to accommodate up to twenty-five thousand families; the strandway, the beaches and the waterways would be altered for commercial purposes; and experimental forms of communication, transportation, housing and recreation would be designed to showcase a bicentennial celebration called EXPO 76. Upset over the danger of radical changes in their traditional neighborhood, the South Boston Residents' Group gathered over eight hundred supporters at a May 1969 neighborhood rally at Marine Park to voice their disapproval of the proposal to center a world's fair in South Boston.

One surprise development, which demonstrated to local residents that their fears were real and their protests not at all paranoid, took place in 1971 when the city of Boston's zoning board approved the construction of a seventeen-story apartment complex overlooking Dorchester Bay in the midst of two- and three-family homes at the corner of G Street and Columbia Road—on the former site of Dorgan's Restaurant. Although neighborhood opposition failed to halt the project, the construction of this complex was a visible example of what could happen if residents did not keep up their guard and let "outside interests" come into the peninsula district and transform a peaceful family community into an area of high-rise apartments and expensive condominiums.

Residents also fought at this time against what they saw as the exploitation by outside commercial interests of the district's excellent location at the expense of the lives and safety of the people. For many years the pastors of St. Brigid's Church (formerly St. Eulalia's)—first Father Mortimer Twomey, and then Monsignor Patrick Waters—led the fight to preserve the open parkland in the City Point area from commercialized amusements and industrial development. They postponed for several decades the construction by the White Fuel Company of holding tanks for inflammable fuel oils, and they also obtained minimum air-pollution controls on the Boston Edison's coal-burning electrical plant. These civic-minded priests struggled to oppose the licensing of additional barrooms in the residential area, and Monsignor Waters even took on "Knocko" McCormack, flamboyant brother of the prominent local congressman, who wanted to obtain a special permit for a nightclub within the boundaries of the parish.

Convinced that they could obtain no effective relief or protection from such ventures from the city government, citizens discovered they could accomplish much more by taking matters into their own hands. Determining their own priorities, assessing their own needs, they would defend their own neighborhoods from outsiders. During the 1960s, South Boston offered a good example of grassroots political power, designed to force the officials of the government and the representatives of business to consider the interests of the people whenever they prepared any future plans involving the neighborhoods. Throughout the United States at this time, political and social activism had taken on a new intensity and effectiveness. People in neighborhoods like South Boston had witnessed black people organize for their civil rights. They had seen college students agitate for educational reforms and demonstrate for an end of the war in Vietnam. Night after night on their televisions, they had watched rallies on Boston Common, demonstrations at the State House and public gatherings at City Hall. Now it was their turn to unite, to organize, to demonstrate, to force the changes they wanted for themselves and their neighborhoods. Using many successful techniques from other reform movements, working-class groups formed community organizations to prevent the destruction of their neighborhoods. Longtime residents and new arrivals, housewives and laborers, men and women, amateurs and professionals, some had considerable backgrounds in community organization, but most had no experience at all.

Determined to take matters into their own hands and use their grassroots political power to force a confrontation with government power and private pressure, many communities formed development corporations to rehabilitate rundown houses, redevelop dying business districts, and even bring light industry into their districts. The South Boston Community Development Corporation (SBCDC) was one of many local agencies that rehabilitated and upgraded their districts to head off government renewal plans. The Massachusetts Urban Reinvestment Advisory Group (MURAG) forced many local banks to invest their money in those neighborhoods in which they were located. Longtime residents sought to preserve the distinctiveness of their old neighborhood with the Beacon Hill Civic Association; local businessmen worked to stabilize their local district with the Mattapan Square Board of Trade; and parents fought for meaningful educational reforms through such coalitions as the Boston Home and School Association and the Federation of Children with Special Needs. Through these and similar associations, community-action groups fought against plans to construct the Southeast Corridor through Roxbury, to develop the Mission Hill district, and to further expand Logan Airport. Sometimes they succeeded. More than often they failed. But in any case, they quickly became a force that could no longer be ignored. "Before you even turn over a rock in South Boston," one real estate developer warned, "you'd better check with Melba Hamilton, the head of the local Community Development

Corporation.'' Coalition politics, a new and alternate source of power
in the city, had a decided influence on how people in the neighborhoods
responded to decisions made by political and financial groups outside
their communities.

The changing character of the national economy also had repercus-
sions at the local level. By the late 1960s the costs of the Vietnam war
had begun to skyrocket, and as the total military budget rose from $51.6
billion in 1964 to $82.5 billion in 1969, Congress cut back sharply on
appropriations for a wide range of domestic programs. Federal monies
dried up, construction projects fell off, and unemployment began to
rise at an alarming rate. By the early 1970s national production was
dropping precipitously, and before long runaway inflation sent food,
clothing, fuel, rent and gasoline prices soaring. In 1977 the inflation
rate was up to 6 percent; by 1979 it was over 10 percent; and by 1980
it had passed 12 percent. A national phenomenon, the recession of the
seventies nevertheless worked some of its most distressing effects upon
the New England region, where unemployment rates climbed to levels
not seen since the Great Depression. In Boston, with its large blue-collar
white population and an increasingly militant black population, the
discouraging economic picture had devastating implications for the social
fabric of the community. The already uneasy relationship between low-
income blacks and low-income whites now became even more
precarious. Racial anatagonisms deepened as people fought for a share
of economic benefits that seemed to be getting smaller every day. The
growing economic tension between racial groups in Boston only ex-
acerbated the other major problem that was beginning to overshadow
the city—the issue of school desegregation and mandatory busing.

For a long time, Boston's small black population had been a negligible factor in city politics. Though black people developed an active local
political network at the turn of the century—after they moved out of
the old West End and settled in the South End-Lower Roxbury area—
they were still not able to develop any citywide influence because of
their relatively small numbers and their isolated location. During World
War II, however, skilled and unskilled black laborers came from all
parts of the country into the New England region to work in industrial
plants, army posts, armories and shipyards. Boston's black population
nearly doubled in only a decade, rising from twenty-three thousand in
1940 to over forty thousand in 1950. Since no new construction had
taken place in the Roxbury area since the early 1920s, the district was
very overcrowded. When the general prosperity of the postwar years

stimulated the heavily Jewish population in North Dorchester and upper Roxbury to seek better housing in the suburbs, black families moved
out of their ghettoes and spread throughout the former Jewish district
with amazing rapidity. By 1960 they had moved all the way down Blue
Hill Avenue to Mattapan Square. From then on, they were moving
beyond the confines of their traditional Roxbury boundaries into the
fringes of such traditionally white neighborhoods as Dorchester, Jamaica
Plain, Roslindale and Hyde Park.

It was not long before the growing black presence ran into white
resistance. Intensely proud of the distinctively ethnic characteristics of
their neighborhoods, the Irish in South Boston and Charlestown, the
Italians in East Boston and the North End, and other residents of traditionally white neighborhoods panicked as they thought of blacks taking their jobs, lowering the standards of their schools, bringing down
property values, and adding to the danger of crime in the streets. "Conflict in intergroup situations is most likely to arise precisely when there
is lack of agreement about the desirability of assimilation as a goal,"
sociologist Richard Schermerhorn has written. "If both groups agree—
either to remain separate and different, or to become as one—the occasion for conflict is reduced." But there was no such agreement in Boston.
The flow of black people into white communities violated the established
neighborhood dictum that different races and nationalities remain in their
own separate localities. Admonitions to "know your own place," "stay
with your own people," "go to your own church" and "marry your
own kind," had conditioned generations of young people to regard racial
and ethnic insularity as practically an article of faith. Many white people saw in the apparent breakdown of this neighborhood tradition a
serious threat to the stability of their society and to the very security
of their lives. As the national and state economic situation went from
bad to worse, working-class whites became even more determined to
keep blacks from getting "too much too soon."

But the economic decline also stiffened the resolve of blacks to ac-
quire an improved standard of living before it was too late. The successes of the national civil rights movement of the 1950s and 1960s
promoted among black people a greater pride in their identity and a
growing consciousness of their distinctive heritage. Black citizens no
longer accepted the social and economic injustices that had retarded
their progress for so many generations. Inspired by the ideals of Rev.
Martin Luther King, Jr., and the well-publicized victories in various
Southern states, black citizens were further buoyed by the enactment

of important civil rights legislation by the Johnson administration. The
Civil Rights Act of 1964 ensured equal access to public accommoda-
tion and prohibited discrimination in employment. In 1965 the Voting
Rights Act encouraged black voter registration, and in 1968 the Open
Housing Act banned discrimination in housing. In Boston, as in other
American cities at the time, the black community set out to see that
their members were accorded equal rights in housing, equal opportunities
in jobs and equal access to a good education.

Focusing on what it called "segregation in fact" in the Boston public
school system, the NAACP demanded that the school committee correct that condition. The all-white committee, however, flatly denied
that any child had ever been deprived of the right of attending any Boston
public school because of his or her race, religion or national background.
If there were schools in Boston that were "imbalanced," Chairwoman
Louise Day Hicks explained, it was because black people happened to
live in certain parts of the city while white people lived in other parts.
Parents naturally sent their children to the closest neighborhood school.
Imbalance, she argued, was a housing problem, not an educational prob-
lem. And if outsiders in the suburbs were so interested in helping the
Negro, Mrs. Hicks remarked, then they should start building subsidized
housing for them in their own commmunities.

Mrs. Hicks's remark made it clear that criticism from people living
in the affluent suburbs was a sore point among working-class people
in the inner city or the neighborhoods. When the state legislature passed
the Racial Imbalance Act in August 1965 it said that any school which
was more than 50 percent black was racially imbalanced. This definition put the onus of desegregation on Boston, where over 60 percent
of its black students attended schools that were at least 70 percent black,
and where some 84 percent of its white students attended schools that
were at least 80 percent white. It left virtually untouched the rural and
suburban areas of the Commonwealth with small black populations and
only a handful of black students in their schools. Residents of Boston,
working with a sizeable black population, deeply resented being labeled
as racists and segregationists by outsiders in the suburbs, whose all-
white schools were formally categorized as "racially balanced" and
whose public officials were not required to come up with plans for increasing the number of black students in their localities. This contrast
between the basic needs of hard-working, tax-paying, native Bostonians
and what they regarded as the fanciful theories of liberal, upper-class
suburbanites was what Mrs. Hicks continued to hammer home as she

announced herself a candidate for mayor of Boston in the spring of 1967. Defending the ideal of the neighborhood school, she opposed any plan to transfer students from one school district to another. She also called for the city to turn its attention away from the downtown area and develop programs that would allow people to walk the streets in safety, prevent subways and playgrounds from becoming "jungles of lawlessness," and halt the alarming flight of white Bostonians out of the city.

Working-class families in neighborhoods like South Boston, who saw themselves facing the full impact of desegregation alone, responded to these words. According to sociologist Richard Meister, ethnic groups can function in both positive and negative ways. Positively, they keep cultural traditions alive, offer opportunities for upward mobility and provide a strong sense of personal consciousness. Negatively, however, they also work to reinforce "exclusiveness, suspicion and distrust." The reaction of the Irish in South Boston confirmed these observations. After all, they had to watch their children bused away from their familiar white neighborhoods into predominantly black neighborhoods while their friends and relatives in the suburbs were free from the prospects of such pressures. They saw themselves as the ones whose husbands, fathers, brothers and uncles were denied jobs or promotions on the police department, the fire department and the public works department in the interests of affirmative action, while doctors, lawyers and bankers in the suburbs were far removed from the impact of such social experiments. Residents of South Boston, Charlestown, East Boston and other ethnic neighborhoods constantly complained that everyone they used to count on—political leaders, social workers, educators, lawyers, judges, churchmen—now seemed terribly concerned with the needs of poor black people; but none of them seemed equally concerned with the needs of poor white people. They felt betrayed, ignored and abandoned—at the mercy of outside forces they could not control.

All these problems provided the background for the mayoralty elections of 1967. Louise Day Hicks presented herself as the outspoken champion of local autonomy and neighborhood schools. The daughter of the well-known and highly respected Judge William J. Day, lawyer, banker, real estate investor and justice of the South Boston District Court, she grew up in a fine three-story house on Columbia Road, directly across from the beach. She attended neighborhood schools, married "Johnny" Hicks during the war, clerked part time in her father's downtown law office and generally lived an uneventful life until her father's sudden death in 1950. The loss of such a powerful influence in her life galvanized Louise into a more purposeful phase of work and public service. Although she was now thirty-six years old, married and the mother of two children, she returned to the Boston University Law School, completed her law degree, and in 1956 passed the bar examination. For a time she went into law partnership with her brother, John, but she soon became active in a number of civic organizations and in 1961 ran successfully for a seat on the Boston School Committee.

After a fairly routine first year in office, Louise was elected chairwoman of the committee for what promised to be an equally uneventful second year. On June 11, 1963, however, the NAACP raised its charges of *de facto* segregation in the Boston school system and demanded immediate remedies. At first Mrs. Hicks appeared sympathetic to the charges of black parents, but then she abruptly changed her position, denied that the school committee had any responsibility for segregation and broke off relations with NAACP leaders. Although she was roundly denounced by angry blacks and white liberals, when she ran for a second term in the fall of 1963 she gained such overwhelming support from the white working-class neighborhoods that she was able to get a staggering 74 percent of all votes cast—a record for a Boston municipal election. From that point on, Hicks became the unquestioned spokesperson for what she called "the little people," the white working-class residents of the city, standing up for their rights and defending their neighborhood schools from the social experiments of black "outsiders" and their ivy-league supporters.

The other major candidate to emerge from the September 1967 primaries was Kevin Hagan White. From a long line of active politicians, White soon established himself as a resourceful campaigner in his own right. A graduate of Williams College and the Boston College Law School, he was acceptable to upper-middle-class groups in the city as a capable and articulate administrator. As four-time Secretary of State of the Commonwealth he was viewed by older members of the downtown Yankee community as an appealing "nonpolitical" candidate in the tradition of John B. Hynes and John F. Collins who could be depended on to keep urban renewal rolling. And as a reputed liberal-minded progressive in the flamboyant style of New York's Mayor John Lindsay, White was more than acceptable to Boston's black community as the only viable alternative to Mrs. Hicks. Recent analysts, however, have attributed his liberal image to hyped-up media coverage. Kevin White betrayed "no recognizable ideology through his early years," wrote J. Anthony Lukas, for whom White took on a much more liberal tinge as he brought aboard such out-of-town liberal advisers as Barney Frank, Hale Champion and Colin Diver. George Higgins agrees that White was *"tabula rasa"* when he first ran for mayor. "He was free to invent himself as he proceeded, and to permit the media to shape him as served expedient to the campaign."

Most political observers agreed that it would be a tight race. Despite the opposition of civil rights groups, black associations, the downtown legal establishment and most newspaper reporters who poked fun at her hats, laughed at her hairdos, counted the sequins on her dresses and dismissed her as a "tea party candidate," Mrs. Hicks more than held her own. She rallied her constituents in support of local autonomy and neighborhood schools ("You know where I stand," she repeated) and won considerable admiration for the way she stood up to the outside forces that threatened to change their lives. Even when *Newsweek* lampooned her and her South Boston followers as "characters in a Moon Mullins comic strip," she was able to turn this to her own advantage by a public display of outrage and indignation that generated even more sympathy and support. So strong a candidate was Mrs. Hicks that the *Globe* broke a seventy-one year tradition by coming out with a public endorsement of White. Although her supporters in South Boston's Ward 6 and 7 gave Hicks a whopping 11,335 votes to a meager 4,489 for her opponent, Kevin White was able to pile up enough votes in the other wards to take the election. Out of a total of 192,673 votes cast, White defeated Hicks by a margin of twelve thousand and began his first term of office during one of the most chaotic and disruptive periods in American history.

Mayor White worked long and hard to keep the city under wraps during those critical years by placating as many of the varied and often conflicting constituencies as possible. He maintained good relations with the downtown bankers and businessmen by pushing ahead with plans for commercial development to modernize further the city and improve its financial standing. He also established contacts with representatives of the various communities, insisting on his concern for neighborhood problems. He set up "Little City Halls" to make city government more responsive to the needs of the people, and he provided better lighting and more police protection to help reduce crime and vandalism. All the while he tried to keep things cool in the city's restless black community. He frequently paid visits to the black neighborhoods, maintained communications with local black leaders, supplied more black policemen to counteract charges of police brutality (as well as to give

blacks the feeling they were full members of the community) and supported a mobile program called "Summerthing" to supply music and
entertainment for young people during the long and dangerous summer months.

After a successful four-year term, Kevin White was again opposed
in 1971 by Hicks, who had just taken over the congressional seat vacated
by Speaker John McCormack on his retirement in 1970. Although Wards
6 and 7 in South Boston once again came to the support of their "Louise"
(but by a smaller margin than in 1967), White buried Mrs. Hicks in
the overall election by capturing 62 percent of the total vote. By the
time he embarked on his second term of office in 1972, it seemed to
many observers that Boston had weathered the worst of the storm. The
Vietnam war had begun to wind down, the antiwar protests had begun
to peter out, and racial tensions appeared to be easing up. By the time
the war officially came to an end in 1973, the city showed signs of returning to a more normal and peaceful routine, with little more exciting
on the horizon than deciding the most appropriate way of celebrating
the bicentennial of the nation's independence in 1975. But things were
not that simple; and they certainly were not that quiet, as the issue of
school desegregation finally came to a head.

For nearly eight years the State Board of Education and the Boston
School Committee had engaged in a running fight over implementation
of the state's Racial Imbalance Law. Year after year the state board
called upon school committee members to come up with some kind of
plan to reduce the number of the more than sixty Boston public schools
classified as "unbalanced" because they were more than 50 percent
black. Year after year, however, the school committee held the line,
refusing to admit that *de facto* segregation existed and insisting that a
situation resulting from housing conditions was not the responsibility
of a committee charged with educating children. The school system,
it argued, already had an "open enrollment" policy that permitted any
student to enroll in any Boston public school where a vacant seat was
available, and it agreed to offer a series of compensatory education programs for black students in their own schools. Residents of South Boston
strongly supported Mrs. Hicks as she stood fast against attempts by "outsiders" to change their neighborhood schools and infiltrate their communities. "We have no inferior education in our schools," insisted
school committeeman William O'Connor of South Boston in 1964.
"What we have is an inferior type of student." With the committee
chairwoman, O'Connor introduced a bill into the legislature calling for

the repeal of the state's Racial Imbalance Act. Whenever Mrs. Hicks told her South Boston audiences "You know where I stand," she was invariably rewarded with standing ovations. It was clear that they knew *exactly* where she stood.

In 1971 the state board called upon the school committee to transfer a number of white children from a nearby school to achieve a "balance" at the new Lee Elementary School in Dorchester. At first the committee, by a three-to-two vote, agreed to balance the school—53 percent white and 47 percent black. Under pressure from irate white parents, however, School Committeeman John Craven later changed his vote, and the white children remained in their neighborhood school. An angry state board ordered a freeze on $200 million worth of new construction in Boston and withdrew $14 million in state aid from the city. Black parents in Dorchester, also outraged at what had happened, arranged with the NAACP for a class-action suit against the Boston School Committee under the name of a mother named Tallulah Morgan. Since James Hennigan was school committee chairman at the time, the case subsequently became known as *Morgan v. Hennigan.*

Early in 1972 the Morgan case made its way through the Federal District Court and was eventually assigned by a lottery system to Judge W. Arthur Garrity, Jr. An Irish-Catholic native of Worcester, a graduate of Holy Cross and the Harvard Law School, a campaign worker for John F. Kennedy and a highly respected member of the Massachusetts bar, Garrity at first seemed to have all the ingredients for being an objective and experienced arbitrator in the complicated school case. For two years Judge Garrity listened patiently to arguments and counterarguments brought forward by the various attorneys and then continued to work on the case for fifteen more months. On June 21, 1974, the last day of the school year, the judge finally handed down his decision. The Boston School Committee, he said, had "knowingly carried out a systematic program of segregation" and had "intentionally brought about and maintained a dual system." For these reasons, he concluded, "the entire school system of Boston is unconstitutionally segregated."

After having spent nearly a year and a half studying the case, Judge Garrity now felt it necessary to come up with a plan to desegregate the schools that would go into effect in September—less than three months away. Sight unseen, as he himself admitted, the judge accepted a first-stage plan worked out by the State Board of Education that would involve the busing of seventeen thousand Boston students. In the meantime he intended to work on a second-stage plan that would go into effect the following year. In developing their first-stage plan (Phase I), professional educators from outside the city, with little or no first-hand knowledge of Boston and its neighborhoods, drew a series of arcs across a map of the city in a mechanical fashion, cutting up the various districts in such a way that each school included the right proportion of black and white children. "When we got to to the ends of the arc," they explained, "we were left with South Boston and Roxbury." Disregarding warnings by Professor Louis Jaffe of the Harvard Law School—who said that since the people of South Boston were known to be "intensely hostile" to black people that community should be excluded from the plan and the plan itself should be "restudied"—the educators decided to go ahead and exchange white students from South Boston and black students from Roxbury in their overall plan to reduce from sixty-one to thirty-one the number of unbalanced schools in the city.

State experts claimed that this decision to cross-bus children between South Boston and Roxbury was objective and impartial, designed to carry out the legal decrees of the court. Critics of the plan insisted it was a deliberate and provocative attempt to humiliate the opponents of busing in South Boston. Whatever the case, the results were clear and predictable when the time arrived for the first day of class on September 12, 1974. "To mix Southie and Roxbury," as Alan Lupo put it later, "to bus students from each into the other, was not to ask for war, for the war was inevitable, but it was to insure that the war would be bloody." Early that warm September morning local residents gathered on G Street in front of South Boston High School, angry, nervous, bitter, waiting for the buses to arrive. Among the five hundred or so were students boycotting classes, mothers pushing baby carriages, fathers who had taken time off from work. This particular morning was the emotional climax of nearly a year of mounting tension and almost continuous planning.

Earlier in the year, even before Judge Garrity's decision, antibusing leaders in the community including Mrs. Hicks and State Representative Raymond Flynn helped form "Massachusetts Citizens Against Forced Busing," a group that soon expanded into an organization known as ROAR—"Restore Our Alienated Rights," in an effort to head off busing in September "in an orderly basis in a legislative way." In February 1,400 parents crowded into the Gavin School to discuss boycotts, alternative schools and other contingency plans. Members of the Home and School Association reported that they had organized South Boston into two hundred "block patterns" with a network of people ready to place calls throughout the district. In March, St. Patrick's Day turned into more of a day of protest than a day of celebration. State Senator William Bulger canceled the traditional dinner and good-natured roasting of political leaders at Dorgan's. During the parade many South Boston residents angrily turned their heads when politicians supporting the Racial Imbalance Law came marching by. The following month brought a "big demonstration" on April 3, when an estimated fifteen to twenty thousand adults and children gathered at the State House as the legislature's Joint Sub-Committee on Education heard testimony concerning the repeal of the state's Imbalance Law. Things calmed down considerably in early May while both sides pondered the ambiguous announcement by Governor Francis Sargent that, while he would not repeal the Racial Imbalance Law, he would try to come up with a better plan to improve the whole educational system, leave the responsibility for the welfare of children "in the hands of their parents" and use "voluntary" rather than "mandatory" methods to achieve desegregation.

With the desegregation decision of Judge W. Arthur Garrity on June 21, however, the antibusing agitation exploded into action once again, taking on an even greater intensity as the Phase I plan made busing a certainty for the coming school year. School Committee Chairman John Kerrigan accused Garrity of selling the people of Boston "down the river" and setting the stage for the destruction of the city's public school system. Mrs. Hicks urged that the federal court's decision be appealed to a "higher court," and Flynn argued that the court had violated the principle of separation of powers by invading an area of government that rightfully belonged to the legislative branch. Appearing on local television in late July, Senator Bulger warned that many families were preparing to leave the city because of a sense of "despair and disillusionment," since they were no longer allowed to "control their own lives or make their own decisions." Despite these cries of protest, however, school department officials moved ahead with their preparations for the desegregation process while the organization of protest activities increased as the first day of school drew nearer. On September 7, five days before the opening of school, antibusing groups staged an elaborate motorcade in South Boston at which City Councilor Albert "Dapper" O'Neil confidently assured the parents that their children would not be bused. "They don't want to be bused. Their parents don't want them to be bused," he said. "So they won't be bused!"

Two days later many of these same parents were among the throng of eight thousand gathered at City Hall Plaza to protest Phase I and agitate for a citywide boycott of classes by white students. Senator Edward Kennedy arrived at the rally and attempted to reason with the demonstrators. Assuring them that he sympathized with their objections to busing, he nevertheless repeated his support for busing as an unpleasant but necessary means to achieve racial desegregation. That was too much for the crowd, which obviously expected more from a member of the Kennedy family they so greatly admired. The demonstrators pressed in upon the senator, shoving, jostling, shouting, cursing, until he had to be hurriedly escorted into the safety of the nearby Kennedy Office Building under a hail of tomatoes and rocks. The excitement of that moment may well have been fresh in the minds of many of the bystanders on that first day of school when they heard the sounds of the engines as the first yellow school buses came lumbering up G Street hill. Hoots and catcalls greeted the buses as they slowly rolled to a stop in front of the high school. Then the angry crowd surged forward to pound on the sides of the vehicles with fists and clubs until the police moved in and cordoned off the sidewalk. The black students quickly filed out of the buses and made their way up the steps into the school. Busing had come to South Boston.

Despite the protests of the parents, the planning of its leaders and the assurances of its politicians, the yellow school buses had brought black students into this traditionally all-white neighborhood for the first time in its history. Month after month, year after year, the buses would become a familiar sight, morning and afternoon, rumbling through the streets of the community with their equally familiar police motorcycle escorts riding alongside. Most school authorities had yielded to overwhelming municipal pressures, reluctantly agreeing to accept the inevitability of the desegregation policy and go through the appropriate motions. But the residents of South Boston would not even go that far. They were determined to maintain their opposition at all costs, regardless of the consequences. Words like ''never'' and ''resist'' were scrawled on walls and fences throughout the district in public defiance of the city's political and legal establishment. But *why*? Why were the people of South Boston so ferocious in their resistance to the busing of school children to achieve the goal of desegregation?

Allowances might be made for the anger, outrage, bitterness and fear of overwrought parents who gathered outside South Boston High School those September mornings in 1974. But no one who heard the ugly chants of "Niggah! Niggah! Niggah!" that filled the air or who read the graffiti scrawled on walls and fences proclaiming "Nigger Go Home," "Boneheads Beware," "Niggers Eat Shit" can have any doubt that a basic hatred of black people supplied a powerful dynamic to the busing crisis. Racism spread its cancer throughout the district until there was hardly a family, black or white, untouched by its insidious presence. Violent words and violent actions marked the coming of school busing from the start and quickly divided black neighborhoods from white neighborhoods so completely that citizens of one color could enter another's "turf" only in fear of their lives. Day after day crowds of youths threw bottles, rocks, cans and bricks at the yellow buses as they made their way along Day Boulevard to or from school. Night after night South Boston was the site of almost continous motorcades, rallies, protest marches and public demonstrations. Black residents of the Columbia Point housing project complained that night-riding bands of youths were driving through their project, hurling insults, intimidating families and causing all sorts of damage. And on September 22, shots were fired into the offices of the *Boston Globe* on Morrissey Boulevard, only a short distance away from Columbia Point.

The emotional ferocity over busing soon forced blacks and whites into two camps and made compromise or accommodation a practical impossibility. In South Boston and Roxbury there was no common ground, no forums where substitute programs could be studied rationally, no commnity leaders who were willing to suggest alternate solutions. Moral absolutes became the rule, militant slogans the rhetoric, and both sides saw any deviation as treason. Anyone who took issue with the majority was ostracized, harassed or intimidated. These were days when those who were not "with us" were "against us," and residents vented their rage against the policemen—most of them Irish Catholic and many from the local neighborhood—who were carrying out their orders to enforce the desegregation process. On Friday night, October 4, local patrons scuffled with members of the Tactical Patrol Force (TPF) outside the Rabbit Inn, a popular barroom on Dorchester Street between Eighth and Ninth Street, across from the Old Colony housing project. The following night, October 5, about sixteen members of the TPF burst into the bar, smashed the furniture, wrecked the equipment and beat up customers in the bar as well as people who had gathered outside. Two days later, not far from the Rabbit Inn, a crowd of whites dragged a black man from his car and nearly beat him to death after he had stopped at the traffic lights at the intersection of Dorchester Street and

Old Colony Avenue. Andrew Yvon Jean-Louis was rescued from further injury only when Patrolman Robert Cunningham fired his revolver in the air and pulled the half-conscious man to safety.

And all the while, events at South Boston High School continued to keep the neighborhood in turmoil. Almost without let-up, there were confrontations in the corridors, fistfights in the lunchrooms, clashes in the lavatories and shoving matches in the lockerrooms. One day white students would walk out of classes; the next black students would boycott. White parents charged Headmaster William Reid with showing partiality toward black students; black parents insisted he was favoring whites. On December 11, 1974, shortly before the Christmas holiday, a white student, Michael Faith, was stabbed in a fight with a black. When news of the incident flashed through the neighborhood, it took platoons of mounted police, special detatchments of MDC police and squads of state troopers in full riot gear to clear the streets of angry demonstrators and permit the terrified black students to board their buses for home.

Observers hoped for improvement as Judge Garrity went to work early in 1975 on an improved plan for Phase II. To help him prepare such a plan, he chose two "experts"—Robert Dentler, the dean of Boston University's School of Education, and Marvin Scott, a black associate dean at B.U. The judge also selected four "masters"—Edward J. McCormack, former Massachusetts attorney general; Jacob J. Spiegel, a retired justice of the state's Supreme Judicial Court; Francis Keppel, former United States Commissioner of Education; and Charles V. Willie, a black professor of education at Harvard. Eddie McCormack had much to recommend him. As an able lawyer and a lifetime member of the NAACP, his strong civil rights stance as attorney general had earned him the respect of Boston blacks. On the other hand, as a native of South Boston, a graduate of the local high school and a favorite nephew of Congressman John McCormack, he was in a unique position to exercise considerable influence in the Irish-Catholic neighborhood.

Under the Masters' Plan these people developed, the city would be divided into nine community districts, which J. Anthony Lukas has likened to slices of a pie. White students would be bused into black neighborhoods at the center of each wedge, and black students bused out to the larger white communities along the edge. Under this new plan, students could elect to attend a school within their own district or one of the thirty-two citywide "magnet schools" that offered specialized programs. In either case, parents would be given greater control over their children's schools through elected district councils. The proposal

to eliminate busing between South Boston and Roxbury in favor of bringing in black students from nearby Dorchester made the new plan more
palatable to local residents. Certainly, not everyone liked the plan. Black
leaders, for example, objected to the exclusion of East Boston; white
leaders complained that the plan still involved forced busing. But many
distraught parents saw it as a compromise between the demands of the
black community for racial justice and the insistence of the white community on the principle of parental authority. That McCormack had
thrown his personal influence behind the plan gave it additional credibility
in his hometown neighborhood.

At the last minute, however, Judge Garrity changed signals. Despite
urgent pleas by Eddie McCormack and Judge Spiegel that he stay with
the original plan, Garrity agreed with arguments presented by the State
Department of Education and the NAACP. On May 10, 1975, he formally outlined the plan for the coming school year, retaining a good
portion of the original Masters' Plan but introducing certain critical
changes. First, he substantially increased the number of students to be
bused, raising the figure from 14,900 to 25,000. Second, he imposed
a much more uniform racial ratio across the entire city, without making allowances for special local differences. And third, he again decided to combine South Boston and Roxbury in the same district. After
all his work in building a consensus for the new plan, Eddie McCormack was furious at Garrity's decision. He was certain that the judge's
revisions had "destroyed the plan's mystique, and therefore its efficacy."
And as schools opened on September 10, 1975, McCormack's worst
fears were realized.

Opening day itself was not too bad. With nearly 1,900 city and state
police deployed across the city, mounted policemen patrolling the approaches to South Boston High School, swarms of motorcycle cops racing through the streets, police helicopters circling overhead and six hundred national guardsmen on the alert at the Fargo Building on Summer
Street, there were none of the racial incidents that had marked the opening of the previous school year. But it proved to be merely the calm
before the storm. The following day a series of so-called Mothers'
Marches were begun, first in Charlestown and then in South Boston.
To dramatize their continued opposition to court-ordered busing before
the large numbers of reporters and newscasters waiting regularly for
some new development, the women of the neighborhood, led at times
by Mrs. Hicks herself, marched in procession through the streets of
the district to church, fingering their rosary beads, intoning the Our

Fathers and the Hail Marys and ending with appeals to "deliver us from
forced busing and the TPF."

By the end of the month violence at the high school had once again
risen to dangerous levels, as reports of fights, brawls, protests and
boycotts filled the newspapers. On October 8 almost all the ninety-two
black students who arrived by bus that morning refused to enter the
high school until they were guaranteed increased police protection. A
week later, on October 16, 250 white students walked out of school,
demanding an American flag in every classroom and the daily recitation of the Pledge of Allegiance. On October 23 trouble broke out at
a football game between South Boston and Dorchester at Franklin Park
as fights erupted in the stands and degenerated into a wholesale racial
brawl. After reading through the reports of such incidents, and after
several personal visits to the school, on December 9, 1975, Judge W.
Arthur Garrity placed South Boston High School under direct federal
control. Although he praised the work of Headmaster William Reid under
the most adverse conditions, he relieved him of his post because the
receivership called for a new administration.

These managerial changes, however, did little to relieve the almost
daily litany of fights, brawls and skirmishes that continued to mark the
decade-long course of court-ordered busing.

Some people questioned whether racism, by itself, would have sufficient dynamism and staying power to generate the fierce and unyielding
resistance that would last more than ten years. They also questioned
seriously whether opposition to court-ordered busing should be
automatically equated with racism, a question already raised by Nathan
Glazer and Daniel Moynihan in their study of urban problems. If a group
of women, they asked, insist that they do not want their children bused
to black schools because they fear for their safety; or if they do not
want blacks bused into their neighborhoods because they fear for the
academic quality of their schools, should we denounce this as "racism"
or recognize that these fears "have a base in reality and deal seriously
with the issues?" For most of the residents of South Boston, the basis
of their fears was indeed real—precisely the point raised by leaders of
the antibusing movement almost as soon as the violence began to escalate.
On Monday, September 16, 1974, just four days after the opening of
school during the first year of busing, Senator Bulger, State Representative Michael Flaherty and Mrs. Hicks issued a "Declaration of
Clarification" that took issue with the prevailing attitude that singled
out South Boston as a hotbed of racism and the worst source of irrespon-

sible trouble in the entire city. Flatly denying the truth of this charac-
terization and insisting that the danger lay in the black community, not
the white community, they asked, "Why is there resistance to busing
in Boston? Simply stated, it is because it is against our children's interest to send them to school in crime-infested Roxbury," a neighborhood
they described as ravaged by "routine, everyday violence." No "responsible, clear-thinking person" would send his child there, and no white,
suburban woman would pass through that community alone, "not even
by automobile." White leaders insisted that their opposition to court-
ordered busing was not based on race at all, but upon well-founded fears
for the physical safety of their children in a high-crime area. To label
such a position as "racist," they charged, was an insult to themselves
and their community. The statement commended the residents of South
Boston for the "restraint" they showed during the first days of
desegregation, urged them to remain peaceful "in the face of the tremendous pressure that has been so unjustly placed upon this community,"
and deplored the "vicious impression" that the people of South Boston
were opposed to black people and their "legitimate aspirations."

A month later, responding to a request by Mayor White to bring in
federal marshals, Representative Flynn wrote a letter to Judge Garrity
complaining that Mayor White and Police Commissioner Robert
DiGrazia had deliberately "singled out" South Boston from the rest
of the city and had "targeted" that particular neighborhood for a
"massive show of force" that provoked a "massive reaction" by the
people of that district. "Force will only beget force," Flynn warned.
"The people of South Boston have a proud tradition. They don't like
to be pushed around, by police, or by federal marshals either."

Local leaders deplored the way the media slanted the news reports
about busing and displayed contempt for blue-collar ethnic groups in
white neighborhoods like Charlestown and South Boston. In *Common
Ground*, J. Anthony Lukas suggested that the opposition of the *Globe*
to Mrs. Hicks in her campaigns against Kevin White was based as much
on consideration of class as it was on the paper's passion for social
justice. To a group of liberal publishers thirsting for national status,
this "huge marshmallow of a woman in her tentlike dresses" obviously represented the "frumpy world of the Irish middle class," and they
ridiculed her physical characteristics in ways that an enlightened feminist
would never have tolerated.

Local residents were well aware that the same condescending attitude
reflected in the well-known *Newsweek* article describing them as a

"comic-strip gallery of tipplers and brawlers" was also shared by their own upper-class neighbors in the Greater Boston suburbs. These so-called yuppies, one journalist wrote, looked down on members of the working class for their "parochialism," for their "obsessive fascination with local lore" and for their lack of interest in "the larger world." Alan Lupo reflected on this tone of social superiority when he described a gathering of liberal Democrats at an ADA (Americans for Democratic Action) meeting during which one well-to-do suburbanite complained that the white residents in Boston's neighborhoods were content to live the same way their grandparents did. "They're not in the twentieth century," she snorted as her friends burst into laughter. If such a remark had been made about black people, Lupo speculated, the woman would have been branded as a racist. "But it seems okay to say such things about whites." George V. Higgins agreed. "It is very easy to be quite contemptuous of the more vocal people who still live in South Boston," he wrote in *Style Versus Substance*, "and that careless, supercilious cruelty is accordingly indulged by otherwise mannerly people who would never think of sneering about blacks or ghetto-dwelling Jews."

This scornful attitude characterized the thinking of most desegregationist leaders and had a significant influence on their plans for school integration in South Boston. Journalist William A. Henry III reported on the insulting expressions *Boston Globe* editors normally used to refer to members of the Boston School Committee. Ione Malloy, a teacher at South Boston High School who later published her diary of the desegregation years, was shocked to learn that Judge Garrity's "experts," Robert Dentler and Marvin Scott, had contemptuously described the faculty at South Boston High School as natives of South Boston "whose ignorance and hostility matched that of the street-corner toughs." And from the bench, even Judge Garrity himself lashed out at what he called "the frenetic, hate-mongering fringe in South Boston." Speaking in the pouring rain before a group of antibusing parents the following March, after they had gone to Washington, D.C., to present their grievances before their congressional representatives, Senator William Bulger angrily denounced the "public contempt and ridicule" to which the people of South Boston had been deliberately subjected, and he condemned the "unremitting, calculated, unconscionable portrayal of each of us, in local and national press, radio and television, as unreconstructed racists." Bulger again rejected the idea that racism was the main force behind the organized opposition to court-enforced busing in South Boston and continued to emphasize parental concern for the welfare of their children. For citizens to "cherish, to foster, to assert the natural rights of parents to safeguard the education of children in their traditional local schools," he insisted, "does not mean...that we bear any ill will to black children or children of other racial strains."

Although the busing crisis brought fear and anger to South Boston, however, it probably did more to unify that community and solidify its sense of purpose than anything else in recent years. Episodes of this kind, sociologist Peter Rose observed, encourage groups to assume a position of what he calls "defensive pluralism," in which such groups reassert their old ties, stress the difficulties of their early beginnings and demand their own forms of affirmative action. This was certainly the case with South Boston. During the fifties and sixties, in the wake of the social and economic changes that took place after World War II, many observers suspected that South Boston, along with Boston's other ethnic neighborhoods, would gradually lose its traditional character and become just another political subdivision in the bureaucratic network. In a perverse way, however, the busing crisis reversed that trend and produced a definite revival of ethnic pride and neighborhood consciousness. Residents countered cries of "black power" with cries of "green power," complete with shamrocks, green tam o'shanters, Irish-knit sweaters, T-shirts, signs and bumperstickers proclaiming that God had made the Irish "number one." While young black students were being encouraged to rediscover their historic roots and their African antecendents, boys and girls of Irish extraction were being urged to study the origins of their own race in Ireland. Faced by what they saw as a serious danger from an outside enemy to their traditional way of life, residents banded together in a conscious effort to revive the spirit of "old" South Boston.

Perhaps the most dramatic example of the way in which the two opposing groups could look at the same event and come up with two completely different conclusions occurred during the summer of 1975, at a stretch of seashore near the Columbia Point housing project known as Carson Beach. On July 27, six black men, identified as Bible salesmen from South Carolina, drove over to South Boston from Roxbury to escape the oppressive heat and cool themselves in the ocean. According to their own account they suddenly found themselves surrounded by hostile whites, who beat them up, sending one man to the hospital, and put the rest of them to flight. The black community saw this as a blatant example of how peaceful and law-abiding black citizens were not allowed

to travel into white areas of the city except in fear of their lives. Blacks
viewed the Carson Beach incident as symptomatic of a persistent racial
hatred that not only caused the segregation of Boston's schools, but also
its parks, its beaches, its streets and its neighborhoods.

The white version was of the incident, on the other hand, was quite
different. Local white residents of South Boston scoffed at the idea that
the two black men were innocent Bible salesmen who "just happened"
to come to Carson Beach. They maintained that the blacks came into
the district looking for trouble and attacked a white youth with a baseball
bat. People from South Boston didn't go into such black recreational
areas as Franklin Park or Houghton's Pond in a provocative manner,
the editor of the *South Boston Tribune* wrote, "We are not looking for
trouble. We are against forced busing." Jim Kelly of the South Boston
Information Center also emphasized the provocative nature of the incident. "We've always welcomed good colored people to South Boston,"
he said, "but we will not tolerate radical blacks or communists." "Good
colored people," he repeated, "are welcome in South Boston; black
militants are not." The fairly common local distinction between so-called
"good colored people" and what were now characterized as "radical
black militants" was put forward to defend the proposition that opposition
to forced busing was not consistent with charges of racism.

The incident at Carson Beach galvanized black leaders, who held news
conferences to deplore this latest evidence of racial violence. The
NAACP blamed Mayor Kevin White for failing to provide adequate
safeguards for minorities in the city, and a commission of inquiry was
set up to document racial harassment in Boston. Black leaders planned
to hold a community picnic or a "wade-in" at Carson Beach to make
the site a test case for the right of every citizen to use public facilities.
On Sunday, August 10, 1,500 black picnickers assembled at Franklin
Park and formed a three-hundred-car motorcade that made its way to
Carson Beach early in the afternoon. A police helicopter circled
overhead, two Coast Guard launches patrolled the water, and over eight
hundred uniformed policemen took up positions along the beach to
separate the black demonstrators from the groups of white hecklers who
gathered nearby. The number of hecklers would probably have been
much larger had not local antibusing leaders taken steps to defuse what
promised to be an explosive situation. Most South Boston people believed
that the "wade-in" was deliberately designed to force a confrontation
and produce a riot. "People do not land on a beach armed with bats,
canes, sticks and rocks if their purpose is to simply spend a day swim-

ming and picnicking,'' Nancy Yotts wrote in the *South Boston Tribune*. Louise Day Hicks angrily charged that the demonstration was a ''deliberate, planned, vicious provocation'' and accused NAACP president Thomas Atkins of yelling fire in a crowded theater. To prevent things from getting out of hand, two hundred neighborhood marshals, organized by Michael Flaherty and Jim Kelly, moved into the beach area to control the violence. At the same time, Ray Flynn organized a ''Southie Pride'' Day at Marine Park, near Farragut Circle, more than a mile away from Carson Beach. Offering a concert and picnic, this event was calculated to keep local residents away from the scene of the confrontation where violence had already erupted.

According to most accounts the first acts of violence were touched off by a group of ultraleftists—members of the Progressive Labor Party, the Committee Against Racism and a small number of the Maoist October League— who had arrived on the scene with rocks and baseball bats ready to fight. Scuffles between the leftists and the white South Boston youths quickly expanded into general violence as rocks, cans and bottles went flying through the air from all sides. Before long Carson Beach was the scene of a wild melee, with whites, blacks, leftists, marshals and police striking out at each other with rocks, fists, baseball bats and billy clubs. Although leftists called upon blacks to ''stay and fight,'' Tom Atkins wisely moved his group of black demonstrators away from the beach area as the police steadily forced the opposing groups apart and restored some semblance of order.

As the months went by the ugly incidents continued. The tensions carried over from one school season to the next, with the warm summer days only serving as a brief intermission between crises. It was a struggle in which neither side would ever yield, but which neither side would really win. Although it seemed destined to go on forever, the more violent aspects began to diminish slightly with every year. For one thing, many white families decided to abandon their old homes in the frightening battleground of South Boston in favor of the quieter surroundings of the suburbs. Although this so-called ''white flight'' out of the city had started at least ten years before the school desegregation controversy, as George Higgins has demonstrated in his study of Boston politics, the policy of school integration certainly did nothing to reverse the trend. Second, a number of families found subtle but effective methods of seeing that their children were safely enrolled in nearby parochial schools. Despite Cardinal Medeiros's solemn assurances that no new students would be taken in if their acceptance would impede school integration, several Catholic high schools in the Greater Boston area took on new life with increased enrollments, either from new families that had just moved into the area, or from nieces and nephews whose parents still lived in South Boston but who registered from the addresses of aunts and uncles in the suburbs. And third, some residents took their children out of the public school system and sent them to South Boston Heights Academy, which had been set up on East Third Street in the old Choate Burnham School. The enrollment in this alternative community school when it first opened its doors in 1975 was 576 students. Although the total number of South Boston students being siphoned off each year into private, parochial and suburban schools was not necessarily overwhelming, it was enough to serve as a safety valve that kept an already explosive situation from erupting into even greater violence. The decrease in local students attending South Boston High School was accompanied by a simultaneous decline in the intensity of the antibusing leadership. Some community leaders got sick and died; some grew old and tired. Some moved away from the old neighborhoods; some went off to fight other battles in new neighborhoods. Some went on to better political jobs; some just gave up altogether and decided to do something more enjoyable with the rest of their lives before it was too late. The behind-the-scenes arrangement Kevin White had quietly worked out with Louise Day Hicks at the start of the busing crisis helped keep the more violent and irresponsible elements of the district under control. The mayor had found places in his various administrations for friends, relatives and political supporters of his former South Boston rival. Mrs. Hicks, in return, did her best to counsel peaceful resistance to court-ordered busing and deflect the more extreme responses among her consituents. In 1980, after she had retired from the city council, Mrs. Hicks was appointed to the Boston Retirement Board; and in 1982 Mayor White assigned her a part-time position in the Public Facilities Department. The lessening of tensions could be seen in small and familiar ways. The number of policemen on duty around the schools grew smaller; the number of racial incidents reported in the *Globe* became fewer; the slogans defiantly proclaiming "never" and "resist" grew fainter as the white paint began to spot and peel on the brick walls and the wooden fences.

And yet it was never really over. Much of the joy, the spontaneity, the familiar happy-go-lucky spirit that had characterized South Boston in the past had now greatly diminished. The pall that lay over the community was reflected in the heavy metal grills now covering the store fronts, the furtive movements along the streets, the sullen looks and sidelong glances that caused many visitors to remark upon how much the siege mentality of the neighborhood reminded them of Belfast. You could sense it—you could almost smell it in the air. After reading about the latest troubles in the newspapers or watching the nightly news on television, former residents would call up their friends and relatives in South Boston and ask anxiously, "Is it safe to come over?" In spite of the years, the sounds of "never" and "resist" still rang in people's ears in much the same way they echo in the minds and hearts of the Catholics of Ulster.

While the crisis over court-enforced busing proved to be a relatively brief episode in South Boston's three hundred-year-old history, it was an unusually bitter and violent one, and marked the community indelibly in the minds of people throughout the nation as a depressed and depraved area where beer-bellied men and foul-mouthed women made war on defenseless children simply because they were black. It was a terrible stereotype, reinforced in all the national media, from which it was difficult if not impossible for the community ever to recover.

Little consideration and even less understanding had been given to the plight of ethnic neighborhoods like South Boston, whose residents found themselves caught in a struggle for survival in which they were deserted by their friends, relatives, clergy and political representatives. Above all it was a struggle in which they saw themselves confronted by a bureaucracy of outside educational specialists, sociological experts and legal authorities who knew nothing about their unique historical background, their distinctive social customs or their religious ideals—and who cared less.

This cold and bureaucratic attitude in great part forced many South Boston people to regard the program of school desegregation and forced busing as only the latest of a long series of schemes designed to transform their beloved neighborhood, even to obliterate it—just as they had seen the old Rosary Parish demolished to make way for the D Street Project. Year after year they had beaten back attempts by planning experts and real estate speculators to update their neighborhood and commercialize its natural resources. They had refused to accept the renewal plans of the BRA, and they had rejected schemes to turn the beaches of the peninsula into amusement parks for a world's fair. They stood against the idea that outsiders had the right to tell them how to build their houses or how to manage their property, and they saw no reason why they should tell them how to run their schools. It was certainly true that most people in South Boston didn't like black people, didn't know them, didn't understand them and weren't comfortable with them. But it is extremely unlikely that the mere introduction of a relatively small number of black children into their schools, by itself, would have sparked the kind of resistance that lasted for nearly a decade. Rather, it was the absolute conviction of local residents that school desegregation was only one small part of an elaborate program—a "conspiracy"—formulated by out-of-town liberals, irresponsible black militants and radical social engineers to redesign social boundaries, introduce new moral values and create a new modern and sophisticated society on the ashes of the old-fashioned and outmoded ethnic neighborhood. School desgregation, as the residents of South Boston saw it, was only the camel's nose coming under the tent. Unless they wanted the huge and ugly beast coming in and taking over their entire neighborhood, it had to be stopped right there.

And so, alone, their backs against the wall, surrounded on all sides by people who called them names and demeaned their motives, the people of South Boston fought back with every resource at their command. They loved their community; they loved it the way it was and had always been. They refused to have it changed by outsiders who looked upon their morals as medieval and who regarded their lifestyles as barbaric. They might well go down—but they would go down fighting! *That* was the South Boston way.

8

LOOKING AHEAD

T HE ELECTION OF RAYMOND L. FLYNN AS MAYOR OF BOSTON IN
November 1983 was both a real and a symbolic turning point
for South Boston after a decade of anger, bitterness and insecurity.
Tensions were by no means over: the school buses continued to roll,
and racial animosity still afflicted both white and black communities.
South Boston continued to be perhaps the most reluctant of all the Boston
neighborhoods to let down its guard and modify its defensive attitudes—
memories are long among the Irish—but even here the worst appeared
to be over, as a more tolerant racial climate appeared in the city.

The mayoral campaign itself reflected substantial changes. For the
first time in the history of Boston a black candidate, Mel King, a former
state representative from the South End, emerged from the primaries
to run against Flynn. Despite the violence of the previous ten years,
the 1983 election was conducted with a surprising degree of civility
and a high level of tolerance. Both King and Flynn took similar positions on the major issues of the campaign—espousing neighborhood interests, proposing liberal housing programs and urging increased
economic assistance for the poor and the disadvantaged. Flynn differed
from King in insisting that Boston's problems were a result of class,
not race. Flynn insisted that *all* people in the city's neighborhoods were
victims of Mayor Kevin White's preoccupation with downtown development, and that *all* poor children—black and white—were being denied
a satisfactory education in their respective neighborhoods.

Although King captured an overwhelming number of the city's black
votes, he got only 20 percent of the white votes. Flynn won an easy

victory by sweeping the predominantly white neighborhoods and taking 60 percent of the total vote. In his victory statement Flynn underlined
the basic theme of the election, promising to generate progress in the
neighborhoods by obtaining for them a share in the economic revitaliza-
tion that was still going on in the downtown area. It was time to tip
the scales in the other direction, he said, by creating a "linkage" between downtown prosperity and neighborhood needs.

On January 2, 1984, voters saw the first person from South Boston
sworn in as the forty-sixth mayor of Boston. To accommodate over four
thousand friends, neighbors and campaign workers, Ray Flynn held the
largest inauguration ceremony in the city's history at the Wang Center
for the Performing Arts. The ceremony reflected his image as a "people's mayor" and his position as a representative of the poor people
in the neighborhoods, in keeping with the well-known populist tradition of James Michael Curley. In his inaugural address Flynn emphasized
his determination to create racial harmony within the city and bring
to an end the hatred and bitterness of the past ten years. "The full weight
of city government will be brought down," he declared, "on all those
who seek, because of race or color, to deny anyone from any street,
any school, any park, any home, any job, in any neighborhood in the
city."

Later that same day, after dashing off to a fire at the New Westin
Hotel in Copley Place, Flynn attended a performance at the D Street
housing project. Speaking briefly to the audience, which included about
a hundred people bused in from public housing projects in Dorchester,
Charlestown and the South End, Flynn reassured them that he would
not forget his neighborhood roots now that he was mayor. "The name
is still Ray," he joked, "and I'm going to come to D Street to play
basketball." The next morning the new mayor showed up at South
Boston High School, from which he had graduated in 1958, to shoot
some baskets in the gymnasium and show his support for the school
by indicating his decision that the school would not be closed down
as many critics proposed. Such forthright statements and frank gestures
eased tensions throughout the city by assuring white communities of
his personal support and sympathies, while at the same time giving to
black communities his official guarantee to protect their political rights
and civil liberties.

And it seemed to work. According to a research poll conducted early in 1987 by the Kennedy School of Government at Harvard, 41 percent of the respondents agreed that race relations in Boston as a whole

had improved in recent years—despite the fact that most of the people contacted lived in neighborhoods in which one race predominated, and half continued to oppose court-ordered busing to achieve racial integration in public schools. Though over 85 percent of the residents polled in South Boston still opposed busing, they were the most optimistic about the way things were going. Some 64 percent of them expressed the belief that race relations had improved over the past five years, although a majority said that black people would not feel comfortable walking through their neighborhood.

The Harvard poll was borne out by the city's Community Disorders Unit, which reported that the number of civil rights investigations in 1987 showed a definite decline since the early days of the busing crisis. "We had 607 ugly racial incidents back in 1978," Police Commissioner Francis M. Roache recalled. "We had firebombings, we had people wearing the ugly robes of the KKK harassing, intimidating people. Those patterns are no longer there." From 607, the incidents steadily went down to 300 in 1980, 200 in 1985 and 157 in 1987. "This is not to suggest that we have reached the pinnacle of race relations in the city of Boston," Mayor Flynn said, "but that we're working very hard at it, and that we take this responsibility very seriously."

The school situation, too, had quieted down, but not with the fortuitous results anticipated by Judge W. Arthur Garrity, Jr., and his educational advisors. On September 3, 1985, on the day Dr. Laval Wilson assumed office as Superintendent of Schools, Judge Garrity closed the file on thirteen years of hearings, consultations and orders dealing with the Boston desegregation case. He turned control of the schools back to the city's school committee, while retaining stand-by jurisdiction over student assignments, faculty integration, the condition of school buildings and parental involvement. While the busing crisis might be considered officially over, however, there were serious questions as to whether or not the effort had achieved its social objectives. "The dream of integration is gone," newspaper columnist Ian Menzies commented, "burned on the crucible of one of Boston's greatest traumas, school busing." Statistics confirmed that somber conclusion. Out of 59,896 students officially recorded in the Boston school system, there were 28,551 black, 15,842 white, 10,760 Hispanic and 4,742 Asian. The number of white students dropped from 45,000 in 1974 to 15,842 in 1987, a loss of nearly thirty thousand in little more than ten years, and the system had become almost 50 percent black, 25 percent white, 16 percent Hispanic and 8 percent Asian.

Although South Boston High School still retained the highest percentage (30 percent) of white students of all neighborhood schools in the Boston system, it also reflected the changing character of the city's population. As of January 1986, the official enrollment at South Boston High School was 952 students—a number that included 189 bilingual students, 168 special-needs students, and 189 students in a special Occupational Resource Center program. The racial mix was 361 blacks (42 percent), 295 whites (30 percent), 170 Hispanics (15 percent) and a growing Asian population that included a significant number of students from Cambodia. A reflection of this diverse makeup could be seen in the school newspaper *The Galaxy/La Galaxia*, which included articles in English, Spanish and Khmer, the language of Cambodia.

South Boston residents also felt more secure knowing that their own neighborhood now had a significant number of well-known native sons in positions of power and influence in municipal government. After years of feeling neglected and abandoned, manipulated by political leaders from other parts of the city, the prospect of having someone from South Boston in a position to influence government policies did a great deal to improve the spirit of the community. Having Ray Flynn as mayor was an obvious point of pride throughout the district. The son of immigrant parents, Flynn had grown up in South Boston and had a life that reflected practically all the major characteristics of the district itself. A longshoreman disabled with tuberculosis, his father "left the house each morning on cold winter days...not knowing whether he could find work," while his mother worked long hard hours as a cleaning lady in downtown office buildings "from eleven at night until seven in the morning." A devoted Catholic, Flynn spent his youth in a typical working-class household filled with the songs and stories of Ireland, the radio tuned either to "The Irish Hour" or the nightly recitation of the Rosary. More than anything else, the new mayor recalled movingly in his inaugural address, his parents had taught him the importance of dignity and respect for others, "no matter what the cut of the coat or the color of the skin."

After graduating from South Boston High, Flynn went on to Providence College on a basketball scholarship. He later married childhood sweetheart Catherine Coyne, who lived only a block away and whose father worked with Ray's father as a longshoreman. For a number of years Flynn spent his days and nights traveling the city as a state representative and city councilor, working with neighborhood groups on a variety of local projects. One of the earliest political spokesmen to oppose publicly the school desegregation program, Flynn took the position that it was an unconstitutional form of judicial activism that had usurped the powers of the legislative branch of government. Despite his vehement opposition to court-enforced busing, however, Flynn was equally adamant in his opposition to violence. On numerous occasions he was present preventing disorder in the streets of South Boston, counselling restraint or offering nonviolent alternatives to more dangerous responses. He personally rescued a black couple chased by whites on Boston Common in 1979 and was the only white politician to attend the funeral of Levi Hart, a black fourteen-year-old killed by a white policeman in 1980. By the end of the decade he had become recognized as a strongly committed political leader with the capacity to see both sides of a troublesome situation—clearly a factor in his strong showing at the 1983 election.

To assist him in administering the affairs of the city Mayor Flynn turned to two South Boston friends whose family origins, religious views and social backgrounds were amazingly similar to his own. To head the department that would improve the level of law enforcement in the city and ensure the kind of racial justice he promised in his inaugural address, Mayor Flynn chose a lifelong friend, Francis Michael Roache—better known as "Mickey"—as police commissioner. The two men had grown up together in South Boston, the sons of longshoremen—"Stevie" Flynn and "Bubba" Roache—who used to work together unloading ships. The future mayor and police commissioner played sandlot baseball together at M Street Park and shot baskets at the South Boston Boys Club and at the Municipal Gymnasium—the "Munie" on East Broadway. Both men graduated from South Boston High School and married South Boston women. Roache courted his next-door neighbor on C Street, Barbara Campers, and after their marriage at SS. Peter and Paul Church moved to K Street, where they began raising their family. Meanwhile, Mickey passed the police examination and joined the force as a patrolman, while taking courses at Boston State College to earn his bachelor's degree and later a master's degree in public management. He worked his way steadily up the ladder in the police department to attain the rank of sergeant, became an administrative assistant to the commissioner and then agreed to head up the new Community Disorders Unit designed to investigate racially motivated crimes and violations of civil rights. Flynn saw Roache as the most qualified person to take over the job as Boston's director of law enforcement at this point in the city's history.

Flynn selected another lifelong resident of South Boston, Leo Stapleton, for the post of fire commissioner. Stapleton came from a strong family tradition in the Boston Fire Department. His father, John V. Stapleton, had been a firefighter for twenty-five years before becoming fire chief from 1950 to 1956, and both of Leo's sons served on line companies. After serving in the navy in World War II, Stapleton returned home, married a local South Boston girl named Doris White, lived in a two-decker on East Fifth Street, and in October 1951 successfully passed the examination to become a firefighter. He spent his entire career as an active firefighter, and during that time distinguished himself as a nationally known expert in respiratory safety. In Leo Stapleton Flynn could be confident in having a well-trained and highly respected professional who had come up from the ranks and acquired a national reputation as a leading authority in firefighting techniques.

Contributing to an even greater sense of political security among residents of South Boston was the fact that another prominent South Boston political leader, William M. Bulger, had risen to the powerful and prestigious post of President of the Massachusetts Senate. Born in South Boston in 1934, Bulger attended Boston College High School, received his undergraduate degree at Boston College and graduated from the Boston College Law School. After serving in the Massachusetts House of Representatives from 1961 to 1970, Bulger moved on to the senate, where he eventually became the eighty-fourth President of that body in 1979. During his time on Beacon Hill he advanced a variety of social and environmental issues, including parole reform and child protection laws, and was instrumental in the creation of the Boston Housing Court. With his acerbic wit, his endless list of anecdotes and his incomparable parodies of James Michael Curley, Bulger presided for many years at the annual St. Patrick's Day luncheon, at which political figures of all parties and from all parts of the Commonwealth were mercilessly roasted. Continuing to make his home on East Third Street with his wife and family of nine children, Bulger was a prominent opponent of court-enforced busing and an eloquent defender of neighborhood schools and the constitutional rights of parents to determine the education of their own children. With Joseph Moakley in the United States House of Representatives, Michael Flaherty as a representative in the state legislature and James Kelly on the city council, the political influence of the district seemed even further solidified. To have such an impressive array of local political talent at both the state and municipal levels was extremely reassuring to most residents of South Boston and did much to relax the defensive attitudes of the previous ten years.

And finally, there was a more positive, up-beat spirit in South Boston itself regarding its social and economic future as a neighborhood. Classified only ten years earlier as a depressed, shabby, run-down district, red-lined by downtown bankers who refused to give mortgages because they had categorized the area as "blighted," South Boston now began to take on new life. Streets were cleaned, houses were painted and sided, trees were planted along principal thoroughfares, flowers were arranged in public places, and the beaches were tended with much more care. In October 1970 Castle Island and Fort Independence were placed on the Register of National Historic Places, prompting a group of interested local residents to form the Castle Island Association to work with the Metropolitan District Commission in upgrading the ancient fort, maintaining the grounds and preserving the history of the island. With its fresh air, salt water, beautiful beaches and long walkways, with its proximity to the downtown area and its access to major highways, South Boston quickly became a major attraction for private individuals looking for homes, apartments and rental properties. Along with other urban communities, South Boston shared in the real estate boom that had been generated by a prosperous Northeast economy, and by the process of gentrification that brought well-paid young professional people out of the suburbs into the old ethnic neighborhoods of the city. South Boston had virtually no vacancies. Housing in the district was so tight that rooms, apartments and houses were turning over "in days, if not in hours." Although the majority of the 14,000-odd houses were made of wood, and most were fifty years old or more, residents had taken full advantage of low-cost federal and city fix-up loans to improve them and make them more desirable. By the mid-1980s real estate prices had skyrocketed to astronomical heights. "Ten years ago, you could have bought a triple-decker for $30,000," said Joe Uhlman, manager of Century 21-Old Harbor Realty on Broadway. "Now, try $300,000 for the same building." "A warehouse or factory that would have sold for a million dollars three years ago is now going for three million. And storefront rents that were three hundred dollars a month three or four years ago, are now eight hundred or nine hundred—sometimes a thousand dollars," Uhlman said.

Developers, planners and entrepreneurs also saw South Boston as a potential site for much more ambitious and expansive projects. With real estate property in the overcrowded downtown area at an absolute premium by the 1980s, Bostonians looked for available open space in localities close to the central city. South Boston was a natural and obvious attraction to public planners and private developers—especially those underdeveloped sections off Summer Street just across the Fort Point Channel. Plans were already under way for developing thirty acres along the waterfront where Pier 4, the new World Trade Center and the Boston Fish Pier would be able to accommodate an ambitious complex of hotels, restaurants, shops, offices, and expensive apartment houses—a project collectively known as the Fan Piers. On the opposite side of Summer Street, between East First Street and Bolton Street, was another sizable tract of useable property. Formerly occupied by stretches of abandoned railroad yards and obsolete maritime activities, it presented developers with space for the construction of office buildings, small factories, light industries and blocks of residential housing. Although plans for the central Fan Pier project itself were sidetracked early in 1988 after a rift between restaurateur Anthony Athanas and the prospective development associates, most observers expected most other projects to move ahead on schedule. Expansion of the underdeveloped Fort Point Channel district, where South Boston meets the downtown area, seemed a foregone conclusion; the World Trade Center promised to proceed with its plans to develop a nearby five-acre site owned by the Massachusetts Port Authority; and the Pappas Management Company prepared to construct an office complex and a 440-car garage along Summer Street.

Government spokesmen argued that these multimillion-dollar commercial projects had much to offer for the future economic prosperity of South Boston, but residents saw them as mixed blessings. Community representatives were divided in their opinions of the projects and the direction in which they should move. Some, like Daniel Yotts, director of the South Boston Community Development Committee, argued that large units of low and middle-income housing would do more to enhance the residential character of the community than industry. Warehouses, factories and processing plants, with increased parking problems and truck traffic, would become part of what he called a "domino theory" for many small businesses in the local district—particularly on West Broadway. "What you have on lower Broadway," he said, "is a very poor section of town that doesn't have a voting coalition." "The upper part of town controls the vote," he complained, and as a result "no elected official cares about lower Broadway." Others, however, including District Councillor James M. Kelly, disagreed with Yotts, insisting that the city would do all in its power to "accommodate" South Boston during development and gentrification. Although some changes were bound to have "negative" aspects, Kelly conceded, he generally favored using open spaces for industrial development rather than for housing programs which would only bring in more "outsiders" and more upper-class "dinks" (double-income, no kids), who would change the basic character of the South Boston population and, with their ability to pay higher rents and meet rising housing costs, drive out older, low-income residents. Admitting that newer and younger businesses might well swallow up older and less affluent establishments along lower Broadway, such changes would be "nothing we can't handle," Kelly insisted. In the long run such new developments could well encourage South Boston residents, who had been going into downtown Boston to do their shopping or driving out to suburban malls, to return to their own neighborhood and patronize local businesses. Still other local representatives, like Thomas Butler, head of the South Boston Residents Group, placed greater emphasis on the construction of light industries, which would fit in with the essentially blue-collar, working-class character of the district and provide welcome jobs for local residents.

In spite of these different opinions, all leaders agreed that these projects were bound to make daily life more uncomfortable for the people who actually lived in South Boston. They emphasized the need for more highway repairs, improved sewerage, better street lighting, increased public transportation services and the reconstruction of bridges and overpasses leading into the peninsula district. But their major concern was traffic. Most residents feared that the multi-million-dollar developments being projected for the lower Summer Street area would inevitably increase the volume of traffic in South Boston. According to the Fan Pier's environmental-impact report, Fan Pier alone will generate an estimated 18,500 to 24,100 vehicle trips per day—many passing through South Boston. Brian Cloherty, head of the South Boston Residents Group's traffic committee, complained that too many commuters were already using South Boston as a highspeed shortcut. Drivers from the South Shore, he pointed out, came off the crowded Southeast Expressway, traveled along Day Boulevard and turned up L Street onto Summer Street to reach the South Station area and their intown jobs. More and more large trucks were also exiting the expressway and cutting through the residential streets of South Boston, to reach their destinations in South Boston itself or get back onto the expressway off the Northern Avenue Bridge. In either case, local residents were so angry about big trucks speeding through their streets with uncovered loads, transporting hazardous materials, carrying overweight loads and loads that were too long,

that they threatened to take matters into their own hands. Complaining
that neither the regular police nor the Registry authorities were giving
them enough support, residents suggested acts of civil disobedience that
would have people "stalling" their vehicles along the much-traveled
L Street, while mothers wheeled baby carriages slowly back and forth
across the same thoroughfare. State and municipal authorities expressed
sympathy with the traffic problem and promised to take steps to remedy
the situation—such as opening up a stretch of Dorchester Avenue near
the South Postal Annex by the Fort Point Channel and establishing a
special by-pass road near D Street to keep trucks out of the residential
streets during the construction period. Residents, however, were not
convinced that adequate supervision would be maintained.

Even more fundamental than traffic jams, crowded highways and
speeding trucks was the question of the long-range impact these proposed structural changes would have upon the traditional character of
the South Boston community itself. A whole new group of people was
moving into the district with little or nothing in common with its historical
social patterns and cultural traditions as a working-class, Irish-Catholic
neighborhood. "People who gentrify don't have the commitment that
people who have been here for generations have," said John Alekna,
grandson of the founder of the Flood Square Hardware on East Broadway. Subsequent studies bear out his point of view. "The next wave
of buyers will have no previous link to South Boston," a real-estate
market study carried out for the Farragut Cooperative Bank reported,
"and [they] will look at properties from a practical and economic view-
point." As real-estate prices continued to reflect the growing demand
for South Boston property, older, working-class residents with smaller
incomes were bound to move out in favor of younger professionals who
could afford the costs of luxury townhouses and expensive condominiums. "Condominium conversion is displacing lifelong South
Boston residents," Mayor Flynn complained. "And they're not only
being forced out of their homes, but in some cases out of their
neighborhoods as well." Dan Yotts, claiming that encroachment by industrial plants would eventually spoil the essentially residential nature
of South Boston, argued that the Fan Pier project on lower Summer
Street would drive out low-income residents with its high prices and
expensive shops. "Where do the blue-collar workers go?" he asked.
"Where's the Stop and Shop?" "Southie's not quite ready for bou-
tiques," commented Joe Keenan, manager of Flanagan's Supermarket
on Broadway, who felt that in the long run the gentrification of his home
town was bound to bring significant changes.

Ironically, however, these developmental changes, with all their potential social, environmental and personal dislocations, are remarkably similar to those changes that first created South Boston as a separate political entity at the opening of the nineteenth century. In 1803 Judge Tudor and his colleagues looked across the channel for suitable property for their financial enterprises, which were outgrowing the limiting confines of the old Shawmut peninsula. Today, real estate developers and financial speculators are looking to expand beyond the downtown area of Boston, which has become so glutted with the towering structures of banks, insurance companies, office buildings, hotels and convention centers that there is simply no more room to build. Slowly, entrepreneurial construction moved from the central portion of the city into nearby residential neighborhoods. Once the overhead MTA elevated structures of the Orange Line are taken down, expansion will inevitably move through the South End and along Washington Street to the Dudley Street area of Roxbury. What industrial construction, high-priced condominiums and increased rents will do to the low-income black population of this particular area is something only time will tell. Similarly, the entrepreneurial movement into South Boston will probably not be stopped or even slowed down. Located so close to the downtown area, it is an obvious and natural place for developers who can extend their activities with a minimum of dislocation. How it will affect the old ethnic neighborhood, whether it will swallow up the entire community, or whether the residents will be able to once again withstand the efforts of outsiders to reshape a community that has successfully prevented similar efforts in the past—this, too, is something only time will tell.

Even as residents of South Boston were weighing the relative advantages and disadvantages a billion-dollar commercial enterprise would have for their district, the painful subject of segregation suddenly flared up again—this time involving public housing. In October 1987 the Federal Department of Housing and Urban Development sent a letter to Mayor Flynn charging that the Boston Housing Authority was maintaining segregation in the projects. The authority's selection policies tended to "exclude or discriminate against minorities," the dispatch said, stating that the BHA actually excluded black people from projects in South Boston on the ground that it could not guarantee their safety. The federal agency warned the mayor that failure to address this problem could result in a federal lawsuit and jeopardize $100 million a year in federal money as well as some $85 million more in state renovation funds.

About a week before the city's mayoral election the following month, Mayor Flynn made a public announcement that he would comply with the demands of federal and state agencies and see that South Boston's public housing projects were integrated. The city administration began drawing up plans to move several black families to the top of the housing authority's waiting list and into the Old Colony project and the Mary Ellen McCormack projects early in 1988. In several years, after substantial renovations were completed. a hundred more black, Hispanic and other nonwhite families were scheduled to be moved into the D Street project.

On November 3, 1987, Flynn won re-election as mayor of Boston in a landslide victory across the city, winning 63,412 votes to Joseph M. Tierney's 30,897 votes and taking twenty out of the city's twenty-two wards with more than 67 percent of the total vote. Flynn's margins were particularly impressive in black sections of the city—in Mattapan's Ward 14, for example, he won by a ratio of fourteen to one. In a shocking turn of events, however, Flynn lost both of his home-town wards to his opponent by nearly 400 of the 10,638 votes cast in that neighborhood. In *The Last Hurrah* the fictional Skeffington observed the "virtually bottomless capacity" of voters for suspicion and ridicule. He had seen popular men, he said, who when suddenly suspected of getting a bit above themselves "had been turned on with a savagery which could scarcely be believed." Ray Flynn was clearly the surprised recipient of such "savagery" from his own friends and neighbors. Almost all political observers interpreted his defeat in the South Boston wards as a deliberate "back-of-the-hand" to their favorite son by residents who were bitter and angry at his public support of integrated housing.

Most residents rejected the idea that their opposition to Flynn's plans for integrated housing had anything to do with race. They insisted that they were disturbed by the compulsory nature of the city's plans and what they saw as an unfair policy of allowing some people to go to the head of the waiting line. "It's not a racial thing," claimed one young man who was interviewed on election day. "People shouldn't be told where they have to live. You can't force this on people." Several young women interviewed at the polls the same day complained that the proposed new housing plan gave preferential treatment to outsiders at the expense of local residents. Mayor Flynn should "take care of the people in South Boston first, " one woman declared; another agreed that "people here should be given the first chance at housing"; a third complained that Flynn was not doing enough for the people of South Boston.

"He should help us, not hurt us!" she exclaimed. Leo Keaney, spokesman for the Old Colony Tenants Task Force, expressed opposition to the program. "It's forced housing," he argued. "It shouldn't be happening. If you force people, they're going to rebel." Barbara Mellan, head of the D Street Tenants Task Force, took a more moderate approach toward integrated housing but warned that local residents must be involved "every step of the way." People don't want anything forced on them, she explained. "As long as no one is moved out, people generally feel better."

On the evening of January 12, 1988, less than two weeks after his second inauguration, Mayor Flynn met with five hundred local residents in the basement of St. Monica's Church to explain his plans to integrate public housing in South Boston. He tried to allay fears that local project residents would be put out of their homes to make room for outside minorities. "No person, especially the elderly, will be displaced from their unit because of any fair housing policy," Flynn promised. "That is a commitment to you." Many residents remained unconvinced, however, and several at the meeting greeted the mayor's promises with yells of "Lies, lies, Flynn lies!" Representatives for the three housing projects argued that South Boston's elderly, handicapped and low-income families must be assured the right to remain in their own neighborhoods. If there was a shortgage of housing for black people, they said angrily, then the city should repair the numerous vacant, boarded-up projects in Roxbury. "Leave us the hell alone. Leave the blacks alone," Leo Keaney said, as the emotional audience shouted its approval.

To defuse this potentially explosive situation, and get out the word that desegragation would not mean the eviction of longtime tenants, Mayor Flynn met with city councilors and administration officials two days later. According to the mayor he and the councilors reached agreement on three major points: 1) No existing tenant over sixty-two would be forced to vacate a unit, even if the unit were larger than the tenant required; 2) Tenants under sixty-two might be moved if they were "overhoused," but only to another unit in the same project; and 3) All 14,500 households currently on the public-housing waiting lists would be guaranteed a fair opportunity for housing in all neighborhoods throughout the city, regardless of race. Clearly, Flynn was trying to avoid breakdown of community relations that had provoked racial hatred and the terrible busing crisis fourteen years earlier. On the one hand, as a South Boston native he was sensitive to the real fears of longtime Irish-Catholic residents, many of them elderly widows, who did not want to leave their friends and relatives in their familar neighborhood to get public housing in a predominantly black neighborhood where they would feel alone and afraid. On the other hand, as an elected constitutional official Flynn was committed to obey public policy in support of civil rights—a policy he publicly agreed was "the right thing to do." Anxious to avoid a bureaucratic resolution of the issue formulated by outsiders, Flynn looked for some kind of workable and mutually acceptable arrangement that would reconcile the civil rights of all citizens with the justifiable desires and expectations of neighborhood residents. "Either we do this the right way," he warned, "or they will do it for us. And there's no guarantee that it will be done as it should be."

In his early discussions, Flynn steered carefully away from the highly sensitive issues of race and ethnicity, focusing more upon the themes of fairness, freedom of choice, and individual preference, themes that lent themselves to open discussion and rational negotiation. James Kelly and William Bulger, among others, agreed that these were important considerations and emphasized the importance of flexibility in any final arrangement with federal agencies so that all citizens could choose the neighborhood in which they would live. "It should be possible for any applicant from any part of the city to have his preference respected," Bulger said, so that such a person could continue to live amid "familiar surroundings." Flynn tried carefully to develop a process that would recognize and safeguard individual preferences, but also be linked to the principle that no family could be *excluded* from living wherever it wished and therefore be denied freedom of choice. In his efforts to develop a workable consensus on public policy, the mayor received strong moral support from leaders of the Catholic Church. On Sunday, January 24, 1988, Boston's Cardinal Bernard F. Law had a six-page pastoral letter read at all Masses in the eight Catholic churches in South Boston, condemning racial bigotry in all forms and urging peaceful integration of public housing. "There is too much at stake for us to let our communities become divided by blind emotion," the Cardinal said. "Every one of us should seek a reasonable, calm, open and fair resolution of the issue affecting public housing in South Boston."

Everyone involved was aware that the issue of integrated housing might re-create many of the same frightening episodes of a decade earlier. The mayor, city officials, state legislators, black citizens in Roxbury and white citizens in South Boston all knew that the housing situation was a tinder box. But there were reasons to hope that history would not repeat itself. For one thing, public housing involves adults, not little children, and emotions are not so easily aroused about such matters. "This isn't like busing where people's kids got taken out of their own schools and sent somewhere else while black kids took their place," one twenty-nine-year-old mother explained. "Sure, there's going to be some trouble," she shrugged, "but there's trouble now." For another thing, the number of nonwhite tenants would be relatively small and introduced at gradual intervals into the area projects located along the outskirts of the neighborhood—quite different from transporting large numbers of students into a high school located in the very heart of the district. The process was also to be conducted by a mayor who stood behind the moral imperative of racial equality but who gave every evidence of conducting the process at a local level with sensitivity and understanding. Despite their "back-of-the-hand" rebuke on election day, most residents of South Boston still admired and trusted Ray Flynn and instinctively counted on him to use his powers as mayor to protect them and their neighborhood from the worst excesses of municipal bureaucracy. Many interviews revealed a sullen acknowledgement that more open public housing was something that had to come—"it's bound to come"…"it's inevitable"…"it's the law…" some of the residents grudgingly admitted—but their anxieties were lessened by Flynn's refusal to allow anything as terrible as forced busing happen to their community again. Finally, the willingness of Cardinal Law and the clergy of the archdiocese to take a public position in the case of integrated housing introduced an important moral influence that was not present to the same degree in 1974. Many community leaders and local residents might express anger and resentment at churchmen "sticking their noses"into political affairs, but a vocal religious influence was simply one of many important considerations that had failed to operate during the earlier controversy over forced busing.

Whether it comes fast or slow, whether it takes five years or ten, whether it takes place at all, integrated housing is only one factor destined to change the character of South Boston and turn the district into more of a nostalgic recollection than a thriving ethnic neighborhood. Almost all of the traditional forces that once provided cohesiveness have either completely disappeared or become almost negligible. The once dominant role of the Catholic Church and the pervasive influence of the clergy have been reduced to largely social amenities in older parishes like SS. Peter and Paul's and St. Augustine's where churches are often empty and services mostly unattended. The pugnacious character of a blue-collar, working-class population has been greatly modified by the changing demands of a high-tech industry and an essentially service-oriented economy. And while a major portion of the community still has strong emotional ties to Ireland, members of the third or fourth generation are much more likely to be searching for their roots in the higher realms of education at Boston College, the University of Massachusetts or even (*mirabile dictu!*) Harvard University.

It appears almost certain that outside forces will slowly but surely transform the social and economic structure of South Boston. As integrated housing brings a more varied population into the projects along Old Colony Boulevard and the lower part of East Eighth Street, the Fan Pier projects will expand along the waterfront across from the Fort Point Channel. The commercial developments will certainly have an impact on the western end of the peninsula and those portions of Summer Street that lead directly into L Street. Different types of people will move into the district, bringing different habits and customs and higher levels of income. How long residents and neighborhood groups can hold out against developers is the only question left.

Before it all happens, before South Boston fades into the mists of history and then disappears even from memory, it seemed important to pass along to future generations some idea of how it "used to be." It was a community of gas lamps and cobblestones, of large families and three-decker houses, of cod-liver oil and rubber boots, of rosary beads and vigil lights, of Midnight Masses and May processions, of streetcorner gangs and rowdy barrooms, of torchlight rallies and Saturday-night baked beans. In so many ways South Boston exemplified the complex characteristics of an Irish-Catholic neighborhood—good and bad, admirable and abominable, memorable and unforgivable. One cannot help but call to mind the reflections of the old Yankee philanthropist, Nathaniel Gardiner, as he walked to his downtown office after Mayor Skeffington's funeral mass. "Skeffington had gone, and it was as if a part of the city itself had gone; a part of the city which Gardiner had both liked and deplored, but most of all a part of the city with which he had grown up, which he knew, and which was as much a part of the city to him as the fine old buildings themselves. And now it was gone, and Gardiner, too, was an old man who would soon be going; the question he asked himself now was: 'Who and what is to follow us?' ''

SOURCES

CHAPTER 1

Older works on South Boston are indispensable to an understanding of the early years of the community. Thomas S. Simonds, *History of South Boston* (Boston: 1857) is especially helpful on the colonial origins and the basic land structure of the peninsula. C. Bancroft Gillespie, *Illustrated History of South Boston* (South Boston: 1900) and John J. Toomey and Edward P. Rankin, *History of South Boston* (Boston: 1901) include photographs of prominent houses and buildings as well as biographies of notable citizens. The Castle Island Association of South Boston publishes a series of occasional papers dealing with the history of Castle Island and Fort Independence. These scholarly studies are done by William J. Reid, Ph.D., a specialist in American history and former headmaster of South Boston High School.

Samuel Eliot Morison, *Builders of the Bay Colony* (Boston: 1930) and Darrett Rutman, *Winthrop's Boston: A Portrait of a Puritan Town, 1630-1649* (Chapel Hill, N.C.: 1965) provide insights into the early settlement of Boston, while Walter Muir Whitehill's *Boston: A Topographical History* (Cambridge: 1959) is invaluable to an understanding of Boston's topographical growth and development. Maud P. Kuhns, *The "Mary and John": A Story of the Founding of Dorchester, Massachusetts, 1630* (Rutland, Vt: 1971) describes the early years of Dorchester; Edward Rowe Snow, *The Islands of Boston Harbor* (New York: 1971) is the standard work on the outlying islands; and Alden Vaughan, *The New England Frontier: Puritans and Indians, 1620-1675* (Boston: 1965) sheds new light on the Native Americans in the region.

Works concentrating on Boston's role in the coming of the Revolution include Bernard Bailyn, *The Ordeal of Thomas Hutchinson* (Cambridge: 1974); Benjamin Labaree, *The Boston Tea Party* (New York: 1964); Edmund and Helen Morgan, *The Stamp Act Crisis* (Chapel Hill, N.C.: 1953); and Hiller Zobel, *The Boston Massacre* (New York: 1970). R. Frothingham, *History of the Siege of Boston and the Battles of Lexington, Concord, and Bunker Hill* (Boston: 1873) focuses on the early stages of hostilities and can be supplemented by William Dillaway's study, *The Evacuation of Boston* (Boston: 1899) and Anna Morris's article, "General John Thomas of Dorchester Heights," *South Boston Journal*, I (Fall, 1978). A dramatic account of the war's end can be found in Myron F. Wehtje, "Boston's Celebration of Peace in 1783 and 1784," *Historical Journal of Massachusetts*, 12 (June, 1984).

The resurgence of Boston after the Revolution can be traced in Thomas H. O'Connor and Alan Rogers, *This Momentous Affair: Massachusetts and the Ratification of the Constitution of the United States* (Boston: 1987); Samuel Eliot Morison, *The Maritime History of Massachusetts* (Boston: 1921); Josiah Quincy, *A Municipal History of the Town and City of Boston during Two Centuries, from September 17, 1630 to September 17, 1830* (Boston: 1852); and Robert A. McCaughey, *Josiah Quincy* (Cambridge: 1974).

Alice Felt Tyler's *Freedom's Ferment* (Minnesota: 1944) and Clifford S. Griffin, *Their Brothers' Keepers* (New Brunswick, N.J.: 1960) are excellent introductions to the social and cultural changes in Boston during the early 1800s. They provide a good background for more specialized accounts, such as Harold Schwartz, *Samuel Gridley Howe: Social Reformer, 1801-1876* (Cambridge: 1956); Gerald Grob, *Mental Institutions in America: Social Policy to 1875* (New York: 1973); and Norman Dain, *Concepts in Insanity in the United States, 1789-1865* (New Brunswick, N.J.: 1964). Martin Green, *The Problem of Boston* (New York: 1966) is a provocative analysis of changing patterns in Boston's cultural life during this same period.

CHAPTER 2

Robert Lord, John Sexton and Edmund Harrington, *History of the Archdiocese of Boston* (3 v., Boston: 1945) not only provides a comprehensive narrative of the Catholic Church in New England but also offers a well-documented history of the people. Annabelle Melville, *Jean Lefebvre de Cheverus, 1768-1836* (Milwaukee: 1958) is a scholarly account of Boston's first Catholic bishop, while Thomas H. O'Connor, *Fitzpatrick's Boston, 1846-1866* (Boston: 1984) is a study of John Bernard Fitzpatrick, third Bishop of Boston, who took office at the time of the Great Famine. An essential source of information throughout this period is the weekly diocesan newspaper, *The Boston Pilot*.

Kerby Miller, *Emigrants and Exiles: Ireland and the Irish Exodus to North America* (New York: 1985) is a modern scholarly study of immigration, and supplements such earlier works as William Adams, *Ireland and Irish Immigra-*

tion to the New World from 1815 to the Famine (New Haven: 1932); Marcus Lee Hansen, *The Atlantic Migration* (Cambridge: 1940); George Potter, *To the Golden Door* (Boston: 1960); and Thomas Gallagher, *Paddy's Lament: Ireland, 1846-1847* (New York: 1982). Cecil Woodham-Smith's *The Great Hunger: Ireland, 1848-1849* (New York: 1962) is a brilliant analysis of the famine years, while Oscar Handlin's *Boston's Immigrants* (Cambridge: 1941) continues to remain the outstanding study of immigrant life in Boston. John A. Krout, *The Origins of Prohibition* (New York: 1925); Ian R. Tyrell, *Sobering Up: From Temperance to Prohibition in Antebellum America* (New York: 1979); and N. H. Clark, *Deliver Us from Evil: An Interpretation of Prohibition* (New York: 1979) investigate the impact of alcoholism in America, while J. R. Barrett, "Why Paddy Drank: The Social Importance of Whiskey in Pre-Famine Ireland," *Journal of Popular Culture*, 11 (1977) looks into the Irish past.

Ray Allen Billington, *The Protestant Crusade, 1800-1860* (New York: 1938) is a good starting point for the study of nativism, which has been updated by such studies as Jay Dolan, *The Immigrant Church* (Baltimore: 1975); Michael Feldberg, *The Philadelphia Riots of 1844* (Westport, Conn.: 1975); and Carleton Beals, *Brass Knuckle Crusade: The Great Know-Nothing Conspiracy* (New York: 1960). For general treatments of Catholics and the slavery issue, see Madeleine Hooke Rice, *American Catholic Opinion in the Slavery Controversy* (Gloucester, Mass.: 1964); Robert Leckie, *American and Catholic* (New York: 1970); and John Francis Maxwell, *Slavery and the Catholic Church* (London: 1975). Differing views of the local abolitionist leader William Lloyd Garrison can be found in Walter Merrill, *Against Wind and Tide* (Cambridge: 1963), and John L. Thomas, *The Liberator* (Boston: 1963).

Such works as Thomas H. O'Connor, *Lords of the Loom: The Cotton Whigs and the Coming of the Civil War* (New York: 1968); Eric Foner, *Free Soil, Free Labor, Free Men: The Ideology of the Republican Party before the Civil War* (New York: 1970); Gerald W. Wolff, *The Kansas-Nebraska Bill, Sectionalism, and the Coming of the Civil War* (New York: 1977) provide a background for the increasing tensions over slavery after 1854. Don Fehrenbacher, *The Dred Scott Case* (New York: 1978); Roy Nichols, *The Democratic Machine, 1850-1854* (New York: 1923); and Dale Baum, *The Civil War Party System: The Case of Massachusetts, 1848-1876* (Chapel Hill: 1984) focus on local political transformations.

CHAPTER 3

William Schouler, *A History of Massachusetts in the Civil War* (2 v., Boston: 1868) is an older work that provides a background for such accounts as Frank Flynn, *The "Fighting Ninth" for Fifty Years* (Boston: 1911) and William L. Burton's article, "Irish Regiments in the Union Army: The Massachusetts Experiment," *Historical Journal of Massachusetts*, 11 (June, 1983). Jack Leach,

Conscription in the United States (Rutland, Vt.: 1952) and Eugene Murdock,
Patriotism Unlimited: The Civil War Draft and the Bounty System (New York:
1967) describe the problems of conscription that led to the New York riots
described in Basil L. Lee, *Discontent in New York City, 1861-1865* (New York:
1943); Irving Weinstein, *July, 1863: The Incredible Story of the Bloody New
York Draft Riots* (New York: 1952); and Adrian Cook, *The Armies of the
Streets: The New York City Draft Riots of 1863* (New York: 1974). An account of Boston's short-lived draft riot may be found in O'Connor, *Fitzpatrick's
Boston.*

The changing character of the South Boston economy in the decades after
the Civil War can be traced in such studies as *Commerce, Manufactures, and
Resources of Boston, Massachusetts, A Historical, Statistical, and Descriptive Review* (Boston: 1883); *Professional and Industrial History of Suffolk
County, Massachusetts* (3 v., Boston: 1894); and Orra L. Stone, *History of
Massachusetts Industries: Their Inception, Growth, and Success* (4 v., Boston:
1930). A booklet published by the South Boston Savings Bank on the occasion of its hundredth anniversary, *A Century of Service* (South Boston: 1963),
provides an interesting glimpse into the economic status of the community;
Sam Bass Warner, Jr., traces the movement of the immigrants out of the inner
city in his fascinating *Streetcar Suburbs* (New York: 1974); and George G.
Crocker shows the changing forms of transportation in *From the Stagecoach
to the Railroad Train and the Street Car* (Boston: 1900). Dennis P. Ryan,
Beyond the Ballot Box (Rutherford, N.J.: 1983) explores the social history
of the Irish from 1845 to 1917, while Hasia Diner's *Erin's Daughters*
(Baltimore: 1983) describes the roles and activities of Irish immigrant women
in the nineteenth century.

The impact of the "new" immigrants coming into Boston from southern
and eastern Europe at the close of the nineteenth century can be viewed in
several lights. Thomas Archdeacon, *Becoming American* (New York: 1983)
describes the interaction between the newcomers and older immigrants; Barbara
Miller Solomon, *Ancestors and Immigrants* (Cambridge: 1956) analyzes the
reactions of native Bostonians to alien influences in the city; and Samuel Eliot
Morison, *One Boy's Boston, 1887-1901* (Boston: 1962) views the changing
Boston scene in autobiographical fashion.

As historians move beyond the written historical works published in 1900,
they must rely increasingly on private diaries, personal memoirs and oral
testimony. The family of Francis E. Birmingham kindly supplied me with his
memories of South Boston in the early 1900s, and the Jesuit Community at
Boston College made available to me the recollections of Rev. Maurice Dullea,
S.J., who grew up in St. Vincent's parish during the same period. Robert P.
Toland, a noted authority on South Boston history, was generous enough to
provide several personal interviews; while Professor Andrew Buni of Boston
College offered the use of a number of taped interviews with South Boston

residents conducted by graduate students under his direction. A fascinating and valuable collection of personal reminiscences can be found in the booklet on "South Boston," one of a series of neighborhood studies in the *Boston 200 Neighborhood History Series* published by the City of Boston during its 200th anniversary observances in 1980.

The *History of the Archdiocese of Boston* continues to be a valuable source of information concerning the construction of churches and the activities of the clergy during this period. In more recent years the work of such younger scholars as James M. O'Toole, Rev. Robert E. Sullivan and Thomas E. Wangler regarding the role of the Catholic Church and its clergy during the administration of Cardinal O'Connell may be found in *Catholic Boston: Studies in Religion and Community, 1870-1970* (Boston: 1985).

CHAPTER 4

Arthur Mann, *Yankee Reformers in an Urban Age* (Cambridge: 1954); Geoffrey Blodgett, *The Gentle Reformers: Massachusetts Democrats in the Cleveland Era* (Cambridge: 1966); Robert Woods and Albert Kennedy, eds., *The Zone of Emergence, 1905-1914* (Cambridge: 1962) are valuable studies of turn-of-the-century Boston, which have been updated by scholarly essays in Ronald Formisano and Constance Burns, eds., *Boston, 1700-1980* (Westport, Conn.: 1984).

William Shannon's *The American Irish* (New York: 1963) is a lively and perceptive analysis that serves as an effective background for such studies of local figures as Leslie Ainley, *Boston Mahatma: Martin Lomasney* (Boston: 1949); Doris Kearns Goodwin, *The Fitzgeralds and the Kennedys* (New York: 1987); Henry G. Pearson, *Son of New England: James Jackson Storrow* (Boston: 1930); and Joseph F. Dinneen, *The Purple Shamrock* (New York: 1949). James Michael Curley's autobiography, *I'd Do It Again: A Record of All My Uproarious Years* (Englewood, N.J.: 1957) will probably always be read against the fictional account of Mayor Skeffington in Edwin O'Connor's classic tale of Boston politics, *The Last Hurrah* (New York: 1956). The diary of George Reed Nutter, together with papers, pamphlets and booklets of the Good Government Association are located in the Massachusetts Historical Society and shed much light on the reaction of native Bostonians to the movement of Irish Catholics into the higher levels of Boston politics.

CHAPTER 5

A record of the activities associated with the erection of the Farragut statue may be found in *A Memorial of David Glasgow Farragut from the City of Boston, with an Account of the Dedication of the Farragut Statue at Marine Park, South Boston, June 28, 1893* (Boston: 1896). Toomey and Rankin's *History of South Boston* also contains information on the Farragut statue. Leo P. Dauwer, *Boston's St. Patrick Day Irish* (Author: 1980) is a nostalgic and anecdotal account of the famous local celebration; and Gillespie's *Illustrated History of South Boston* has numerous photographs of well-known houses, mansions, schools and churches in the district.

City of Boston, *Report on Free Bathing Facilities* (City Document No. 102: 1866), and G. W. Hangar, "Public Baths in the United States," *Bulletin of the Bureau of Labor* (Washington, D.C.: 1904) provide vital historical information on bathhouses, while Jane A. Stewart's article on "The Boston Experience with Municipal Baths," *American Journal of Sociology*, 7 (November 1901) offers a local view of the enterprise.

Fredrik Barth, ed., *Ethnic Groups and Boundaries* (Boston: 1969); Leo A. Depres, ed., *Ethnicity and Resource Competition in Plural Societies* (The Hague: 1975); John Higham, ed., *Ethnic Leadership in America* (Baltimore: 1978); William Newman, *American Pluralism* (New York: 1973); and Milton G. Gordon, *Assimilation in American Life* (New York: 1964) focus on the numerous complexities of immigrant groups moving into pluralistic societies.

CHAPTER 6

The pages of the local newspapers, the *Boston Globe*, the *Boston Herald-Traveler* and the *Boston Post* contain details of the progress of World War I and the activities of the Yankee Division. Frederick Palmer, *America in France* (New York: 1918) describes the engagements of the American expeditionary forces, while the official citation to Private First Class Michael J. Perkins (Deceased) is reprinted in *The Book of Salutation to the Twenty-Sixth ("Yankee") Division of the American Expeditionary Forces...Also the Official Program for the Divisional Parade, April 25, 1919* (Boston: 1919).

Joseph E. Persico, "The Great Swine Flu Epidemic of 1918," *American Heritage*, 27 (June, 1976); Francis Russell, *The Great Interlude* (New York: 1964); *Carney Hospital: Diamond Jubilee, 1863-1938* (Boston: 1938), courtesy of Sister Grace Collins, Archivist, Carney Hospital; Edward Parks, "Without Warning: Molasses in January Surged Over Boston," *Smithsonian Magazine*, November, 1983; James Green and Hugh Donahue, *Boston's Workers: A Labor History* (Boston: 1979); and Francis Russell, *City in Terror: 1919, The Boston Police Strike* (New York: 1975) all shed light on the social and economic changes of the postwar decades.

Once again, the author is indebted to local residents for personal recollections of South Boston during the 1920s and 1930s. The short-lived publication of the *South Boston Journal* under the direction of Frank Alcorn provided an opportunity for valuable articles by Jack Canavan, Tim Caulfield, Eddie Kelley, Charles Satkewich, Martin Slobodkin, Bob Toland and Mary Lou Ward. A series of essays by Marie H. Crowley, "One Girl's South Boston, 1910-1930," published in *The Irish Echo* (May, June, 1986), added further material on the period, while Leo Dauwer's *I Remember Southie* (Boston: 1975) contributed more nostalgic anecdotes about the district. Two young scholars from South Boston have been generous in sharing with me the results of their ongoing research. Christine Canavan submitted a sociological study of South Boston as a senior research paper at Smith College in 1986, and Rev. James DiPerri completed an M.A. thesis analyzing the social and political attitudes of the clergy in South Boston.

The best professional account to date of the Curley administration is Charles H. Trout, *Boston: The Great Depression and the New Deal* (New York: 1977). George Q. Flynn, *Roosevelt and Romanism: Catholics and American Diplomacy* (Westport, Conn.: 1976) explores the interrelationship of religion and politics during the New Deal era; and John F. Stack, Jr., *International Conflict in an American City: Boston's Irish, Italians, and Jews, 1934-1944* (Westport, Conn.: 1979) focuses on the isolationist views of the Boston Irish during the wartime years. From 1943 to 1946, the Commercial Filters Corporation of South Boston compiled newsletters with excerpts of letters from former employees serving in the armed forces during World War II. A complete file of these letters can be found at the South Boston Branch of the Boston Public Library.

CHAPTER 7

Social Facts by Census Tracts, Federal Census Data, South Boston District, analyzed by the United Community Planning Corporation, 1950, 1970, 1980; *Rehousing the Low Income Families of Boston: A Review of the Activities of the Boston Housing Authority, 1936-1940* (Boston: 1941); Deborah Bluhmin, *A Study of Crime in a Boston Housing Project*, The Mayor's Safe Streets Act Advisory Committee (Boston: 1973) are among documents that provide essential statistical information on the changing character of the city after 1945.

Paul Wright, *John W. McCormack* (U Mass/Boston, Occasional Papers: 1985). This monograph, prepared for the dedication of John W. McCormack Hall at the University of Massachusetts at Boston, April 26, 1985, should lead to a much-needed, full-scale biography of the South Boston statesman. Murray B. Levin, *The Alienated Voter: Politics in Boston* (New York: 1960) is a professional analysis of the mayoral election of 1959, when John Collins upset John E. Powers. Boston Redevelopment Authority, *South Boston General Neighborhood Renewal Plan* (Boston: 1962); and *EXPO Boston 76* (Planning Pamphlet, Official Project Description: 1976) are documents which show plans for public projects in South Boston.

George Higgins, *Style Versus Substance: Boston, Kevin White, and the Politics of Illusion* (New York: 1984) offers a contemporary analysis of the White administration; Alan Lupo, *Liberty's Chosen Home* (Boston: 1977) is a perceptive account of the first days of busing against the background of race and class distinctions in Boston; Ione Malloy, *Southie Won't Go: A Teacher's Diary of the Desegregation of South Boston High School* (Urbana, Ill.: 1986) is a passionate first-hand account of busing by a concerned teacher; and

J. Anthony Lukas, *Common Ground* (New York: 1984) is a kaleidoscopic, Pulitzer Prize-winning novel of the busing crisis as seen through the eyes of three Boston families. Jon Hillson, *The Battle of Boston* (New York: 1977) is a report on the busing crisis by a black jounalist and civil-rights activist; J. Michael Ross and William M. Berg, *"I Respectfully Disagree with the Judge's Order": The Boston School Desegregation Controversy* (Washington, D.C.: 1981) offers a view more sympathetic to the opponents of forced busing.

INDEX